T0246304

THE ARMY THAT NEVER WAS

Also by Taylor Downing

1942 – Britain at the Brink

1983 – The World at the Brink

Breakdown

Secret Warriors

Night Raid

The World at War

Spies in the Sky

Churchill's War Lab

Olympia

Cold War (with Sir Jeremy Isaacs)

Battle Stations (with Andrew Johnston)

Civil War (with Maggie Millman)

The Troubles (as Editor)

THE ARMY THAT NEVER WAS

GEORGE S. PATTON AND THE DECEPTION OF OPERATION FORTITUDE

TAYLOR DOWNING

PEGASUS BOOKS
NEW YORK LONDON

THE ARMY THAT NEVER WAS

Pegasus Books, Ltd.
148 West 37th Street, 13th Floor
New York, NY 10018

First Pegasus Books cloth edition November 2024

ISBN: 978-1-63936-754-2

10 9 8 7 6 5 4 3 2 1

Printed in the United States of America
Distributed by Simon & Schuster
www.pegasusbooks.com

ACKNOWLEDGEMENTS

This book has been immensely enjoyable to research and write as it deals with so many remarkable characters and so many stories that read more like fiction than fact. The accounts of the complex planning for the invasion of Europe and of the actual assault on D-Day and what followed are amongst the most powerful in the Second World War. And the inventiveness and creativity of the deception teams has been a magnificent story to tell. But as always the historian is reliant upon the support and encouragement of the archivists who store, preserve and make accessible the raw material of history.

I would like to thank especially Andrew Richards at the Imperial War Museum who pointed me in the direction of many memoirs and personal accounts of those caught up in the deception campaigns around D-Day. The IWM archives are still second to none when it comes to researching the world wars. The archivists at the National Archives in Kew are always courteous and efficient and I'm grateful to them all. The material held at the Mass Observation Archive at the Keep in Sussex is a rich source for anyone studying the social aspects or reactions to events in the Second World War. And the role of the photo interpreters at RAF Medmenham is crucial in understanding the deception operations around D-Day. The Medmenham Collection is lucky in having Ruth Pooley and Tim Fryer providing access to the treasure trove of material about aerial photography and photo intelligence in the Second World War.

I'm grateful to several friends and colleagues who over the years have helped and inspired me in discovering D-Day stories. Among many others they include Sir Jeremy Isaacs, David Edgar, Chris Going, Paul Nelson and James Barker.

I'm grateful to Andrew Lownie for picking up on this project with enthusiasm and for Duncan Heath, Connor Stait and Steve Burdett at Icon/Amberley for their support and wise advice.

Finally, as always, thanks to Anne who supported and encouraged me as I re-lived the momentous events of 1944.

Taylor Downing,

CONTENTS

PROLOGUE

Britain was in the middle of a long, hot spell. At the end of May 1944 high pressure had descended on southern England and the Channel. For day after day the weather was warm, dry and without strong winds. The hottest day of the year so far came on 28 May, reaching what in those days was recorded as 88 degrees Fahrenheit (31 degrees Celsius). Ideal weather in which to launch an invasion. But the Allied armies were still gathering. Equipment was still being prepared and men being trained. The Deceivers were still spinning their webs of deception. They were not yet ready for D-Day.

On 29 May 1944, General George S. Patton Jr gave a speech in the south-east of England to a group of men from his army, the First US Army Group. A platform had been erected at the base of a slight hill. Men arrived and surrounded the platform, and then as more came along they spilled up the hillside, creating a natural amphitheatre. Before his arrival the scene was alive with anticipation. Silence fell as his black Mercedes finally appeared with flags flying, and he emerged surrounded by an escort of Military Police. A band played stirring marches as he strode onto the podium. All the soldiers present jumped to attention. At the centre, General Patton stood there tall and with a rod-like straight back, resplendent in a smartly tailored uniform, the epitome of a great commander. He was a three-star general who proudly displayed his trio of stars on his helmet, his shirt collar and his shoulder pads. The bevvy of medals glittering on his chest included the Distinguished Service Cross awarded 'for extraordinary heroism' in the First World War. He wore knee-high leather cavalry boots, complete with spurs, so heavily polished that they positively shone in the bright sun. He stood in immaculately creased riding breeches held up by a hand-tooled leather belt sporting a gleaming brass buckle. He also carried a holster which boasted a white pearl-handled revolver visible to all. He stood there facing his men, formal and totally formidable, every inch a warrior. Alongside him, standing perfectly still, as though at attention and mimicking the General, was his white bulldog terrier, Willie.

When he began to address the troops he spoke in a rather high-pitched voice, not the deep drawl that might have been expected to come from such a striking figure. But the words he used silenced everyone. In hushed anticipation every man present strained to hear what this magnificent-looking figure had to say. First he told them, 'At ease,' and that they could sit down. Then, after a pause, he began his peroration, which was full of profanities. But he was accustomed to inspiring his listeners on the eve of battle.[1]

He spoke first of the American desire to win, whether in sport or at war. 'Men … when you were kids, you all admired the champion marble player, the fastest runner, the big league ball players, the toughest boxers,' he began. 'The Americans love a winner, and cannot tolerate a loser. Americans despise cowards … That's why Americans have never lost and will never lose a war, for the very thought of losing is hateful to an American.' He talked about how all men show signs of fear when they first experience combat. 'But the real man never lets fear of death overpower his honour, his sense of duty to his country, and his innate manhood.' He told his audience that every one of them had to be alert at all times. If not, 'some German sonofabitch will sneak up behind and beat you to death with a sockful of shit.' This roused a laugh and a cheer.

Patton carried on: 'All the real heroes are not storybook combat fighters either. Every single man in the Army plays a vital part. Every little job is essential to the whole scheme.' He spoke of the truck drivers who continued to bring up supplies despite being under fire, of the quartermasters who delivered the food and clothing, and of the cooks and washers-up who kept the men fed and watered. He talked of a man whom he discovered in the heat of battle up a telegraph pole under heavy fire, repairing a wire. He asked him if it wasn't a little unhealthy up there now. '"Yes, sir," the soldier replied, "but this goddam wire has got to be fixed."' The General continued: 'Each man must not only think of himself, but think of his buddy fighting alongside him. We don't want yellow cowards in the Army. They should be killed off like flies. If not, they will go home after the war, goddam cowards, and breed more cowards. The brave men will breed more brave men.' A few men were shocked by this. But most applauded loudly.

As he continued Patton bellowed out proudly, 'We have the finest food, the finest equipment, the finest-spirited men in the world.' Then he rose to his crescendo: 'Why, by God, I actually pity those sons of bitches we are going up against – by God, I do.' The men clapped and cheered. Giving his words a Shakespearian tone reminiscent of Henry V's speech on the eve of Agincourt, Patton concluded, 'Thank God that, at least thirty years from now, when you are sitting around the fireside with your grandson on your knee and he asks what you did in the great World War Two, you won't have to say "I shoveled shit in Louisiana."' The men roared with approval. They loved the earthy prose, the profanities and the sense that everyone relied upon everyone else. It made them feel good, part of something big and important. Patton knew how to command men and marshal his words for battle.

On 23 May, a short while before Patton gave his rousing speech, another general addressed a group of his officers, who were part of the 21st Army Group. He was speaking in the south-west of England. This commander was General Bernard Law Montgomery, the great victor and hero of Alamein and North Africa. He too was a great orator who had the ability to get through to his men. He did not use swear words, however. He spoke in short, staccato sentences. He called on God to support the Allied mission and spoke with an evangelical passion, almost as though he were leading a crusade. He expressed his faith in the good and righteous in their struggle to overcome the bad and evil. He was shorter and far less physically impressive than the American general. Nor did he dress flamboyantly. Unlike Patton, he wore simple khaki battledress like his men and usually sported a plain black tanker's beret. The traditional view of British generals, mostly left over from the First World War, was that they were rather pompous and stiff, and lived behind the lines grandly in splendid chateaux. This was not the case with Montgomery, universally known as Monty. He lived very simply, and when in the field he used a set of caravans which comprised his map room, his office and his bedroom.[2]

From January 1944 onwards, Monty had carried out a series of visits to the troops under his command. This was part of a campaign he called 'Salute the Soldier', and these visits were intended to raise the morale of fighting men whom Montgomery realised were growing weary after four years of war. They needed a lift before the upcoming new offensive. Most of the men in his Army Group had never met their new commander before. His fame preceded him, but they did not know what it was like to be in his Army. He wanted to impress every one of them with a sense of mission. Monty had a dedicated train on which he travelled up and down the country to give dozens of talks. Sometimes he spoke to a battalion, sometimes a regiment or a brigade. On occasions he spoke to an entire division. Monty would address up to 30,000 men in a single day. The purpose of the talks was for his men to be able to see and hear him as much as it was for the General to meet them.

The sequence of events usually followed the same pattern. He would arrive at a unit in a humble jeep and summon the troops around him by loudspeaker. He would then walk down the ranks of the assembled men, staring into their eyes. Army Intelligence reports had concluded that many soldiers expected to die in the invasion of Europe. So Monty would often begin by picking out a single infantryman and asking him, 'What is your most valuable weapon?' The soldier would always reply, 'My rifle, sir.' Monty would respond, 'No, it isn't, it's your life, and I'm going to save it for you. Now listen to me …'[3] He would usually conclude his speeches with encouraging words. 'We're going to finish the thing off … you and I together … with God's help we will see the thing through to the end.' One journalist who heard some of his talks said that he 'made the soldiers feel that they were embarked upon something which made them larger and finer and more commanding human beings than they were before.'[4] A junior officer who heard one of Monty's pep talks probably summed up the view of many when he wrote, after hearing him, that 'I fell completely under his spell and had no further doubts about the outcome of the war in Europe.'[5]

In addition to speaking to the troops, Monty also addressed industrial workers, who were facing more austerity and another bleak year of restrictions and drabness. He spoke to railway workers, miners, dockers and munitions workers. He visited factories and football grounds. At Hampden Park in Glasgow he was cheered when he entered the ground. To everyone he urged further effort to sustain the final struggle that was still to come. 'Keep on working,' he encouraged them. 'We British have had many disasters in this war; they have been due to neglect.' He said Britain had not been properly prepared for war when it came in 1939, and to the country's shame 'we sent out soldiers into this most modern war with weapons and equipment that were hopelessly inadequate ... We must never let that happen again. Nor will we.'

Such was his crusading charisma that his message went down well everywhere. Posters went up in city centres showing him smiling down. But in Westminster, people began to wonder if this was not a military campaign but a political one. Did Monty have his eye on Downing Street after the war? The papers were told discreetly to stop reporting his factory visits. The BBC did not ask him to broadcast on the radio. When it was suggested he should stop the lecture tour, he refused. He insisted his talks were doing good and said, 'I will go through with it because I am informed that it will be of value in heightening morale.'[6]

Monty's exact words on 23 May 1944 were not recorded, as Patton's had been. But from his notes we can get the gist of what he said to the senior officers present. He told them, 'We are going to be involved in great events.' He said that everyone must know each other and what their task was to be. He added that it was also, 'Very important that you should know my views on things. In the business of war, very clear thinking is required.' He put great emphasis on training and on having men who were at the peak of their condition. He underlined what he called 'the Human Factor,' telling his officers, 'It is the man that counts and not the machine. If you have got men who are mentally alert, who are tough and hard, who are trained to fight and kill, who are enthusiastic ... and you give these men the proper weapons and equipment – there is nothing they cannot do. Nothing. Nothing.'

As he approached his peak, he went on: 'If you tell the soldier what you want and you launch him properly into battle, he will always do *his* part – he has never let the side down. The British soldier is easy to lead; he is very willing to be led; and he responds at once to leadership. Only from an inspired nation can go forth an inspired army ... And then as the sap rises, the men will feel themselves to be the instrument of a new-born national vigour.' Returning to his Christian theme he concluded: '"Let God arise and let His enemies be scattered" ... The Promised Land is not now far off; if necessary we have got to hazard all, and give our lives that others may enjoy it.' He finished with an analogy of pulling on a rope. 'How long will the pull last? No one can say for certain; it may last a year; it may take longer. But it will [end in] a magnificent party. And we shall win.' All the officers who heard Monty's talk felt invigorated, enlivened and, most importantly of all, confident in victory.[7]

Despite the very different way in which the two generals expressed themselves, in reality Patton and Montgomery shared many characteristics. Neither man lacked in personal confidence when it came to the rightness of his beliefs. Both could be stubborn and vain. Both men believed totally in their command abilities. The two generals went to great lengths to be seen and heard by their men, and both sought to build a cult of personality around themselves. In the Eighth Army in North Africa from August 1942 onwards, and in the 21st Army Group in the run-up to D-Day, all soldiers came to know they were part of Monty's Army. And in Sicily in spring and summer of 1943, every soldier in the US Seventh Army knew they were one of Patton's men. Both generals sought publicity, dressed distinctively, if very differently, and were happy to pose for photographers. Their armies had fought battles alongside one another. Indeed, over the previous year the two generals had become rivals.

Apart from the very different tones of the speeches from the two commanders, there was another big difference. Montgomery was speaking to men who in a little over a week would be splashing ashore on the beaches of Normandy to launch the invasion of Occupied Europe. Patton, however, was in command of a hoax army. He was addressing an army that didn't exist.

Concealment has always been an essential part of military strategy; whether concealing from the enemy your own plans, like where you intend to attack, or not allowing the enemy to know your real strengths or weaknesses, concealment can make the difference between victory or defeat. The lesson was always to keep the enemy in the dark about your intentions. Through concealment an army could exploit the benefit of surprise. And surprise was behind many of the great victories in history, from Napoleon's advance into Italy in 1796, surprising the Austrians and Piedmontese, to the launch of the German attack upon Belgium, Holland and France in May 1940. 'Surprise,' wrote the great theorist of war Carl von Clausewitz, 'becomes effective when we suddenly face the enemy at one point with far more troops than he expected. This type of numerical superiority is quite distinct from numerical superiority in general: it is the most powerful medium in the art of war.'[8]

In the Second World War, due to a remarkable set of circumstances, the process of concealment and surprise was very effectively taken a stage further into deception. Army commanders came slowly to realise that if they could deceive the enemy into believing an untruth, if they could convince Axis commanders into thinking one thing while they were actually planning another, then they could hopefully gain an advantage that would help bring victory on the battlefield. But a successful deception relies on several factors being in alignment. It requires an understanding of the psychology of the enemy, what they are *likely* to believe and what they would never accept. Additionally, it requires complete control over the sources of intelligence that the enemy are likely to pick up and interpret. This is incredibly hard, almost impossible, to achieve. There were various ways in which the Nazi intelligence establishment could gather information about Britain during the war. These included aerial reconnaissance, communication intercepts, open sources like contemporary newspapers and broadcasts, and, of course, the statements from agents or spies in Britain.[9]

However, Britain enjoyed a high level of security during the war in which the country's island status became a key feature of its defence, not only against invasion but also in the control of information.

Britain's coast was to all intents and purposes impenetrable. Also, despite pretences of independence and objectivity, its press and public broadcasting system were in fact carefully controlled by the Ministry of Information. As we shall see, the agents that were sent into Britain by the enemy were almost all 'turned' and reported back only what British intelligence bosses wanted the enemy to hear. These circumstances were unique, however. They never prevailed, for instance, in the decades of Cold War that followed on from 1945.[10]

The final element of deception that was unique to the latter part of the Second World War was that the code breakers at Bletchley Park, initially aided by the Poles and the French, had managed to decrypt the cyphers used by the German government and its military high command. As a consequence, British commanders were able to read and to understand German plans and objectives, both strategic and tactical. From this they were able to build up a deep understanding not only of what Axis capabilities in Europe were, but also of how the German leaders and the nation's military chiefs thought. And in one further and vital development, they were able to read how the misinformation that was being fed to them was being received and interpreted. This was such an unusual circumstance that it gave the Allies an extraordinary advantage. When a deception campaign was conducted it was possible to see if the enemy were taking it up, if they were believing it or dismissing it, how they were reading the disinformation that was being fed to them. As it was once reported to Churchill, Allied intelligence could see if the enemy were or were not swallowing it 'rod, line and sinker.'[11]

The story of the double agents who played a central role in deceiving the enemy in the run-up to D-Day has been excellently told in several popular histories.[12] Their activities will, of course, form an essential part of this story. But the central element of *The Army That Never Was* lies elsewhere, in the brilliant and ingenious use of other remarkable devices to deceive the enemy.

All of this did not come about by accident. It was the result of the extraordinary achievements of a remarkable group of men and women. They were inventive, creative, hard-working and often eccentric. They had the sort of brains that didn't always follow the rule book. They had the ability to think up entirely new scenarios and to work them through step by patient step. One of the pioneers of deception in the Second World War was Colonel Dudley Clarke, who ran 'A' Force, based out of Cairo. We will hear a good deal about him and his achievements. In the mid-1950s he wrote up his memoirs, but publication was prohibited by an establishment that still cherished its secrets. In his unpublished memoirs Clarke wrote of what he called a 'Secret War' that was 'waged rather to conserve than to destroy … and the organisation which fought it was able to count its gains from the number of casualties it could avert.' He further wrote that this Secret War 'was a war of wits – of fantasy and imagination, fought out on an almost private basis between the supreme heads of Hitler's Intelligence (and Mussolini's) and a small band of men and women.'[13]

It is the story of this small band of men and women, from a variety of different backgrounds, and of their inventiveness that is at the heart of this book. If some of it reads like a fiction, that's because it seemed like one at the time and still does today.

Chapter 1

DECISION

'I have never seen him in better form. He ate and drank enormously all the time, settled huge problems, played bagatelle and bezique by the hour and generally enjoyed himself.'[1] So wrote a future British prime minister about his predecessor at the Casablanca conference in January 1943. Harold Macmillan, Minister in charge of Mediterranean affairs at Allied Headquarters, wrote these words after observing Prime Minister Winston Churchill and US President Franklin D. Roosevelt getting on famously and planning wartime strategy for the year ahead.

Churchill had had a torrid twelve months. Initially, when the Japanese attacked the US Pacific Fleet at Pearl Harbor in December 1941, he was euphoric. He was convinced that with the United States in the war as an ally and with the Soviet Union engaged with Nazi Germany in some of the biggest land battles in history, victory was inevitable. What he had entirely failed to realise was how bad the situation would become first, before reaching the long road to final victory. Only three days after Pearl Harbor, the Royal Navy lost two of its most powerful ships, the battleship HMS *Prince of Wales* and the battlecruiser HMS *Repulse*. They were sunk in the sea off Malaya by Japanese torpedo bombers, with massive loss of life. Moreover, it was Churchill who had ordered the two warships to proceed to Malaya without an air escort as a sign of British naval power and as a deterrent to the Japanese. 'In all the war I never received a more direct shock,' he later wrote of his reaction to the news.[2]

One disaster followed another. The Japanese army fought its own form of blitzkrieg down through the Malayan peninsula, surrounding, isolating and forcing into retreat tens of thousands of British imperial troops. In a matter of weeks the Japanese had reached the mighty fortress of Singapore. This had been built up as a naval stronghold for nearly twenty years, a symbol of British power in the region. But its big guns pointed out to sea, and when the Japanese attacked they came from the landward side. After a week of fighting, a British-led force of nearly 100,000 men surrendered to a Japanese force of about one quarter that number. Photos of Lieutenant-General Arthur Percival, the commander-in-chief, walking out to surrender accompanied by a white flag went around the world. As well as being the largest British surrender in history, it was an imperial humiliation of epic proportions. Britain's power and prestige in Asia was shattered for ever. Churchill did not make light of the disaster, saying in a speech to Conservative party members, 'Singapore has been the scene of the greatest disaster to British arms which our history records.'[3]

Another humiliation came when three German warships sailed up the Channel and through the Straits of Dover in broad daylight. Despite attacks from the navy and the air force, and shelling from the heavy guns in Dover, the *Scharnhorst*, the *Gneisenau* and the *Prinz Eugen* got through and finally reached their Baltic ports. The press were up in arms. The normally loyal *Daily Mail* led the attack, comparing the Channel Dash with the Spanish Armada nearly four centuries before. Sir Francis Drake had stopped the Armada then; why couldn't the Royal Navy stop just three ships in 1942? Sir Alexander Cadogan of the Foreign Office wrote in his diary,

'The blackest day of the war yet ... We are nothing but failure and inefficiency everywhere.'[4]

And so it went on. The biggest defeat in British history was followed by the longest retreat, as the Japanese army pushed imperial forces back 900 miles across Burma. Another Asian capital, Rangoon, fell in March, and imperial troops retreated across the mountains, reaching the borders of India in May. The Japanese Navy moved into the Bay of Bengal and attacked merchant shipping, sinking more naval vessels there, including two cruisers, a light carrier and a destroyer. Mostly these were old ships, and once again they had gone into action off the Ceylonese coast (today Sri Lanka) without sufficient air escort. It was another embarrassment for the Royal Navy and resulted in the loss of many more lives at sea.

In North Africa, vast reinforcements were sent out to the newly created Eighth Army, but at the Battle of Gazala in May–June 1942, Rommel outwitted Lieutenant-General Neil Ritchie, captured Tobruk and forced the Allied troops to retreat at speed into Egypt. Churchill was in a meeting at the White House with Roosevelt when news came through that the large garrison at Tobruk had surrendered to a much smaller Axis force. Once again, Churchill felt humiliated, but this time in the presence of the President and his chiefs of staff. 'I did not attempt to hide from the President the shock I had received,' he later wrote. 'Defeat is one thing. Disgrace is another.'[5]

Across Britain, the opinion-recording organisation Mass Observation reported a tsunami of hostility rising up towards the government, who were held responsible for the humiliations. And for the first time Churchill himself, who had been lauded for saving the nation two years before during the Battle of Britain, became the focus for much of this hostility. A young WAAF officer on an RAF station in Lincolnshire recorded for Mass Observation that, 'Up to now the government has been criticised often, but always with the reservation "Churchill's all right". But now Churchill is condemned with the rest.' One of her friends was reported as saying, 'He roars all right in his time, but he's outlived it.'[6] A fifty-year-old man was recorded commenting, 'I reckon Churchill's got too much on his hands to conduct the war properly.'[7] There were hundreds of similar accounts of such thoughts being overheard.

In addition, there was a vote of no-confidence in the House of Commons at the end of January and a vote of censure in June. Churchill won both easily. It would have been remarkable if he had not. But both debates allowed the opposition to Churchill to air its voice and for literally dozens of MPs to express the general sense of grievance felt across the country. Churchill had only himself to blame. Uniquely, when appointed Prime Minister in May 1940, he had also appointed himself Minster of Defence. So, at this point, there was no one else to blame for military failures. In the House of Commons debates, many MPs called for the appointment of a new minister of defence, or at least a minister of production to buck up a national war effort that was demonstrably overstretched and failing in so many directions. Churchill himself, of course, shared some of this sense of frustration, openly humiliating his Chief of the General Staff in front of Cabinet colleagues by demanding forcefully, 'Have you not got a single general in that army who can win battles? Have none of them any ideas? Must we continually lose battles?'[8]

This *annus horribilis* all changed when Lieutenant-General Bernard Montgomery finally did bring a resounding victory, at the Second Battle of El Alamein in early November 1942. And four days after this success was reported, US troops entered the war for the first time in a vast amphibious landing in north-west Africa known as Operation Torch. Three large naval task forces brought men and materiel from the United States and the United Kingdom to co-ordinate landings on three separate beaches, near Casablanca in the west, and at Oran and Algiers further east on the Mediterranean. Some 125,000 men stormed ashore on the first

D-Day of the war in the west. It was a genuine Anglo-American combined operation, another first of the war. The Royal Navy supplied most of the escort vessels and the US provided most of the invasion troops. The landings were successful, and within a few days all three cities and their surrounding airfields were in Allied hands. Now they could start to move eastwards across North Africa. And a few days later, Montgomery's Eighth Army, advancing westwards through Libya, recaptured Tobruk. The Allied armies were on the march and Churchill ordered the church bells to be rung again. They had been silenced at the beginning of the war, and in 1940 their ringing would have been a signal of a German invasion. Now their tolling was a sign of victory.

In Britain, confidence was once again restored in Winston Churchill as war leader. Mass Observation noted a boost in morale and that 'cheerfulness changed to an optimism that was often exaggerated. There was talk of the end of the war being in sight.'[9] An opinion poll in December indicated that satisfaction in his leadership had risen to an extraordinary 93 per cent.[10] Now, at last, maybe the Allies could plan for victory.

It was in this context that Churchill and Roosevelt, with their substantial military entourages, travelled to Casablanca to plan strategy. At last the Allied leaders felt they could choose the time and place to take the war to the enemy. Although there was still a lot of fighting ahead in North Africa, Rommel had been resoundingly defeated and the ultimate expulsion of Axis forces from that continent looked increasingly certain. Additionally, the Red Army was in the process of surrounding and cutting off the mighty German Sixth Army at Stalingrad. In the Pacific the wave of Japanese expansion had been stopped, and although fighting was still raging in Guadalcanal, the prediction was that enemy forces would soon be expelled from the island.

The warm winter sunshine in Casablanca brought relief to the atmosphere within the closely guarded villas where the Allied political and military leaders met. 'Bright sunshine, oranges, eggs and razor blades,' wrote John Martin, Churchill's principal private secretary, describing items that were in abundance in Casablanca but which were in short supply in wartime Britain.[11] The genial social atmosphere, however, could not hide deep divisions between the two Allies.

The British military brass was led by Chief of the Imperial General Staff General Sir Alan Brooke. He was a tough Ulsterman who came from a family that had a long tradition of army service. He was single-minded and determined to do the best thing for the British Army, of which he was effectively the head. He was as tough as nails and his nickname in the Cabinet Office was 'Colonel Shrapnel.' Moreover, he was one of the few generals who could stand up to Churchill's bullying and interference in military matters. No detail was too small to attract the Prime Minister's interest. Churchill was, in today's parlance, a micromanager. But Brooke felt that Churchill meddled in detail of which he did not have full knowledge or competency. Aides frequently reported hearing a shouting match coming out of the room in which they were meeting. But despite raised voices, both men still held each other in great respect. Churchill admired Brooke's professionalism and never overruled him when faced with a clear, determined and persuasive case. Moreover, Brooke not only had the courage to stand up to Churchill but had the capacity for, as one observer noted after a particularly bruising encounter with the Prime Minister, 'shaking himself like a dog coming out of water,' recovering quickly and carrying on without holding a grudge.[12] And Brooke knew that Churchill had extraordinary qualities of leadership that marked him out from other politicians. After one especially loud and infuriating encounter Brooke was overheard to murmur, 'That man!' But then with a sigh to continue, 'But *what* would we do without him?'[13]

Brooke, along with Air Chief Marshal Sir Charles Portal and Admiral Sir Dudley Pound, the chiefs of the RAF and the Royal

Navy, had prepared their position well for Casablanca. They had discussed their views repeatedly and at the conference were in agreement with the Prime Minister. The British position was that 1943 should see a continued emphasis on the fighting in the Mediterranean theatre in the hope of knocking Italy out of the war and undermining the Axis alliance. This would force Germany either to abandon its southern flank or to bring in reinforcements to shore up the Mediterranean and weaken the fighting forces on the Eastern Front, thus helping Stalin's Red Army in its titanic struggle.

The American position was instead to plan for a cross-Channel invasion in northern Europe as soon as possible. General George C. Marshall, the Chief of Staff of the US Army, was a cool customer by comparison to his British equivalent. There were no shouting matches when Marshall was around. But he had a sort of quiet charisma that made other military men listen to him and follow his lead. He inspired men and had a clear vision of how to achieve victory, but he also knew that the President, as Commander in Chief, always had the final say. On a couple of occasions in the war to date, Marshall had disagreed with Roosevelt but still went along with what the President had resolved. His clear sense of duty always overcame his own feelings or beliefs. Marshall's principal conviction was that to defeat Hitler it was essential to launch a major landing in Occupied Europe, almost certainly France, and then sweep through France and advance into Germany. Only this could strike at the heart of the German war machine and bring victory over Nazism. Everything else he regarded as something of a sideshow to what he called 'the main plot.' On the other hand, Admiral Ernest J. King, the Chief of Naval Operations for the US Navy, argued that if agreement over strategy in Europe could not be reached then priority should be given to the war in the Pacific, and shipping resources, in particular landing craft, should be diverted to this theatre. The British chiefs met daily at the Casablanca conference, and the Americans and British chiefs met together twice a day. Both sides reported back to their political bosses every evening.

For several days the British and American military leaders were locked in disagreement. The British argued forcefully that 1943 was too soon to mount a cross-Channel invasion. Firstly, the U-boat menace in the Atlantic had to be defeated so that sufficient supplies of men and materiel could be brought across the Atlantic from America to launch an invasion of France. Secondly, aerial supremacy over northern Europe needed to be won. Attempting a dangerous amphibious operation without securing these two factors would without doubt spell disaster, they argued. Brooke believed the Americans did not yet realise the strength of the German enemy that they were up against. Marshall resented Brooke's arrogant attitude. In his diary, General Brooke recorded 'very heated' meetings with the American top brass that seemed to be 'making no headway.' On the fifth day he wrote, 'A desperate day! We are further from obtaining agreement than we ever were!'[14] The British feared that the Americans would give up on the European theatre and concentrate on the Pacific. The Americans thought the British obsession with the Mediterranean was some sort of imperial hangover in which its leaders were preoccupied with their traditional concern to protect the Suez Canal and the route to India. Making light of these fundamental differences, one senior member of the British military delegation concluded that all they had to do 'was to convince the Americans that ours [ideas] were right and theirs were wrong.'[15]

Meanwhile, Churchill and Roosevelt were getting on wonderfully well in their seaside villas surrounded by palm trees and sweet-smelling bougainvillea. They discussed a wide range of issues. Roosevelt suggested that the ultimate war aim of the Allies should be the 'unconditional surrender' of their enemies. Churchill agreed. Sensing that the Americans were fearful that Britain would pull out of the war after the defeat of Hitler, Churchill on his part agreed to commit to the war in the Pacific after the war in Europe was over. Surrounded by his generals and in daily contact with the President, Churchill was in his element. And Roosevelt seemed less concerned about continuing the war in the Mediterranean than his chief of staff.

After a week of intense arguments, Field Marshal Sir John Dill managed to negotiate a compromise between the British and American military chiefs. Dill was a brave soldier and an inspiring leader of men. He had been Chief of the Imperial General Staff earlier in the war but Churchill found him too cautious and ungenerously nicknamed him 'Dilly Dally.' The Prime Minister eventually sacked him and sent him to head up a liaison unit with the Americans in Washington. Dill both understood the US position and was well respected by the Americans, but he also realised that a premature cross-Channel invasion in 1943 would spell disaster. The compromise thrashed out still put the defeat of Germany as the first priority for the Allies. It was decided to continue with the war in the Mediterranean, and it was agreed that the alternative of a cross-Channel assault was not viable during the next twelve months. After the defeat of the Axis forces in North Africa and the capture of Tunisia, there would be an invasion of Sicily, initially scheduled for July. There was no formal agreement as to what would follow the occupation of Sicily, but the British hoped that it would be an advance on to the Italian mainland with the intention of knocking Italy out of the war.

The build-up of American troops in Britain had so far only brought a small number of American soldiers and airmen across the Atlantic to sample British weather, English hospitality and warm beer. And many of these had now been sent on to participate in Operation Torch.[16] But it was agreed that the build-up should continue and scale up considerably during the next twelve months. Additionally, a new plan for stepping up the bombing of Germany was endorsed. RAF's Bomber Command and the US Eighth Army Air Force would carry out a combined bombing offensive to destroy the German 'military, industrial and economic system' and undermine German civilian morale to the point at which it would be 'fatally weakened'.[17]

The military agreements were rapidly endorsed by Churchill and Roosevelt. It was the high-water mark of British influence over the planning of the war. From this point onwards the vast scale of the US war programme would begin to dwarf Britain's. Whatever Brooke and the other military chiefs felt about the Americans and their failure to understand wartime strategy, Churchill and the British chiefs would soon become junior partners in the relationship. But at Casablanca the American commanders still felt they had been outmanoeuvred, and so finally a momentous decision was made, as something of a sop to them. It was agreed that preliminary planning would begin for a cross-Channel invasion of northern Europe in the spring of 1944.

Although the British war leaders went along with this decision, the Americans felt that their hearts were not really in it. It would be a recurring issue in American thinking that while they were convinced that the Allies had overwhelming firepower and final victory was certain, the British were scared of an invasion that might fail. Nevertheless, the decision to start planning for a major cross-Channel amphibious operation was a crucial moment in shaping the future strategy of the war in Europe, not just for 1943, but for the remaining years of the conflict.

Following the Casablanca conference, a small planning unit was to be established to report to the Combined British and American Chiefs of Staff. Brooke argued that no field commander could be appointed this far ahead, but that a chief of staff could begin planning and that 'a man with the right qualities ... could do what was necessary in the early stages'.[18] The search for the man with the right qualities began almost as soon as the chiefs of staff returned from Casablanca.

Major-General Sir Frederick Morgan was one of the few senior figures in the British Army who did not come from a family with a military background. His father, a wood trader, decided his eldest son should join the army as a sapper because this was the only part of the Edwardian British Army where the pay was sufficient to cover an officer's expenses. Following his father's wishes, Morgan was commissioned into the Royal Field Artillery in 1913 and survived four years as a staff officer on the Western Front, serving in Flanders and on the Somme but suffering nothing more than mild shell shock early in the war and a bout of influenza, Spanish flu, at its end. After the war he volunteered to stay in the army and served in India for many years. Morgan was clever and witty, with a fine sense of humour and a willingness to consider techniques that were new and unorthodox in an army that was still governed by an obsession with tradition. He also had a fine mind and the ability to see issues clearly and to plan ahead effectively. In the late 1930s, as he rose through the ranks he chaffed against the army and the War Office, who seemed to be marching complacently towards war. He later wrote that as an officer not yet in the highest ranks, 'It was not ours to reason why. There was a mighty job to be done in trying to get my little army fit to meet whatever it might be called upon to meet.'[19] And that was what he concentrated on as the clouds of war gathered.

In 1940, Morgan led an artillery brigade that was sent to France to try to rescue the main force of the British Army that was retreating hastily to Dunkirk. It failed miserably and had to evacuate via Cherbourg. Back in England he was promoted through a round of tasks: preparing to throw any invaders who got ashore in Kent back into the sea, defending the coast of Norfolk, commanding British forces in Devon and Cornwall and preparing them to repel any invaders in the south-west of England. Then he was given command first of a division and then of a new corps, I Corps, that was formed to provide support for the Torch landings in November 1942. They were not needed, and despite his extensive planning for amphibious operations in the Mediterranean, despite learning how vital were details like the slope of landing beaches and the range of the tides, and despite having worked alongside senior American generals, including General Dwight D. Eisenhower, his corps was disbanded and Morgan found himself surplus to requirements.

In early 1943, Morgan was put on a list of senior officers looking for roles to fulfil. Being asked by the chiefs of staff to outline the qualities he thought the chief planner for an upcoming invasion should have, he chatted away to them happily about the need to work with the Americans in a truly combined operation and the necessity of coming up with a plan that was detailed, sound and do-able, and not simply a theoretical paper for future debate. It was not just a map problem, but what was needed was a realistic plan of action. He talked of the necessity of formulating an effective organisation of command and ensuring there was a totally reliable supply system backed with adequate stocks of everything that would be needed in such a complex operation. He spoke honestly and forcefully, drawing upon his own recent personal experiences of planning for the Torch landings, but with no thought that he was actually being interviewed for the job himself. However, he clearly articulated exactly what the chiefs wanted to hear, and to his great surprise Morgan was offered the position. This was confirmed after a lunch with the Prime Minister at Chequers. No longer a conventional soldier with a rising career, Morgan was being thrust forward to the cutting edge of the war, reporting to the highest military grouping among the Allied forces. His life was about to change for ever.

Morgan was given the somewhat cumbersome title of Chief of Staff to the Supreme Allied Commander (Designate), which was better when abbreviated as COSSAC. There was no Supreme Allied Commander at this point and would not be for many months to come. But it was assumed that he would be a British general and so his chief of staff, in the normal run of things, would also be British. Morgan seemed the ideal man for the job.

Among the bountiful oranges and warm winter sunshine of Casablanca, a historic decision had been made. The Allies would begin to plan in earnest for the liberation of Europe and an end to the war with Nazi Germany. The plan would soon be named Operation Overlord. It would be one of the biggest, most ambitious and most daring operations of the war. Brooke was still uncertain as to whether it was viable and said to Morgan after his appointment, 'Well, there it is. It won't work but you must bloody well make it.'[20] A plan to invade northern Europe would need to draw on all the tricks of the trade to pull it off successfully.

Chapter 2

DECEPTION

Despite the enormity of the task that lay ahead, Morgan initially was given the barest of resources. In fact, to begin with, the team alongside him consisted of just one aide-de-camp and two batmen. He also inherited a car and driver from his previous position in the headquarters of I Corps. It was a slow start. But he was joined in early March by his deputy, an American, to represent the US in this multi-national operation. General Ray W. Barker had fought in the First World War and, like Morgan, was an artillery man. He was also an anglophile and rapidly came to understand British eccentricities like their passionate diffidence, the habit of understatement and an abhorrence of enthusiasm. American qualities, on the other hand, included a strong spirit of can-do and a passion for talking up a project and displaying great outgoing support for it. Morgan and Barker got on well together and made a splendid team. Before long Morgan was accused by British officials of having 'sold out to the Yanks,' while Barker earned the reputation among his compatriots of being 'sold out to the British.' Thus the two men worked in double harness and created a genuinely combined Allied team.[1]

COSSAC was given premises in Norfolk House in St James's Square, a fashionable corner of London's West End near the headquarters of MI5 and the Secret Intelligence Service, MI6. There were huge decisions that General Sir Frederick Morgan and his small staff had to make. From the beginning he took the view that COSSAC was not just a planning operation but had an executive function to prepare an effective plan of action. He told his team, '"Planning staff" has come to have a most sinister meaning – it implies the production of nothing but paper. What we must contrive to do somehow is to produce not paper: but action.'[2]

Morgan's unit soon began to grow like Topsy. Within weeks it consisted of five branches, for the Army, Navy, Air, Intelligence and Administration. Each branch was made up of both British and American planning staffs, and before long the team had grown to several hundred. They were relatively self-contained in Norfolk House and its satellite buildings. Everything about the unit was, of course, Top Secret, which meant no one could tell their friends or family what they were doing. For some this level of secrecy came easily. For others it was a continuing struggle. COSSAC had its own mess and bar, which was important, as everyone could enjoy a good, well-lubricated meal within the security curtain. It helped to bring cohesion to the unit of many disparate talents, and Morgan remembered that 'pre-prandial and post-prandial discussion seemed at least as productive as more formal sessions round the conference table.'[3]

The problems ahead were enormous. The landings in Europe would prove to be the biggest amphibious operation ever mounted. They would require vast supplies of men and all the materiel of war, including everything needed to feed a growing army and care for the wounded. There were multiple political problems to address. How would the liberation of conquered territory be handled? But most importantly there were the three leading military questions of When, Where and How to launch the invasion?

To the first question, 'When,' they had been given an answer by the decisions reached at the Casablanca conference: the spring of

1944. 'Where' was a massive question. There were options all the way from the Norwegian coast, through Denmark and Holland, to the Pas de Calais and the entire French coast westwards, including Normandy and Brittany, down to the coastline along the Bay of Biscay, from Bordeaux to the Pyrenees. There had been a disaster at Dieppe the previous August, when an ill-planned Anglo-Canadian operation had gone disastrously wrong, leading to the death, wounding or capture of two thirds of those who landed. The fiasco had taught the planners many lessons. These included an appreciation of the need for split-second co-ordination of timing, excellent intelligence and, most of all, the impossibility of trying to seize a well-defended major port town.[4] After an appeal for people to send in personal photographs, picture postcards or other memorabilia about the beaches from Bergen to Bordeaux, the planners were overwhelmed with a mass of evidence showing the slope of the beaches, the scale of the promenade and the existence of seaside buildings, shops, cafes, hotels and villas along the coast. Added to this was an abundance of aerial photographs that were being collected. As well as studying beach defences and the construction of German fortifications along the coast, the photo interpreters were able to assess the steepness of the beaches with the tides in and out, and the ability of the shoreline to support armoured vehicles and supply trucks. It was the beginning of a huge operation to survey from the air hundreds of miles of coastline.[5]

The question of 'How' was even bigger and more challenging. The initial concept was to get something like 30 divisions or 450,000 men ashore over a period of several days. With them would be needed all the materials required to keep an army on the move – ammunition, vehicles, fuel, food and medical supplies. Much of this had to be transported across the Channel in landing craft of one sort or another, not the most seaworthy of vessels, in sometimes stormy seas. The naval support required to protect the invasion fleet from enemy attacks, whether on or below the surface of the water, had to be considerable. And the air cover necessary both to weaken the defences in advance of the landings and then to cover the beaches and the bridgehead as the troops made their way inland was enormous. Would the resources needed for such a combined operation ever be available? The scale of the problems facing Morgan and his growing team of planners was immense.

Several areas could be ruled out quickly as potential landing zones. The Norwegian coast with its mass of fjords would be an impossibly difficult area to land huge numbers of troops. Likewise, the Danish and Dutch coasts, behind which were areas of great sand dunes, would make it difficult to move troops off the beach to advance inland, and in any case they were also out of range of fighter escorts. The Belgium coast offered relatively few good landing opportunities, as did Brittany, where high cliffs favoured the defenders. And the beaches along the Bay of Biscay, although good for possible troop landings, were, again, out of range of the fighter aircraft that would be needed to cover a landing. That left two possible stretches of beach, the Pas de Calais and the Normandy beaches around Caen. The Pas de Calais, the stretch of coast from Calais to Boulogne, had the advantage of offering the shortest crossing route over the Channel and a good starting point for a liberation of occupied France and passage into Belgium, Holland and ultimately into Germany itself. But it was strongly defended from cliffs that overlooked many of the possible landing beaches. Normandy had the disadvantage of being further to get to across a choppy Channel and posed a longer route for an army to advance into the heart of the Third Reich. But its beaches were more suitable for landing men and machines, and there were gaps in the dunes for an army to progress inland. Additionally, on the Cotentin Peninsula, there was the possibility of capturing a port, Cherbourg. After pouring over the details it was clear to Morgan and his team that the choice was between the Pas de Calais and Normandy. After Dieppe, the Allies knew that making this decision was crucial. The right choice could provide a clear route to victory over Nazi Germany and an end to the war in Europe. The wrong choice could realise British fears that a failed invasion would prolong the war for some years.

To assess the number of men that were needed for a successful landing proved an even more tricky calculation. Partly it required an intelligence assessment of the size of the enemy forces that would be defending the beaches. But how could that be predicted one year in advance? Who could guess what numbers would be needed to overcome the unknown? Another way of looking at it was to assess how many landing craft would be available, ranging from smaller LCIs (Landing Craft Infantry) capable of bringing a single platoon of men ashore, to the large LSTs (Landing Ship Tank) that brought armour, vehicles and supplies onto the beaches. From the assumed availability of these vessels it could be calculated how many men could be carried ashore. General Barker wrote that the 'Provision of landing craft ... constitutes a continuing bottleneck which ... must be overcome.'[6] Looking at the challenges from this angle resulted in a scaling down of the landing operation to ten divisions: six to land on the beaches and four airborne divisions to protect the flanks, more like 150,000 men. By the late spring of 1943 some pragmatic refinements to the original plan, with a focus on areas for the invasion, were slowly coming into focus.

Morgan and Barker received their formal orders from the Combined Chiefs of Staff in April. They were tasked with three principal objectives. Firstly, to prepare a 'full scale assault against the Continent in 1944.' Secondly, to make plans for a 'return to the Continent in the event of German disintegration at any time from now onwards with whatever forces might be available at the time.' And thirdly, they were charged with creating 'an elaborate camouflage and deception scheme over the whole summer with a view to pinning the enemy in the west and keeping alive the expectation of large-scale cross-Channel operations in 1943.'[7] So, from the very beginning, camouflage and deception were part of the central plan for Operation Overlord.

By 1943, the British military were becoming very familiar with deception planning. In the early part of the war there had been attempts at several deception operations, necessarily of a defensive nature. Colonel John Turner was the first to actively promote the idea of deception at a senior level. He was an unlikely figure in this science. He had served most of his career in India as a civil engineer before joining the Air Ministry as Director of Works and Buildings in 1931. He was closely involved with the planning and construction of new RAF airfields in the rapid re-armament of the late 1930s and finally retired from his career as a bureaucrat in 1939. Outwardly, his career had been entirely conventional and, frankly, rather dull. But he had several qualities of imagination and vision of which only those who had worked with him closely were aware. Turner was called out of retirement on the declaration of war to run a programme to build decoy airfields to distract enemy bombers. His newly created unit was so secret that it was given no name, simply being called 'Colonel Turner's Department.'

Turner soon became a passionate advocate of deception and came up with a variety of imaginative plans to construct decoy sites away from RAF airfields. Initially, senior figures in the RAF were uninterested in his work, and Air Marshal Sir Hugh Dowding at Fighter Command was positively hostile to what he saw as a distraction to his principal task. He wanted to build real airfields and not decoys, what he called 'substance' not 'shadows.'[8] But Turner was nothing if not determined. His nickname because of his beak of a nose was 'Conky Bill,' and the novelist Dennis Wheatley, who worked with him, described him as a 'quite exceptionally forceful and determined personality.'[9] He drove through the construction of a large number of dummy airfields to divert Luftwaffe attacks from real airfields. They were particularly effective at night, when lights could be switched on and moved around to signify the movement of RAF aircraft on the ground. Several thousand ground crew were trained purely to run these dummy airfields. By the end of 1941 there were about a hundred such sites across the countryside, and they had attracted about 350 attacks away from actual airfields.[10] The only people who were not so happy were the local farmers. On occasions, farm workers asked to be billeted in local towns, which they took to be far less dangerous than being out in rural areas near a dummy airfield.

Not all such deceptions had been a success. Prime Minister Winston Churchill was known for the minutes that he dictated, sometimes several a day, demanding answers or encouraging action. Often he stamped them with his red 'Action this Day' sticker, which meant the recipient had to stop what they were doing and address the issue the PM had raised.[11] Churchill had a real interest in camouflage, and in October 1940 he sent off a minute encouraging his chiefs of staff to use smokescreens to distract bombers from identifying valuable military or industrial targets, as he had seen smoke used very effectively in the First World War. Various experiments were tried, but when the smoke created by burning oil in cannisters combined with a local fog it produced an oily mixture that made workers, often from the factory being protected, cough, feel nauseous and say they could not work. Many complaints were made, and when local anti-aircraft gunners and searchlight operators also complained of developing severe headaches, the use of smokescreens in industrial areas was abandoned.[12]

The first more offensive-orientated deceptions came in the war in North Africa. In December 1940 a new unit was created by the Commander in Chief Middle East, General Archibald Wavell, to concentrate on deception. Wavell was an exceptional man and quite unlike most senior figures in the British Army. He was a brave soldier who had fought in the Boer War, had lost an eye on the Western Front at Ypres and had commanded troops in the troubled mandate of Palestine in the 1930s. But unlike his brother officers, most of whom were inward-looking and rarely took an interest in issues outside the surrounds of their regiment, Wavell had a fertile mind and a multitude of other interests that marked him apart. He loved poetry, and even published an anthology of verses he had learned by heart over the years, *Other Men's Flowers*.[13] He read widely and enjoyed classical literature, had a powerful intellect and was somewhat academic in his approach, delivering a series of lectures on 'Generals and Generalship' at Cambridge University in 1939. He spoke several languages, including Urdu, Pushtu, Persian, French and Russian. He represented the British Army at Soviet Army exercises in 1936 and accompanied Churchill on some of his later visits to Moscow, where he amazed the Soviet military leaders by addressing them in fluent Russian. But he was often a man of few words and could come across as taciturn and withdrawn. One staff officer remembered that having joined his headquarters, he was soon required to accompany Wavell on a long car journey. 'When did you join?' Wavell asked the officer as they set off. Thinking he meant when did he join the army, the officer replied, 'In 1916, sir.' About an hour passed in total silence, and as they approached their destination Wavell turned to the officer again and said, 'I meant when did you join this headquarters?' Anyone working closely with Wavell had to get used to the long silences.[14]

Most of the time Wavell's silences were not an issue and many of his subordinates respected him for them, but his manner didn't work when in the company of a man like Churchill. The Prime Minister's constant talk and ebullience overwhelmed Wavell and left him tongue-tied. This did not impress Churchill, who was usually a good judge of character, but he interpreted Wavell's silence as timidity, and it did the General no good at all.

At the end of 1940, Wavell's Middle East command included the defence of Egypt, East Africa, Palestine (Israel and the West Bank), Iraq and Persia (Iran). He also had responsibility for

Greece and the Balkans. It was an enormous area to command, and Wavell had barely 90,000 men to defend British interests. In contrast, the Italians had more than half a million troops in the region. However, since he had studied the campaigns of Lawrence of Arabia in the First World War, Wavell had developed an interest in unorthodox warfare, and particularly in deception.[15] When Italy joined the war in June, Mussolini believed Britain was on its knees and ordered his army in Libya to advance against the much weaker British forces in Egypt, to aim for the Suez Canal and to cut Britain off from its direct imperial route to India, Asia and the Far East. Wavell set up what was called 'A' Force, and Lieutenant-Colonel Dudley Clarke was brought out from England to become its commander.

Clarke was another able soldier with a highly inventive mind and a puckish talent for deception. He had been born in South Africa, but his family came back to England when he was young. He joined the Royal Flying Corps in 1916 and flew out of Egypt for the rest of the war, building up a love for that country and the Middle East in general. After the war he joined the Royal Artillery and served in Mesopotamia (Iraq), Transjordan (Jordan) and Palestine (Israel and the West Bank) under General Wavell. While there he was put on a death list by an Arab Palestinian hit squad and developed the habit of always sitting in a restaurant with his back to the wall. He attended Staff College at Camberley and after war was declared in 1939 he went undercover in Ireland to research contingencies in case the Germans should invade that country. In 1940 he helped to set up the Commandos as a new force and took part in the first raid on the French coast three weeks after Dunkirk. His sister Dollie was a journalist and author, and his brother Tom went into filmmaking, writing the scripts for some of the finest post-war Ealing Studios comedies, including *Passport to Pimlico* and *The Lavender Hill Mob*.[16]

Dudley Clarke was fair-haired and blue-eyed, had a great sense of humour, was a talented raconteur and had the rather spooky ability to suddenly appear in a room without anyone having noticed him come in. Dennis Wheatley, who worked with him later in the war, described Clarke's 'quiet chuckle which used to make his shoulders shake lightly', but was most impressed by his 'fertile imagination and tireless energy' and the fact that many of his subordinates saw him as a 'near genius'.[17] It was his talents as a creative mastermind, however, that laid down the foundations of Allied deception in the Second World War.

In December 1940, having been called out from London to Cairo by Wavell, Clarke immediately set about planning operations to deceive the enemy. The Italians under Marshal Rodolfo Graziani had advanced cautiously into British-controlled Egypt in September 1940, while Britain was otherwise preoccupied with fighting the Battle of Britain. They advanced only about 70 miles to Sidi Barrani and then stopped, to fortify their position. In the month that Clarke took control of 'A' Force, the Italians were led to believe that there were substantial British troops to their south and they built new defences to protect themselves. Then General Richard O'Connor, following Wavell's orders, launched a counter-attack. It was a stunning success, helped by the fact that the Italians had reduced their front-line defences in order to protect themselves from troops that did not exist. By early February, O'Connor had advanced 500 miles, throwing the Italians out of Egypt, passing through Cyrenaica well into Italian Libya. Some 130,000 Italian troops, along with 400 tanks and 1,200 artillery pieces were captured, and back in Britain cinema audiences cheered as they saw newsreel film of apparently endless lines of Italian prisoners winding off into the distance. It was the beginning of Clarke's success as a principal deception expert.

Clarke's 'A' Force was initially a tiny unit, but there was no room for it in the vast Army GHQ in Cairo, so it was situated alongside a brothel in the busy centre of the city. Even this was a deception. Clarke calculated that no spying eyes would be surprised to see British officers entering a brothel and so no interest would be shown in what they were up to. As there were so few in the deception team to begin with, Clarke allowed the ladies to continue plying their trade on an upper floor.

Wavell decided that with his forces covering such a large area and being so thinly spread, he would use Clarke's deception unit as often as possible to try to boost his limited chances of success. But not every attempt worked as intended. Wavell decided that after his triumph in Libya he would attack Italian forces in Abyssinia. He resolved to attack from the north and so Clarke responded by providing many hints that the assault was coming from the east. In Cairo rumours were circulated, leaks of information were arranged and faked documents were allowed to go astray. The Italians picked up these leaks, but instead of taking troops from the north to reinforce the east, they clearly decided that an attack from the east would be successful and so they withdrew troops and moved them to the north where they could counter-attack when they were ready. This was, of course, entirely the opposite of what was intended. But Clarke learned from this a valuable lesson in deception warfare. In order to succeed, a deception plan must be based not on what you want the enemy to think but on what you want him to *do*. In a later campaign in Abyssinia, Clarke ensured that the Italians knew exactly where the British assault was coming from, and this resulted in there being almost no opposition as they moved all their troops away from the area where the assault was due.[18]

Clarke had striking success in another aspect of his deception work by inventing forces that did not exist in order to exaggerate the size of the Allied armies. Knowing that the Italians expected the British to use parachute forces in Italy, Clarke invented a unit of 500 paratroopers who were apparently being trained to drop behind Italian lines. Photos of troops with parachutes began to appear in the press and rumours spread about the existence of this new unit in areas of Cairo where Clarke was certain they would soon get back to the Italians. They did. He even invented a new name for this unit, the 1st Brigade of the Special Air Service. At the point of its creation no such force existed, but when a few months later Major David Stirling suggested the creation of an unorthodox commando force that would drop behind enemy lines to create havoc at airfields and depots, Clarke supported the formation of the unit as long as it took the name of the force he had invented, the SAS. Having already helped to establish the Commandos, Clarke was involved in the creation of two unorthodox units in the war.

This was only the beginning of his techniques for inventing an Order of Battle that would consistently inflate the size of the Allied armies to deceive the enemy intelligence staff. After inventing brigades, he soon moved on to creating phantom divisions, and then even imaginary corps and entire armies. His ability to create armies out of nothing would later fool not only the Germans but other Allies as well. For instance, two years later, during the early advance in Italy in autumn 1943, there was an urgent need for more men. The Americans were annoyed by the fact that the British appeared to have two armies still stationed in the eastern Mediterranean doing very little, the 9th and 10th, that were urgently needed in Italy. They complained to Eisenhower who was, to put it mildly, irritated to learn that his staff had been deceived. They were simply fake units Clarke had created to deceive the Germans about British strength in the region.[19]

Clarke's contribution to the world of deception had been and would continue to be considerable. He remained a figure who kept himself very much in the shadows, except for one remarkable incident. There was a feeling in intelligence circles that Lisbon and Madrid should be developed as neutral cities where disinformation could be passed on directly to agents sympathetic to Germany. Clarke was asked to investigate the prospects in person. He spent a month living in a luxury hotel in Estoril, just outside Lisbon, in the guise of a British journalist, and made about sixteen separate contacts with German agents. He then went on to Madrid to continue this operation, specifically to target the German military attaché in the Spanish capital. It was here, while working as an undercover agent in rather obscure circumstances, that one of the more bizarre features of the deception game unfolded.

On 20 October 1941, the Spanish police arrested Clarke, who was dressed entirely in female clothing, right down to underwear and high heels. They put it out that they had arrested Wrangel Craker, a journalist for *The Times*. He was soon released and made a rapid retreat to his desk job in Cairo. Exactly what had been going on was never really established. It raised some questions in the formal world of British intelligence, but a quick survey concluded that Clarke was still sound in mind and body and should continue with his work. But among his colleagues, Clarke's curious cross-dressing in Madrid only added to his reputation as a master of deception, disguise and espionage.[20]

In early 1941, Hitler sent his most daring general, Erwin Rommel, to North Africa to help out his Italian ally. With him came a couple of divisions of armoured troops, the basis of what would grow into the Afrika Korps. Thus began the long see-saw war across North Africa, or more precisely across a narrow strip of desert scrub never extending more than about twenty miles inland from the sea. Rommel soon threw the Allied troops, consisting of Australians, New Zealanders, South Africans and Indians as well as Brits, back almost to where they had started their advance the previous December. To add to the humiliation, General O'Connor and his headquarters staff were all captured in the process. Wavell prepared a counter-attack, Operation Battleaxe, in June. But Rommel put up stiff resistance, and after a few days the offensive was called off. Wavell was sacked by Churchill, who was unimpressed by what he saw as Wavell's lack of drive and taciturn nature, which the PM mistakenly interpreted as a sign of weakness and lack of charisma.

Wavell's great contribution to the Allied cause in the war had been to appoint Clarke and give him free rein to develop his ideas on deception. After leaving the Middle East, Wavell was sent by Churchill to India as commander-in-chief. He realised that by the time of his departure, Clarke was doing such good work in the Middle East that he would have to leave him behind. So on arrival in India, Wavell appointed another officer to head up deception operations for him in South-East Asia. This was yet another colourful character, Lieutenant-Colonel Peter Fleming. Fleming had been to Eton and Christ Church, Oxford, and was a traveller, adventurer and best-selling writer. During the 1930s he had been on a river expedition to central Brazil and was also *The Times* correspondent in Peking. At the outbreak of war he returned to the UK and explored the possible uses of irregular warfare, including the training of Home Guard commandos to attack the rear of an invading army. In New Delhi he dreamed up various schemes to deceive the Japanese. Peter Fleming is thought to have helped provide inspiration for his brother Ian's fictional character James Bond.

Back in Egypt, Clarke and his 'A' Force now had to work with a new commander, General Claude Auchinleck. He was less committed to deception as a tactic, but Clarke proved his worth in Auchinleck's first major offensive, Operation Crusader, in November 1941. As Auchinleck prepared his actual offensive along the coast, Clarke created a fake armoured division in the south around Siwa and Jarabub. Trucks were disguised as tanks by fitting a canvas sunshield over the top in order to exaggerate the amount of armour that was available. And, to achieve the opposite effect, canvas shields were fitted over tanks to disguise them as lorries when the intention was to hide the location of armoured squadrons. Fake camps were constructed out of simple camouflage, and tank tracks were artificially created in the desert to make it look from the air as though large numbers of armoured vehicles were gathering. Captured German documents revealed that German intelligence had spotted this and believed it to be real, but it probably did not make much impact on the distribution of their defences. As it was, Crusader was a great success, and imperial troops advanced about 200 miles into Libya, lifting the long siege of Tobruk as they passed the port town. Despite the success, Clarke was not entirely happy with his deception operation and concluded that in order to be effective, a deception plan needed to be worked out in real time alongside the planning for a genuine assault.

The military success was only brief, as Rommel once again took the initiative and recaptured most of the territory that had been lost. After another defeat in the spring of 1942 for the imperial force now called the Eighth Army, Rommel advanced once again far into Egypt, until running out of steam at a small railway halt at El Alamein, only 60 miles from Alexandria. As GHQ prepared to evacuate Cairo, Clarke planned his most ambitious operation yet. Key to this was his remarkable ability to deceive the enemy and make them believe that there were far more Allied troops available than was actually the case. When on the defensive, it might be appropriate to pretend the defending army was weaker than it was to encourage an attack that could be beaten off and so end in disaster for the attacking force. When on the offensive, it was likely to be more effective to exaggerate the strength of the forces available to deter the enemy from making a counter-attack. Preparing a new offensive now came to involve the creation of a comprehensive Order of Battle deception plan.

During 1942, Clarke's 'A' Force grew more and more successful in inflating the strength of British-controlled forces in the Middle East. In spring 1942 the Order of Battle in the region stood at five armoured and ten infantry divisions. Clarke's team set about convincing enemy intelligence that this was actually eight armoured and twenty-one infantry divisions. This was an intricate and complex deception to plan. It involved inventing units that had to have their own insignia and 'existence.' They had to arrive on the scene credibly, by boat or rail transport. If they were within radio interception of the enemy, they had to create sufficient radio activity to fool listeners about their existence. And once created they had to stay in existence, or some plausible explanation for their disappearance had to be invented. Documents captured later that year showed how successful this had been. German intelligence had overestimated the strength of British armoured units by 40 per cent and the infantry strength by 45 per cent. It was a tremendous achievement that resulted in the Axis intelligence believing they were outnumbered and outgunned far more than they actually were.[21]

However, 'A' Force was by no means successful in all its attempts at deception, as we have seen. With Malta's three airfields and deep harbour, the RAF and the Royal Navy were able to use the island as a base to intercept shipping between Italy and North Africa and disrupt supplies to Rommel's forces. So, in the first half of 1942, Axis forces put the island under siege. The relatively small island of Malta had the dubious reputation of being the most intensely bombed place on earth in the spring of that year. Several relief convoys were arranged to get vital supplies of fuel, ammunition and food through to the island. 'A' Force repeatedly tried to deceive the enemy as to the route and objective of these convoys, but not one of the deceptions worked. One convoy had to turn back under repeated Axis naval and air attacks, and another came within a hair's breadth of failure. Also, later in the year, 'A' Force tried to make German intelligence believe that an attempt to retake the island of Crete was about to be made. Leaks were made that units were gathering in Cyprus with the intention of launching an amphibious operation against Crete. However, this had no effect at all on Rommel's planning. He refused to allow any of his units in the Afrika Korps to be diverted to the defence of Crete. Strategically, Rommel believed that the key battle with the Allies would take place in the Western Desert. And, of course, he was correct.

When battle finally came towards the end of October, Montgomery had a clear offensive plan for the reinvigorated Eighth Army he led. The main attack was to take place in the north by XXX Corps, with a series of feints by Indian troops in XIII Corps along the south of the line. Accordingly, 'A' Force tried to make it seem that the opposite was the case. In Operation Bertram, dummy pipelines, supply depots and storage camps were located in the south and camouflaged, but in such a way that enemy reconnaissance would be able to pick up what was going on. About 2,000 dummy vehicles were also assembled along the southern front, while in the north, ammunition dumps and the tanks of XXX Corps were camouflaged as much as possible. The armour was moved into assembly positions at night and hidden by morning.

In a second aspect of the deception plan, everything was done to hide the date of the offensive and make the enemy think it was coming later in November. A summit was publicly arranged, in which all the military heads were supposed to be in Tehran at the time the attack was due. Also, hotels were booked out in Cairo for senior officers, whom it was said would be on leave from their units for a series of sporting competitions. It was assumed that rumours of all this would soon reach the ears of German intelligence. And they did.

Both deceptions were successful. Rommel was away in Germany when the offensive at El Alamein was launched. Believing this to be some sort of diversion, it took Hitler 24 hours to realise it was a major assault and to order him to return at once. Meanwhile, Rommel's deputy, General Stumme, had believed that the attack in the north was only a prelude to a bigger attack in the south, and he left a panzer division and an Italian armoured division facing the southern sector of the line. However, when Rommel returned it only took him a few hours to assess the situation correctly and to decide to concentrate all his armoured units in the north. But by this time, Allied forces had thrust well into the Axis lines, and although the battle went back and forth for another week, in the end the superior firepower of the Allied forces led to a breakout and sent Rommel's army into a rapid retreat along the coastal road.

The Second Battle of El Alamein became one of the turning points in the Second World War. A captured German general, Wilhelm von Thoma, confessed to interrogators that he had been certain the attack would come in the south and had argued to leave the two armoured divisions there, keeping them away from what proved to be the critical confrontation in the north.[22] In his report to the House of Commons on the victory on 11 November, Churchill told the House, 'By a marvellous system of camouflage, complete tactical surprise was achieved in the desert. The enemy suspected, indeed knew, that an attack was impending, but where and when and how it was coming were hidden from him.'[23] Deception had proved its worth on the battlefield. It was only Rommel who seemed impossible to deceive.

By this time 'A' Force had expanded considerably, to about a hundred officers, and, having outgrown its early premises, was relocated to a disused suite in GHQ. Clarke was regularly away, travelling to Iraq or Persia, to East or South Africa, as well as those occasional forays travelling incognito to neutral Lisbon and Madrid, making use of some of his more elaborate disguises. Spending so much time away, he desperately needed a deputy. But the normal process of recruitment of senior officers was not for Clarke. He needed someone he could trust implicitly, and that meant someone he knew and had already worked with.

Noel Wild was a busy staff officer in GHQ. Like Clarke he had joined the army in the First World War, and had ended up in the 11th Hussars, an elite cavalry regiment that had fought in some of the great nineteenth-century engagements at Waterloo and in the Charge of the Light Brigade in the Crimea.

Like Clarke, Wild stayed on in the army post-war and helped the Hussars transition to a motorised unit, and he became a specialist teacher at the Army Tank Driving and Maintenance School at Woolwich. By 1942 he was serving as a staff officer, playing a vital role administering the operational requirements of the Armoured Corps in the Western Desert.

One evening in April 1942, Wild popped into the famous Shepheard's Hotel in Cairo, a well-known meeting place and drinking hole for British officers, to cash a cheque. He was told by a porter that someone wanted to see him at the bar. There he met Dudley Clarke, his old friend with whom he had worked in Palestine in the 1930s. But as the work of 'A' Force was top secret, Wild had no idea what his old pal was up to in Cairo. Clarke offered to buy him a drink. He then proposed a toast to Wild's promotion. Wild was naturally surprised and asked what he was talking about. Clarke explained that he was offering Wild the post of his deputy. Wild explained that he already had a senior job but enquired what the work would involve. Clarke refused to tell him and said he would only find out when he had accepted the job. Wild was clearly sceptical about the offer at first, but it seems that after an evening of drinking at Shepheard's he became convinced and at some point that night accepted the offer.

A couple of days later, sitting in his office still supervising the affairs of the Armoured Corps, the general in command stormed in and gave Wild a severe telling off, announcing that he was giving up an important position and going to a dead-end job where he would play no further significant role in the war. But it was too late for Wild to change his mind. Clarke had the man he wanted, and Noel Wild began with 'A' Force in May 1942.[24]

Wild served as Deputy to the often absent Clarke for the rest of 1942 and throughout 1943. He picked up invaluable experience in the arts of deception. During this time 'A' Force ceased to be an independent unit reliant upon the inventive mind of its commanding officer, and became integrated into a global system with links to London and to intelligence units in Italy, India and South-East Asia. The overall supervision of its activity was no longer in the Middle East but with the Chiefs of Staff and the Joint Intelligence Committee in Whitehall. By 1943, the British Army was learning a lot about the techniques of deception.

Chapter 3

XX: DOUBLE CROSS

A group of Oxford dons enjoy an amiable dinner in college, as they are accustomed to several evenings a week. There are tensions between them, but over the years they have got used to living with each other in their very closed world. After dinner they pass the port and savour the company of a visiting Viennese lawyer and criminal specialist, Professor Ernst Brendel, who is in Oxford to give a series of lectures on criminal law. He tells the dons stories about various gruesome murders he has solved. They hang on his every word, asking questions about each case he reveals. A few minutes after everyone retires for the evening one of the dons is found dead in the Dean's college rooms, murdered. When the Senior Tutor reports his death, an investigation begins. Over the following days, the police are stumped and can make no progress, despite mapping out exactly where everyone was in college in the minutes following dinner. The President is distraught, imagining that the reputation of the college will be ruined. The only outsider in college that night, Professor Brendel, starts to pursue his own inquiries. Soon every Fellow at the dinner becomes a suspect. It seems that in this small, insular world of an Oxford college they all had a motive to kill their colleague. Finally, the visiting Austrian professor tracks down the person he is sure is the killer. He takes the Senior Tutor to him in order to reveal the conspiracy. But what follows is not what they had expected.[1]

If this sounds like the plot of a novel, that's because it is. John Cecil Masterman, a tutor at Christ Church, Oxford, wrote the novel called *An Oxford Tragedy* in 1933. It displays an inventive mind, a wonderful sense of story-telling and an ability to convey the twists and turns of a drama in a compelling way. It also established a new genre of crime fiction based in and around Oxford, a tradition that carried on via Edmund Crispin to Colin Dexter and his Inspector Morse.

John Cecil Masterman's inventive and conspiratorial mind equipped him well for the task he was appointed to in 1941. But his background did not obviously point to a central role in the playing out of Britain's military deception planning. Masterman has been described as 'a cold fish'.[2] He was certainly a serious intellectual and by no means a conventional extrovert, but he was widely admired by those with whom he worked closely. Brought up in a naval family, his father intended for John to follow in his footsteps, but his son quickly realised this was not for him and he dropped out of the Royal Naval College in 1908. In the following year he won a scholarship to read modern history at Worcester College, Oxford, and it was clear that the academic life better suited him. After obtaining a first-class degree he went on to do post-graduate research in Germany and, unfortunately for him, he was there when war broke out in 1914. Consequently, he was interned and spent the whole war at Ruhleben camp, outside Berlin, which he regarded as four wasted and rather shameful years. Post-war he returned to Oxford and rose rapidly up the academic ladder at Christ Church. His work as a historian was combined with a talent for sport, and he played tennis at Wimbledon in the 1920s. But his real love was cricket. He enjoyed the game that was subtle yet sophisticated, played to a set of gentlemanly rules but requiring a meticulous understanding of your opponent. Very much like espionage, in fact. His cricket and his senior position in one of Oxford's most traditional haunts helped him to become what was later described as a 'quintessential Establishment figure'.[3]

In June 1940, Masterman was called up to the War Office, where he became secretary of a committee and must have done an excellent job, as he was seconded to MI5. Thus the Oxford historian moved seamlessly into this secret world that was populated by gentlemen, many of whom he had tutored at Oxford over the last twenty years. Then in January 1941 he was selected to chair the XX Committee, the only grouping using Roman numerals for its title, a pun on Double Cross. This committee would control the information that captured agents would feed the Germans for the rest of the war, so becoming 'double agents', that is agents who pretended to spy for one side but were in fact controlled by the other. Masterman was an amateur in espionage but would lead and co-ordinate a team of professionals.

The use of agents to spy and reveal what the enemy is up to is a common form of intelligence gathering and has been used for centuries. In the years leading up to the Second World War, the first agent that was 'captured' by MI5 was a hard-drinking, Welsh-born engineer named Arthur Owens travelling under a Canadian passport, who settled in England in 1933. The company Owens worked for did secret work for the Admiralty, but his job also involved many trips to Germany. It seems most likely that German military intelligence, the Abwehr, asked him to provide information on his Admiralty contracts at some point in the mid-1930s. But in 1938 he reported this to the Secret Intelligence Service and confessed to his activities for Nazi Germany. SIS allowed him to keep up his German activities, and on the pretext that he was an extreme Welsh nationalist and hostile to England, his reputation grew within the Abwehr. In the summer of 1939 the Abwehr sent him a radio transmitter and informed him he was their principal agent in Britain. On the declaration of war, MI5, whose responsibility was to protect the country from all security risks including overseas spies, decided to take no chances and imprisoned him and his radio transmitter in Wandsworth prison. But MI5 encouraged him to send messages to Germany as though he was still a free man, giving him the codename Snow. Over the next year he received occasional messages and requests for information from the Abwehr, and a small network of agents were sent out to work with him. All of them were captured on arrival and most were 'turned,' that is persuaded to work for British intelligence. But the Abwehr did not give Owens's spying much of a priority until Hitler's blitzkrieg invasion of Belgium, Holland and France left Britain isolated and facing a real threat of being next. The Germans were therefore in desperate need of hard and detailed information about the state of Britain's defences. They needed to get more spies quickly into the United Kingdom to assist Owens.

In the summer and autumn of 1940, several German agents were sent into Britain. Some were dropped in by parachute, some landed by boat, others came as refugees. Most of them came with an introductory link to Snow, so MI5 found it relatively easy to track them down and round them up. Even if they had no link to Snow these enemy agents were pretty easy to spot. Few of them had any real training in espionage or preparation for life in Britain. One Dutchman, who crossed the Channel in a small dinghy at night, wandered into the nearest village and, knowing nothing of British licensing laws, went into the village pub at 9am and asked for a bottle of cider. The landlady reported the stranger to the local police, who immediately arrested him. Another agent, a Swede, was dropped by parachute, but the radio he was carrying around his neck struck his chin during his descent and knocked him out. He staggered around on the ground for a bit and then collapsed. A local farmhand spotted his feet sticking out from under a bush, and the Swede admitted being a spy and seemed pleased to be handed over to the police.

The arrested spies were all taken to an interrogation centre located in a large Victorian house at Ham, near Richmond Park in Surrey, run by MI5.[4] Here they were rigorously interrogated. After this they were given a choice. Either they would be executed as a traitor, or they could turn and work for the British. Among the 25 agents sent to Britain in the autumn of 1940 there were a few determined Nazis who refused to work for Britain. They were either executed or imprisoned for the rest of the war. Most of the other agents, however, knowing what their fate would be, agreed fairly quickly to be turned and to pass on information as instructed to do so, in other words to become double agents.

As the Battle of Britain turned into the Blitz, the British intelligence establishment had to work out how to use double agents like Snow and his network. Firstly, there were the practical details to work out, like the provision of safe houses, the use of properly monitored communications and how to supply credible access to information that was intended to be passed on to the enemy. Most agents were asked to spy on British military installations or the movement of troops, all of which were usually secret. So the agent had to be given some believable way of finding out what was happening, like supposedly being given a job as a waiter in an officers' mess where he could pick up gossip, or a junior clerical role in some government department that would offer an opportunity to gather stray nuggets of information. All of this had to be carefully supervised by a case officer who was also required to maintain something like a 24/7 watch on the agent, as their trustworthiness and reliability could not initially be relied on.

But then there were the far more difficult challenges. In order for an agent to be believed by the enemy he would have to be able to pass on accurate information, but using details that would not harm British interests. This was called 'chickenfeed' in the trade. But this had to be carefully controlled. If asked, as one agent codenamed Tate was, to provide information about which factories in Coventry had been put out of action by the bombing of that city and which were still functioning, what should he pass on? Lives were at risk here. If he reported that one particular factory was still in production it might prompt a return of the bombers to destroy it. If, on the other hand, he reported that all factories had been destroyed but German aerial reconnaissance was able to report that several were still active, then his credibility as an agent would be undermined and his value to Britain as a double agent destroyed.[5]

The branch of MI5 that dealt with the double agents was called B1A. Its head was one of the more dynamic and colourful figures working in the intelligence establishment. Lieutenant-Colonel Tommy Argyll Robertson was universally known, even by his subordinates, as 'Tar', after his initials. He was a larger than life figure, with matinee-idol good looks and was 'immensely personable … with a charm that could melt an iceberg' according to one of his colleagues.[6] He was often to be spotted puffing on a pipe, wearing the distinctive tartan trousers of his former unit, the Seaforth Highlanders. Robertson had been the first to point out that imprisoning or executing captured spies provided no long-term value to British intelligence. Instead, if they could be turned they would be of immense help to the Allies. If a dialogue could be set up with their controllers in Germany then the questions they were asked would be a useful guide as to what the Abwehr wanted to know, and the answers they gave could become a vital part of any deception campaign. It was clear that a live spy could be a lot more use than a dead one, even if they were a lot more trouble.[7]

Robertson needed a team of dedicated and adroit operators to control the double agents. Once a man had agreed to work for Britain, his case officers had to deliver regular reports to the Abwehr. These reports had to have a basis in new, reliable and accurate 'chickenfeed' to make them trusted, but were served up with lashings of deception. It was a subtle and skilful art for the minders of the double agents to maintain this balance. They had to know the agents they controlled and write in a style or fashion that was consistent with what the Germans expected from them. They had to know about psychology and understand what motivated a man or woman to spy. They had to encourage and cajole without alienating the agent they were working with. They had to understand the fine line between truth and falsehood. And they had to know what truthful information could be revealed in order to sustain the Germans' faith in their agents. The work and inventiveness of some of the minders would become as remarkable and intriguing as the deceptions they were asked to put across.

However, Robertson himself did not have the authority or the knowledge to decide what information could be passed on to the enemy and what could not be. This required direction from a more senior organisation. The problem was that the military themselves had a tendency to want nothing whatsoever revealed to the enemy and to prefer that all operational matters remained top secret. However, this clearly did not meet the needs of the intelligence establishment, who wanted to run credible agents. As a consequence, two separate groups were set up in January 1941 with the remit to decide what could be revealed as 'chickenfeed'.

Firstly, there was W-Board, which consisted of the directors of intelligence of the Army, Navy and Air Force, and the directors of both MI5 and MI6 and other senior figures. Its secretary was Lieutenant-Commodore Ewen Montagu. But this group was too senior and its members were too busy to handle the day-to-day supervision of what information could be revealed to the double agents. So, secondly, the XX Committee was formed to carry out this role, with Masterman its chairman.

There were still several bureaucratic hoops for the XX Committee to jump through before it could become truly effective. There had to be some sort of political approval for the idea of passing information on to the enemy via agents who were, in theory, working for enemy intelligence. When Churchill was consulted on this, in a meeting that was never minuted so those present could deny it had ever taken place, the Prime Minister instructed the representative of the committee that 'obviously there was a job to do and he should get on with it'. But if ever there was a row, they would never be able to claim official authorisation for the committee's actions.[8]

As a consequence, the official structure to manage double agents slowly came into place during 1941, in which W-Board effectively deputised to the XX Committee decisions about what could be passed on to the enemy. Masterman later wrote that 'Nothing in the nature of a charter or even a directive was given to the Committee', which made it 'institutionally unsound'.[9] But in a strangely British sort of muddled way, this turned out to work well. The committee would meet in absolute secrecy every week, on Thursday afternoons at MI5 headquarters, 58 St James's Street, in the centre of London's 'clubland', until the end of the war in Europe in May 1945. Its members worked closely together. At first there was a tendency for tension between MI5 (internal security) and MI6 (external security) as to who should ultimately control double agents. MI5 wanted control when the double agents were in the UK and MI6 wanted to control them if they travelled abroad to meet their controllers. This took some time to resolve but was finally sorted out. Everyone came to know what everyone else in the intelligence establishment was doing, and Masterman wrote that 'the control of the double agents system was an example of harmonious working between a large number of services and different departments'. Masterman concluded: 'Bad men make good institutions bad and good men make bad institutions good.'[10] Clearly the right men were in XX Committee, and the decisions they reached were passed on to B1A, where Tar Robertson and his team of minders actually handled the double agents. But there was still a problem. If the double agents were to be fed information or disinformation to deceive the enemy, someone still had to decide what strategy was going to be implemented in order to resolve which deception to feed to the Germans. While the war was primarily defensive this was barely an issue. But as the war progressed and planning began for offensive strategies, an overall policy was desperately needed.

So one final piece of the bureaucratic jigsaw was required to complete the process of setting up an effective strategic deception policy. As we have seen, in the Middle East, General Wavell had instructed Lieutenant-Colonel Dudley Clarke to form his 'A' Force in Cairo to control deception planning in the region. This was already working well when Clarke had to come to London in October 1941. The Joint Planning Staff took advantage of his visit to ask him to report on what he had been doing. They were so impressed they decided to establish a similar organisation in London. Its Controlling Officer would not be like a committee chairman to co-ordinate views, but instead a senior officer who had the authority to prepare plans and to execute them. The chiefs of staff approved and the first Controlling Officer appointed was Colonel Oliver Stanley. After a distinguished military career in the First World War, Stanley had gone into politics and was President of the Board of Trade in Neville Chamberlain's government, and from January 1940 Secretary of State for War. Despite having both highly relevant political and military experience, his title 'Head of the Future Operational Planning Section of the Joint Planning Staff' did not really signify to others the importance of his role. He was given little support from the intelligence chiefs and was never even told of the existence of the double agents.

Stanley had one success when he encouraged a deception plan in December 1941 to misinform the Germans that an attack was going to be made on the Norwegian coast. Troops were reported to be in training and Norwegian interpreters were openly sought out in London. Hitler was always sensitive about possible attacks on his northern flank in Norway, but whether the misinformation leaked to the Abwehr about an imminent operation had any impact on diverting troops to the Norwegian front was not clear. In any case, Stanley felt frustrated in his role and stepped down in April 1942.

His resignation coincided with the first joint military plans with the American chiefs of staff and the pressure from them to consider an invasion of northern Europe (pressure which, as we have seen, Churchill and the British chiefs successfully deflected until the Casablanca conference). Stanley's replacement would therefore arrive at a critical moment in war planning. The man chosen as the new Controlling Officer was Lieutenant-Colonel John 'Johnny' Bevan. Educated at Eton and Christ Church, Oxford, Bevan had fought in the First World War and had won the MC on the Western Front. Churchill met Bevan in 1918 when he had presented to the Allied political and military leaders an intelligence assessment of the German Order of Battle following Russia's withdrawal from the Great War after its revolution. He had correctly predicted the number of troops the Germans would divert from the Eastern to the Western Front, and Churchill remembered being much impressed by him. In the 1920s and '30s, Bevan had become a successful stockbroker, first for Hambros Bank and then for his father's City firm. In 1939 he had returned to the military on the outbreak of war and had gone on to work in MI5. He was a workaholic who brought great energy to his new position as well as a creative mind and the confidence to take the initiative. Dennis Wheatley, who would work closely with him, later wrote: 'His most remarkable feature was a very fine forehead, both broad and deep; and one of his greatest assets an extraordinarily attractive smile.'[11] During periods of intense pressure, he suffered from insomnia and would come to work exhausted and irritable. At times like these he could be rude and curt to those he was working with. But most of his staff found it easy to forgive these lapses of behaviour, and for the rest of the time he was charming, modest and great company at lunch or dinner when taking time off from a weighty workload. He was also very well connected. His wife was the daughter of the Earl of Lucan, one of two sisters, and the other was married to General Sir Harold Alexander, who thus became Bevan's brother-in-law. And he was a good friend of General Ismay, Churchill's liaison with the chiefs of staff, and with General Alan Brooke, the Chief of the Imperial General Staff, with whom he shared a passion for birdwatching. So Bevan could comfortably move in privileged and high social and military circles. In May 1942, Bevan took over the organisation that was now to be called simply the London Controlling Section, seeking even to deceive its own importance by its anonymous-sounding name.

The chiefs of staff decided to make the London Controlling Section the central body for the planning of British deception operations around the world. The body that helped to bring it into existence, 'A' Force in Cairo, would now be its junior and report to it. The London Controlling Section was directed to: 'Prepare deception plans on a world-wide basis with the object of causing the enemy to waste his military resources.' Its specific brief said it was 'not to be limited to strategic deception alone but [was] to include any matter calculated to mystify or mislead the enemy wherever military advantage may be so gained.'[12] As if to emphasise its central role, the London Controlling Section was moved to the basement under the War Cabinet Offices at Storey's Gate, in the area known as the War Rooms.[13] Bevan would enjoy close proximity to the various groups that would control Britain's war effort – not just the chiefs of staff and the Joint Intelligence Committee, but also, of course, to the Prime Minister and his staff. And the Americans agreed to set up a similar operation in Washington that would be called the Joint Security Control, to work in close liaison with this group in London. The process of deception in Britain ranged widely from getting articles into newspapers to mislead the enemy, to planting questions in the House of Commons that Churchill could answer by providing further disinformation. And in one final detail, Bevan was also given the task of ensuring that Churchill's many travels across the Atlantic, to the Middle East and later to Russia, all took place under cover and were not revealed until they were over.

Around Bevan there gathered a talented and imaginative staff of eccentric conspirators and deceivers. They included Ronald Wingate, an ex-Indian Civil Service commissioner and cousin of both Lawrence of Arabia and Orde Wingate, one of Churchill's favourite commanders, who led the Chindits in daring operations behind enemy lines in Burma. Ronald Wingate had enjoyed a dazzling career as an agent of Empire, negotiating treaties giving Britain a series of protectorates over the oil-rich sheikdoms of the Gulf and taking senior positions in Rajputana and Quetta in India. He ended as Governor of Baluchistan, in which he would ride in a carriage escorted by a troop of lancers. But he also had several homely pursuits, which included golf, fishing and polo. He spoke Arabic, Urdu and French and became close to General de Gaulle. He was a great bon vivant who knew many of the finest restaurants in Europe, and he was excellent and entertaining company. When he joined the London Controlling Section he was 54, the oldest member of the team, and within months he was cleared for access to the deciphered Ultra Intelligence and was appointed as Bevan's deputy.

Also in Bevan's office was another author, Dennis Wheatley, who brought the ingenious mind of a thriller writer to all the operations he dreamed up. He had served in the Royal Artillery in the First World War but had been invalided out after being gassed at Passchendaele. He ran the family wine business for many years until becoming a full-time writer in the 1930s. His thrillers and novels about the occult and satanism soon became bestsellers in Britain and around the world. One of them was turned into a film produced by Alfred Hitchcock in 1934.[14] At the beginning of the war Wheatley wrote a series of papers for the War Office, and it was after a meeting there that he was invited to join the team that would start planning schemes to deceive the enemy, as an honorary RAF officer. His appointment was unusual in that he was already a well-known figure, although probably few senior military men had actually read any of his thrillers. Initially, when he joined at the beginning of 1942, there was little to do, and Wheatley was known for taking long, wine-fuelled lunches that sometimes went on for much of the afternoon. Wheatley was something of a snob who loved, with his wife Janet, to entertain important and influential colleagues at his flat at Chatsworth Court in smart Kensington. He was a great lover of the London club scene where many senior figures took lunch. Top civil servants would head for White's, Boodle's or the Garrick. Senior officers were members of the Senior, the Cavalry or the RAF Club. Bevan and Wingate were members of Brooks. And not happy with the drab surroundings of his basement office, Wheatley brought in his own oval dining table and Chippendale chairs and about £800 worth of silk Persian rugs to cover the government-issued linoleum.[15] But the leisurely pace of life in deception planning all changed when Bevan took over in May 1942. The whole pace of inventive scheming went up a gear and Wheatley was at the heart of many of the operations over the next few years, some so fantastic they would seem far-fetched even in fiction.

Another piece in the intelligence jigsaw was based at the Secret Intelligence Service, or MI6, headquarters at Broadway Buildings opposite St James's Park underground station. MI6 collected information about foreign affairs for the British government by gathering information abroad about political, economic, aviation, military and naval matters. The organisation also tapped the telephone lines of foreign embassies in London. MI6 usually operated abroad inside the countries where it was gathering intelligence. But from 1940 onwards much of Europe was cut off from MI6, and so Section V of the organisation began to listen in to radio messages between enemy intelligence services. In this group was another Oxford man who had also been an undergraduate at Christ Church, the young historian Hugh Trevor-Roper. In 1940, Trevor-Roper published a highly regarded book on Charles I's Archbishop of Canterbury, William Laud. Later that year he moved from studying the seventeenth to the twentieth century by joining the Radio

Security Service of MI6. He would soon build up an immense knowledge of the workings of the Abwehr, and this gave him a close understanding of how the German intelligence system operated. Trevor-Roper was a rather intense intellectual who soon became known as a bit of a troublemaker within MI6. He was not impressed with the calibre of most of the intelligence professionals within the organisation and did not hesitate to let his views be known. His outspokenness gained him many adversaries inside MI6. Many of them accused him of being too close to the 'enemy,' by which they did not mean the Germans but rather their intense rivals in the intelligence establishment, MI5. Sir Stewart Menzies, known as 'C,' the head of the Secret Intelligence Service, believed in Trevor-Roper and admired his talent, and it was his support that probably kept him in post. Another ally in these troubled bureaucratic wranglings proved to be the head of the MI6 section dealing with Spanish affairs, a man who was highly regarded in all sections of the intelligence establishment at the time, Kim Philby.[16]

Philby had been a journalist before the war, working for, among other publications, *The Times*, for whom he had reported on the Spanish Civil War. It was in the mid-1930s that, having dallied with communism at Cambridge, he began to work as an agent for Moscow and sent the Soviets many reports from Spain. In 1940 he got a short-lived job with MI6 training potential saboteurs, but that part of the organisation was transferred to the Special Operations Executive (SOE) later in the year. In 1941 Philby transferred to Section V of MI6, the branch concerned with counter-intelligence, and because of his knowledge of Spain and Portugal was put in charge of the unit that dealt with Iberian affairs. Unlike Trevor-Roper, Philby fitted in wonderfully well at the heart of British intelligence. He was charming, hard-working, efficient, admired by everyone he worked with and was later called 'the blue-eyed boy of the establishment'.[17] Everyone imagined him to be a loyal

British patriot, but in reality he was passing on information to his NKVD (the forerunner of the Soviet KGB) controllers. He passed on details of, among other operations, the use of double agents by MI5. The only problem with the information he passed on was that much of it was not believed in Moscow. The NKVD could not believe that the British had allowed a man with previously known communist sympathies to take a senior role within MI6. Also, the fact that Philby and the other members of the Cambridge Five spy ring (Anthony Blunt, Guy Burgess, Donald Maclean and John Cairncross) were all passing on similar intelligence made the NKVD believe that they were double agents who had been turned by the British and were sending them identical disinformation. It was only at the end of the war that Philby began to supply the Soviets with intelligence that really excited them.

Looking back on this 80 years later, it is remarkable how many of those who entered the world of intelligence during the war were from Oxford. And indeed it is even more surprising how many had attended Christ Church or had been students of J.C. Masterman. These were the days when the old school or college tie still counted for a lot and was usually seen as a badge of honesty and respectability. When staff had to be recruited quickly, knowing a man's college was usually thought to be a sign that he could be trusted. Trevor-Roper told another ex-Christ Church man in intelligence with a certain degree of self-mockery that 'although sensible people *can* be found who have come from other colleges … it is my settled conviction, or prejudice, that one can be sure of Christ Church men. Indeed in the hour of battle, I only really feel safe if I have a Christ Church man on my right and on my left.'[18] It was, of course, this sort of prejudice that meant someone like Kim Philby escaped suspicion for so long. Although a Cambridge man, he had the same qualities and was, as it would later be expressed, 'one of us' and so it was believed he *must* be loyal and reliable.

Equally remarkable is that within a group who outwardly appeared to be such quintessentially conventional and establishment types, there emerged so many varied and inventive ideas. From the fertile minds of the intelligence teams tumbled all the plans and schemes needed to sustain the imaginative deception operations that followed. Britain had of necessity become a creative place during the war years. People had to find ways of making do with what they had and improvise accordingly. This was true on the Home Front, where everyone shared similar deprivations and had to be able to 'Make Do'. It was the case in the military, where the enemy had a massive superiority of men and materiel and every trick was needed to gain an advantage. And it was also true in the field of science, where many astonishing advances were made in the areas of short-wave radar, aviation, operational research and communications. The whacky or eccentric boffin became a stereotype during the war, depicted in films and popular culture as someone whom few people could understand but everyone could accept was coming up with new ideas for the technology that could help to win the war.[19]

This same spirit of inventiveness and of embracing new and different ideas also ruled in the shadowy worlds of intelligence gathering and deception planning. It was certainly also true in the field of aerial reconnaissance and photo intelligence, where by simply studying two-dimensional black and white photographs, the inventive minds at RAF Medmenham created a whole new science of observing, measuring and creating three-dimensional worlds with which to interpret what the enemy was up to. To a degree this creativity came from the top, and Churchill certainly gave considerable encouragement to his military commanders and scientific boffins to explore every avenue that would potentially provide some gain or advantage against the overwhelming power of the enemy.[20] But it's frankly difficult to imagine that today so many conventional figures would be so willing and eager to engage with and encourage new thinking and radical ideas.

During the first two years of war, in Washington, the chiefs of staff had yet to be convinced of the value of large-scale deception operations. Despite this, prompted by the Brits, they had established the Joint Security Control. Its task was not simply to manage deception, but also to control security and prevent leaks relating to upcoming military plans. In October 1942, the first top-level conference was held in London, and a couple of months later John Bevan followed this up with a visit to Washington. It was agreed that the British would manage deception operations in Europe, the Mediterranean and the Middle East, where plans were already being made and operations being run. The United States would take on all deception operations in the Pacific, the Far East and China. India and Burma would remain in the British sphere of activity.

The key figure in Washington when it came to the development of deception planning was Lieutenant-Colonel William Baumer, who had grown up in the Midwest as part of a down-to-earth family who believed in hard work and the simple things in life. Baumer had leapt at the chance of a cadetship at West Point and flourished there, not only in his military training, but he also discovered a skill for writing. He would write sports reports and later continue to freelance as a writer for the *New York Times* on different aspects of army life. He returned to West Point as a lecturer on military history in 1938, and while there got to know General George Patton well. In 1942, Baumer was transferred to the central army planning staff, and towards the end of that year he moved into offices in the newly constructed Pentagon building. At the beginning of 1943 he was allocated to deception planning, which he described as 'fascinating work' but as 'something new to the War Department and to our Army: the British have a start on us of perhaps a year ... No one knows where it will lead.'[21]

Baumer studied everything he could find about deception and the various British operations, and soon became convinced of its value. He would continue to argue the case for deception for two years, often against his more sceptical bosses in the Pentagon.

Meanwhile, back in Britain during 1940–41, the number of double agents being recruited was growing. And none of them came from Oxford or Cambridge. In December 1940 a Yugoslav businessman, Dusan 'Dusko' Popov, arrived in London from Lisbon. Popov was rich, something of a dilettante who loved partying, and was deeply attractive to women, a fact of which he was very aware and happy to exploit. Through his import-export business he had the ability to travel around parts of Europe. Popov was recruited into German intelligence early in 1940 by an old university friend, Johann 'Johnny' Jebsen, who worked for the Abwehr, almost as a favour to act as an agent and spy in Britain. Popov was allocated a handler whom he knew as Major Ludovico von Karsthoff. Von Karsthoff seemed to enjoy the same sort of lifestyle as Popov and the two men got on well. Von Karsthoff instructed Popov in the use of codes and in the value of photography and the ability to disguise what was being photographed, for instance by having a pretty girl stand in front of an object or building to avoid attracting suspicion. But Popov had always been an anti-Nazi, and in Belgrade he contacted MI6, who had recognised his value and suggested he should keep up his contacts with German intelligence. Before long he was recruited as a double agent. On arrival in Britain he was assessed by MI5. They were initially suspicious of Popov, thinking he might be a genuine German agent trying to deceive them. But finally they were persuaded he was genuine, although they were concerned about his excesses. They thought he was lazy and too drawn to the high life and the pursuit of glamorous women. Nevertheless, MI5 took him on and eventually allocated him the codename Tricycle.[22]

Popov had been paid well in US dollars by the Abwehr, who had given him a long questionnaire with a list of points they wanted information on in Britain. Regarding the Home Front, the Germans wanted to know where the principal food depots were and they asked him to explore the general state of morale in Britain. Regarding the Army, they wanted details of coastal defences, the locations of military headquarters and the order of battle of troops in Britain. For the RAF, they wanted details of aircraft construction and the location and output of key factories. For the Navy, they wanted to know what ships were being built and where; how many ships had been damaged by mines and what was coming from the United States and where it was arriving. Popov was fed a certain amount of information by his B1A case officer, Bill Luke, some accurate and some false, and he went back to Lisbon on several occasions over the next six months to hand this on to Von Karsthoff. Popov started to live a weird double life, partly in a smart Lisbon hotel, the Palacio in Estoril, passing on information to his German minders, and partly at the Savoy in London, discussing what he could reveal with Bill Luke. However, from his German meetings, B1A learned a good deal about the Abwehr operation in neutral Lisbon. They also invented two sub agents for Tricycle. Balloon was supposedly a former army officer with a grudge who provided economic and industrial intelligence, and Gellatine was a lady well connected in London society whose indiscretions revealed much high-grade political gossip. Neither of them, of course, existed in reality. The Abwehr seemed pleased with Tricycle, but to MI5's disappointment the Germans decided to send him to America in August 1941 to establish a network of spies there.

MI5 managed to get agreement from the FBI to continue to 'run' Tricycle but all did not go well. Popov was an erratic figure whose extravagant lifestyle was tolerated by MI5 but did not go down well with the rather more puritanical FBI, and after a while they refused to hand over any more chickenfeed. The Abwehr lost confidence in Popov and ordered him back to Lisbon for questioning. After a tense encounter, they decided to return him to Britain, fortunately for MI5. Tricycle would turn out to be an unpredictable individual but a thoroughly reliable double agent.

Another European who had experience of living in Occupied Europe was Roman Czerniawski, an ex-Polish intelligence officer who had fled to France after the fall of Poland. He was short in stature but big in personality, with an attractive face and smiling eyes. As a Polish patriot he hated both the Germans and the Russians with a great intensity. In occupied France he had formed a French Resistance group that had grown into a large network known as the Interallié. It soon included about 50 agents, including railway workers, policemen, ex-French Army officers, criminals and housewives. Czerniawski wanted to spy on everything, German troop deployments, ammunition dumps, radio and radar installations, every aspect of the German war machine in France. Long and detailed reports were smuggled out to the Polish government in exile in London, where they were passed on to MI6. But in November 1941 an informer passed on names and details of the Interallié to the Gestapo. Czerniawski was arrested in his flat on Montmartre and imprisoned. He was repeatedly interrogated by Hugo Bleicher, the head of the Abwehr in Paris.

His imprisonment lasted for over eight months, and Czerniawski was certain on several occasions that he was about to be tortured and then shot. But Bleicher had all the names he needed of the Interallié and had rounded them all up. He had other ideas for Czerniawski. He wanted him to spy for the Abwehr. In a bizarre negotiation Czerniawski said he would spy for Germany only if he was assured that the Nazis respected Poland's identity and would restore its independence after the war. When assured of this he agreed to act as an agent for the Germans. In October 1942 he was allowed to leave prison and was smuggled out of France into Britain, where he was interrogated by Polish intelligence officers. For six weeks he kept up a facade that he had escaped from the Paris prison and had found an underground network to smuggle him to England. Then he handed over a report to his Polish minder confessing that he had agreed to spy for Germany and now wanted to become a British double agent. He called this 'the great game'. In despair they handed him over to MI5, where Christopher Harmer, one of the unit's case officers, spent four days assessing Czerniawski to decide whether he was truthful in now wanting to spy for Britain and if he could be trusted as a double agent. He concluded that he was genuine and was motivated as 'a loyal and patriotic Pole' to fight Germany in whatever way he could. Others in the intelligence establishment were more wary. J.C. Masterman at the head of the XX Committee was particularly suspicious of Czerniawski's motives and wrote that it was 'in all respects a complicated case'.[23] Finally, Harmer's arguments prevailed and Czerniawski began work as a double agent. He was given the codename Brutus, one of the great betrayers of ancient Rome who had been the last to stab his commander, Julius Caesar. Clearly, by giving him this codename Harmer was still uncertain about Czerniawski's reliability.[24] But he would turn out to be an invaluable agent for Britain who, as a Polish officer, could appear to operate at a relatively senior military level within the Allied planning apparatus.

Another European recruit was Juan Pujol Garcia, a Catalan chicken farmer who had grown up in a wealthy, liberal Spanish family.[25] He later claimed to be completely apolitical. But Pujol held a deep hatred of extremism and of tyrants who wanted to impose their extreme views on others. During the Spanish Civil War he had joined the Republican side. However, he hated service in the army and defected to the Nationalist cause in an attempt to escape the horrors of front-line service. He later claimed he had done this in order to avoid the injustices and the bullies he found in the Republican military system. Pujol was, in reality, a mass of contradictions. He was a graduate of Spain's most distinguished poultry school but hated chickens. He was fascinated by the military but detested military service. He went along with Franco's fascism but was more inclined to support liberal values.

When the Second World War began Pujol sided with Britain in its struggle against the oppressive Nazi regime. Feeling his life had been nothing but disappointments and failure, he vowed to help the Allied cause and so visited the British Embassy in Madrid to offer his services as a spy. But 'walk-ins', as they were called, volunteers who just turned up and said they would spy for you, were notoriously unreliable, as it was so easy for them to be enemy plants. So no one showed any interest in the Catalan chicken farmer. Pujol decided he would be given a better welcome if he were already spying for Germany and could offer to become a double agent. So he turned to the Abwehr office in Madrid, whose officials again showed little interest at first in his offer to spy for them in England. By now he was determined to proceed and persuaded the Abwehr officials that he had a visa to travel to London as a Spanish diplomat. They at last decided to take him seriously and gave him instructions in the use of invisible ink and set up a system for getting letters back from him via Lisbon. They gave him the codename Arabel and instructed him to recruit a network of sub-agents when he got to London.

But Pujol had no visa for England; he had simply invented this as a ruse to be accepted as a spy. Instead, he pretended to be in Britain, while he was sending letters to the Abwehr from a flat in Cascais, just outside Lisbon. Armed with a Baedeker's tourist guide to Britain, Bradshaw's railway timetables and a copy of a Portuguese book about the Royal

Navy, he wrote long, vivid descriptions that he thought were the sort of thing a spy in a foreign country would come up with. His style was long-winded and intensely verbose, full of sub-clauses and long asides.[26] Pretending to be travelling around the country, he reported from his tourist guide on the locations of imaginary military camps, and from his naval book he described the coming and going of ships from British ports, being careful not to name the ships in case the Germans had already sunk them. From information he found in a library book about pre-war British industry, he listed the locations he said he had discovered of what he claimed were various war factories. Sometimes, however, his fertile imagination ran away with him. He reported that foreign embassy staff would decamp to Brighton in the summer to escape the oppressive heat of London. And in one remarkable letter he claimed that he had made friends with a group of Glaswegian workers, whom he obviously thought were just like Spanish workers, and reported that they would 'do anything for a litre of wine'.[27]

Both Pujol and his wife Aracelli tried once more to interest the British in taking him on as a double agent. But again there was little interest, and Aracelli walked out of a meeting with a man from MI6 in Lisbon who patronised her terribly. Pujol was left frustrated and angry. He later wrote that he simply could not understand 'why the British were so difficult when the Germans were so understanding and co-operative'.[28] At this point the Americans intervened, sensing that Pujol had credibility with the Abwehr, and eventually persuaded MI6 to look again at the prospect of taking him on. Unfortunately, the recruitment of Pujol as a double agent was delayed for several months by a dispute between MI6, who felt they should handle him in Lisbon, and MI5, who wanted to get him to England where they could turn him and send reports under his name back to the Abwehr. Finally, this internal dispute was resolved and, after being smuggled from Lisbon to Gibraltar, Juan Pujol

Garcia arrived in Britain on a military flight on the afternoon of 24 April 1942. He was met by two men from MI5, Cyril Mills, the son of the circus owner, who later gave him the codename Garbo, and Tomás Harris, who would become his case officer or minder. After interrogating him thoroughly to be certain of his loyalty, they set him up in a safe house in Crespigny Road in Hendon. It had taken Pujol nearly eighteen months to beg the British intelligence establishment to take him on. Finally, he had made it.

MI5 wanted to keep Garbo's identity a secret even from other members of the organisation, so they hired a room above a shopping arcade between Jermyn Street and Piccadilly, just around the corner from the main MI5 headquarters. From this small office Pujol, known in England as Juan Garcia, would write his long letters about business dealings, which were filled in between the lines with his verbose secret messages in invisible ink.

Behind Garbo all the way was Tomás Harris, his MI5 controller. Harris was himself a remarkable figure who had easily slipped into the curious world of espionage. From his Spanish mother he had learned to speak fluent Spanish, a necessity for dealing with Pujol, whose English was poor. From his father, an art dealer who owned a gallery in Mayfair, he acquired a love of Spanish art, especially the Baroque, which he studied as a post-graduate. Harris followed his father's line of business and travelled extensively in Spain, buying paintings and *objets d'art* from fleeing Spanish refugees in the Spanish Civil War. In 1940 he was recruited to MI5, where he cut a raffish and bohemian figure with his neatly trimmed beard and penchant for hand-rolled black tobacco cigarettes. He and his wife were great party-givers in their West End home, and regular visitors included other shady figures from the world of British wartime intelligence, including the infamous Kim Philby, Guy Burgess and Anthony Blunt. But Tomás Harris, in guiding Garbo and helping to write his long-winded reports, was a round peg in a round hole. He had the energy, imagination and creativity to develop a consistent character for Garbo and to constantly invent ways for him to observe or discover remarkable stories about Britain's wartime intentions and strategies. In time the work was so time-consuming that Sarah Bishop joined Harris and Garcia. She had been a secretary in the Cabinet Office who disliked the work and transferred to MI5. She was fluent in French and Spanish and came up with several of the characters who would become part of the extensive network of spies reporting in to Garbo. Harris was always aware of how near the edge he was pushing the German belief in Garbo, but he kept up his deceits with intelligence and vigour and made a remarkable success of it. Garbo would go on to become the person later described as 'the greatest double agent of the Second World War'.[29]

Running and controlling double agents was a game that needed to be played for the long run. It was in many ways like making a set of long-term investments. Some of the investments would produce a dividend, others might not. Some might drain further reinvestment funds and still come to nothing, but others might yield a fortune. But all of them required time and attention in ensuring the enemy had confidence in their agent's reliability. As Masterman wrote later 'you cannot expect in any case to draw a fortune unless you pay, and pay in freely, first'.[30]

It had taken two and a half years, but deception had now been placed at the very centre of the military planning of the war. A set of organisations had been created, with the London Controlling Section deciding on overall policy, the XX Committee settling what should be revealed to the enemy, and MI5's B1A section in day-to-day control of the double agents. In July 1942, MI5 was sufficiently confident of its success to report that it completely controlled the only German spying network of any significance inside the UK. This meant that deception of the enemy on a large scale was now possible. To complete the bureaucratic framework for this, Johnny Bevan was made a member of the XX Committee. This meant he was fully appraised of the double agent system and its potential. So, with the whole deception system fully linked up by the end of 1942, all that was needed was a clear military strategy for the years ahead and an agreement of what objectives the deception policy should aim for.

Chapter 4

BODYGUARD

The arguments between the British and the Americans about global strategy continued to rage throughout 1943. Churchill was still concerned that the US chiefs of staff were not fully on side with the Mediterranean strategy and that they wanted to bring the date of the cross-Channel invasion forward or even reallocate supplies from Europe to the war in the Pacific. He telegraphed Harry Hopkins, Roosevelt's closest advisor, on 2 May: 'What is essential is that our plans should be made and thrashed out and decisions taken as at Casablanca.' He went on: 'I am conscious of serious divergences beneath the surface which, if not adjusted, will lead to grave difficulties and feeble action in the summer and autumn. These difficulties we must forestall.'[1]

Churchill effectively invited himself to Washington for another summit with Roosevelt in the spring of 1943. All the chiefs of staff and other senior figures like General Wavell, by now Commander-in-Chief in India, would accompany him. The party left Greenock on the Clyde on the afternoon of 5 May on board the *Queen Mary*, the giant Cunard cruise liner that had held the Blue Riband for the fastest crossings of the Atlantic since 1938. On board this huge vessel, now adapted as a troop carrier, were also

5,000 German prisoners of war, captured in North Africa, who were being taken to camps in Canada. The liner sped across the Atlantic, zig-zagging its way westwards accompanied by a fast cruiser and escorted overhead for the first part of the journey by a Sunderland flying boat. But no voyage like this was without risk, and in the previous couple of months up to 70 U-boats had been operating in the Atlantic and two convoys had been attacked by a 'wolf pack' of 38 U-boats who succeeded in sinking a quarter of the Allied merchant ships.[2] At least once on the journey the Prime Minister was warned that a German U-boat was up ahead and evasive action was being taken. Churchill joked to Averell Harriman, the American diplomat who was also on board, that if he were forced into a lifeboat he would at least insist that it had a machine-gun fitted so if threatened with capture he would go down fighting. Harriman was more sensitive to the risks of the ocean crossing and seems not to have appreciated the joke.[3]

On the second day of the crossing the chiefs of staff met on board the *Queen Mary* to review their position. As they prepared to meet the American chiefs of staff again, General Brooke noted in his diary how disagreements with the Americans kept recurring. 'Casablanca has taught me too much,' he wrote. 'Agreement after agreement may be secured on paper but if their hearts are not in it they will soon drift away again.' He was worried that 'unless the Americans are prepared to withdraw more shipping from the Pacific our strategy in Europe will be drastically affected ... in spite of all we have said about defeating Germany first!'[4] However, the core fact was that there was simply not enough shipping available to support all the plans made at Casablanca. With this severe restraint continuing to limit Allied activity there was a constant need to re-address priorities and set new targets. And with every front across the globe calling for action it required the most senior Allied leaders to make key strategic decisions.

At the conference in Washington in May, codenamed Trident, the British asked to postpone a major amphibious operation against Burma that would have coincided with the monsoon and the height of the malaria season. There were not enough ships or landing craft to mount a landing. But there were other reasons for postponement in this forbidding corner of the global war. Churchill said, 'Going into swampy jungles to fight the Japanese was akin to going into the water to fight a shark.' It was agreed that the operation should be postponed.

In May 1943, during the Trident Conference, North Africa finally fell to the Allies. Churchill and Roosevelt were naturally delighted, and the news improved the mood of the summit no end. It was confirmed that the decision taken at Casablanca would be adhered to and the Allies would next invade Sicily. But there was no agreement as to where the Allied armies should go after this. The British argued forcefully that with the Italian mainland only a few miles from Messina on Sicily, it was the obvious next step. Knocking Italy out of the war would not only undermine the Axis alliance, they argued, but it would force the Germans to replace the 25 Italian divisions in the Balkans and Greece or surrender southern Europe right up to the Danube. But for General Marshall and the American chiefs this once again seemed like the British wanting to continue fighting in the Mediterranean when all available resources should be gathering to fight the war in northern Europe with the cross-Channel invasion. Churchill countered by saying that as the invasion was not scheduled until spring 1944, they could not justify having an entire victorious Army group sitting around doing nothing for the best part of a year and they had to take the fight to the enemy where they found him. 'They could not possibly stand idle,' Churchill told the President, 'and so long a period of apparent inaction ... would have a serious effect on relations with Russia, who was bearing such a disproportionate weight [of the struggle against the German war machine].'[5] But to the frustration of the British, no final decision was reached at Trident as to where the Allies should go after Sicily.

The confirmation of the plan to invade Sicily now presented the Allies with the challenge of mounting the biggest landing on enemy territory so far in the war, known as Operation Husky. The first plan was to invade over a wide range of landing sites around the island in order to seize ports and airfields. Montgomery, with his attention very much focused on the fighting in North Africa, threw out the plan in February 1943, claiming it left the Allies too dispersed and not strong enough to repel determined counter-attacks. A new plan was made to land British troops on the south-east coast around Avola, and American troops on the south-west around Gela. Both landings would be supported by parachute drops. But the fighting in Tunisia only came to an end in May, with military victory and the surrender of about 240,000 Axis troops, including nine generals, even greater than the German surrender at Stalingrad. This left precious little time for training troops who had been fighting in the desert on how to embark and disembark on landing craft, and to make plans for the vast naval fleet of about 2,500 ships to assemble, including two aircraft carriers, six battleships, fifteen cruisers and dozens of escort and support vessels. Some ships were to come from the UK, some direct from the US and some from bases in the Mediterranean. The timetables for this armada to load up, sail and draw up in the right order was itself immensely complex. The landing beaches had been selected from a detailed examination of aerial photos, but the models made in Britain of the landing beaches to assist the troops did not arrive until after the landings had taken place.[6] All the planning had an air of last-minute haste about it that once again left lessons for the even bigger cross-Channel invasion.

However, the British were by now learning how important deception was becoming. And the planning of the invasion of Sicily included one of the best-known deception schemes of the war, Operation Mincemeat. It stemmed from the fertile minds of Flight-Lieutenant Charles Cholmondeley of MI5 and Lieutenant-Commander Ewen Montagu, who was a member of a secret naval intelligence committee as well as secretary to W-Board. The story of the Operation Mincemeat deception is that a dead body, supposedly of a Royal Marine Major whose plane had crashed at sea, was left floating in the Mediterranean. It was released into the sea on 30 April from a British submarine off the Spanish Andalusian port of Huelva in a strong current where it was known it would wash up on the coast. The body was actually that of a poor, unemployed Welshman who died by taking rat poison, probably as an act of suicide. On the body were a series of private documents and mementos that created a false identity for the Major, right down to recent bills, a letter from his bank warning the Major he was overspending and a love letter with a photograph from a supposed girlfriend. Handcuffed to his arm was a briefcase containing fake letters from two senior generals in London, General Nye, the Vice Chief of the Imperial General staff, and Admiral Mountbatten, the head of Combined Operations. The two letters were to commanders in North Africa, telling them about plans to invade Greece and Sardinia and explaining that the preparations to invade Sicily were only a ruse to fool the enemy.

Although Spain was neutral, Huelva had been selected because it was known that an efficient German agent operated there. It was hoped he would get hold of the briefcase and pass on the details of its letters to his chief in Madrid, who would then inform the Abwehr in Berlin. They would hopefully accept that the next step in the Allied campaign in the Mediterranean was not as they had expected to Sicily, but was actually to be against Greece or Sardinia. It was a daring plan full of risks that could go wrong at several points. As indeed it did. However, Mincemeat was accompanied by a series of sabotage operations carried out in Greece mostly by the Special Operations Executive. Forty-five attacks were made against road and rail links, and a major viaduct carrying the main railway from Salonika to Athens was destroyed, hinting to the Germans that an invasion was coming. Eventually, the concept that the preparations to invade Sicily were only a feint did manage to penetrate German military thinking. Between March and July 1943 the number of German divisions posted to the Balkans, including Greece, rose from eight to eighteen. Whereas only two German divisions were sent to Sicily.

After several anxious days of not knowing if the deception plan had succeeded in getting through to the Germans, Bletchley Park intercepted a 'Most Secret' message from the German High Command to units in Greece ordering a series of measures to reinforce several points along the Greek coast that had been named in the letters attached to the body. In London there was elation, and a telegram was sent to Churchill in Washington on 14 May telling him, '"Mincemeat" swallowed rod, line and sinker by right people.'[7] A major deception plan had succeeded magnificently and once again had shown how a military campaign could be aided by misleading the enemy.[8]

If Mincemeat reduced the numbers of Germans defending Sicily, it still could not turn a complex amphibious operation into a walkover. In addition to the two German divisions on the island there were nine Italian divisions, a mix of second-rate coastal militias that could not be relied on and better-quality mobile units, some of which had had experience of fighting in North Africa. The landings went reasonably smoothly but the airborne drop was a disaster, as strong winds blew the transport aircraft wildly off course. Some paratroopers landed as much as 50 miles from their drop zones and many gliders were even dropped in the sea. Casualties were alarmingly high. The disasters of this day could have spelled the end of the use of airborne troops dropping behind enemy lines. But highly motivated and well-trained elite British and American paras redeemed themselves by fighting with extreme vigour, even if they were in the wrong place.

After 38 days of hard fighting, Allied troops crushed all resistance and Sicily came under Allied occupation. In Rome, the government of Mussolini collapsed. King Emmanuel appointed Marshal Badoglio as the new Prime Minister and all fascists were thrown out of government. Badoglio tried to negotiate but the Allies would only accept unconditional surrender. When Badoglio pulled Italy out of Hitler's war, the Germans responded by occupying Rome and then the rest of the country. Although there was a long, slow slog through Italy ahead, southern Europe was now opened up to Allied troops. And, equally importantly, Operation Husky had been an invaluable dress rehearsal for the even bigger show to come in spring 1944.[9]

In April 1943, General Frederick Morgan of COSSAC had been given his orders, which included running a deception campaign not only with regard to the full invasion scheduled for spring 1944, but also to deceive the enemy about plans for 1943. Churchill himself further defined these orders in instructions to Morgan that he was to prepare 'an amphibious feint to bring on an air battle' and to develop 'Camouflage and pretence on a most elaborate scale to ... pin down the enemy in the West by keeping alive the expectation of invasion.'[10] This deception plan was to run alongside a tentative plan to actually land troops on the Cotentin Peninsula in a substantial raid in August 1943. It was not a popular operation with the chiefs of staff, who wanted to concentrate on their Mediterranean Strategy, but the Prime Minister, always keen to maintain an aggressive stance, kept the prospect of it alive.

The deception plan for 1943, Operation Cockade, finally evolved into three phases. Firstly, there was the deception in which fourteen British and Canadian divisions were notionally to be landed near Boulogne in September. Secondly, there was a follow-up to fool the Germans into thinking that US forces would land in Brittany to seize the city of Brest at the end of September. Thirdly, there was a plan for an imaginary attack upon Norway at Stavanger. For German intelligence to believe that any of these assaults were possible, it was necessary to inflate the Order of Battle in Britain. The actual total of British Army units in the UK at the end of September 1943 was twelve infantry divisions, four armoured and one airborne. The London Controlling Section instructed the double agents to feed German intelligence information that the Home Forces Field Army consisted of 24 divisions and that there was an expeditionary force of another 15 divisions available for landings near Boulogne and Brest. This was more than doubling the number of actual available British troops. As for American troops in Britain, that was more complicated, as it was impossible to invent forces that did not exist since the Germans would have a record of the number of convoys that had crossed the Atlantic. So the double agents started to send back exaggerated figures for the numbers of men who arrived in each convoy, bringing forward the arrival of units that were not due for some months. By August, when 330,000 American troops had arrived, German intelligence was led to believe that more than half a million were in the UK. Moreover, from intercepted German communications, there was clear evidence that these figures had been accepted as the correct numbers.[11]

During the summer of 1943, most of the double agents available to the XX Committee were used to persuade German intelligence of the fake plans in Operation Cockade. Two attractive ladies with a wide range of friends in fashionable London society reported back on military and diplomatic gossip about upcoming events. Two Norwegian agents reported on the threat to Norway. The agent Tricycle started to report a mass of misinformation about the assemblage of British, Canadian and

American troops in different parts of the country, from Scotland to the South West. He also reported that he had discovered a new system for the construction of landing craft, in which the parts were made in inland workshops and then transported to the coast, where they were rapidly assembled. This could help to explain how the large numbers of landing craft and barges that were being reported along England's south-east coast had suddenly come into being. But the jewel in the crown was Garbo and the notional group of sub-agents who reported to him. Under a constant bombardment of questions from his Abwehr controller in Madrid, he reported on units gathering for exercises in south Wales. In August he visited Scotland and reported on troop build-ups there. Then he rushed back to the south coast to report on great concentrations of troops around Southampton. He calculated that seven divisions of troops and a large number of landing craft had been assembled. In order to maintain his credibility his minders told him to send back a note of warning that the successful occupation of Sicily might lead to the operation being called off. But then he sent more urgent messages that men had been confined to barracks and that an operation was scheduled for 8 or 9 September. Then he reported back that it had all been cancelled. 'Troops surprised and disappointed' he noted.

An actual event did take place on the morning of 9 September when thirty vessels crossed the Channel to within ten miles of the French coast. Then, under the cover of a smokescreen they withdrew. The hope was that they would draw out the Luftwaffe into an area where the RAF would be waiting for them. But the Germans did not rise to the bait on this occasion. The German High Command rightly concluded that the thrust of Allied activities would be in the Mediterranean for some time to come. German intelligence was also beginning to get suspicious about the amount of information that seemed to be falling into the hands of their trusted agents. One intelligence report wrote of 'somewhat too obvious preparations for attacking the Channel front' and that the preparations seemed 'conspicuously slow in reaching completion.'[12]

The events of 9 September coincided with real landings in Salerno, south of Naples, to open the Allied campaign in mainland Italy. The British deceivers were naturally disappointed that their plans had not succeeded in fooling the Germans along the Channel. The secret branch of British intelligence that monitored the German Army, MI14, concluded that the reactions of the enemy with regard to Cockade 'can only be described as disappointing in the extreme.'[13] However, they need not have worried excessively. The Germans secretly concluded that the build-up in the Pas de Calais area might have been a dress rehearsal for a landing along the French west coast, as another aspect of Cockade intended. Until winter ruled out any realistic prospect of an assault, fears of an imminent invasion were sustained. And more success was achieved in Scotland, where the four divisions actually stationed there in training had been inflated into a force of seven divisions that were intending, with considerable naval and air support, to seize an airfield just outside Stavanger in Norway. In Oslo, the German headquarters announced that they expected a landing in early September. Then the British let it be known that the operation had been stood down and the naval support vessels returned to their bases at Rosyth and Scapa Flow. It did not take much to convince Hitler that Norway lay under threat of invasion, and the Germans left twelve divisions stationed there throughout the year, despite the demands for more troops to be sent to the Mediterranean and the Eastern Front. So, without being a stand-out success, Cockade had certainly kept the Germans guessing as to what British, Canadian and American troops were up to in southern England while the main thrust of their war effort was concentrated on the Mediterranean.

At the next Anglo-American summit in August 1943, this time in Quebec and codenamed Quadrant, Operation Overlord was again one of the major items on the agenda. Churchill crossed the Atlantic once more in the *Queen Mary*, where an unusual scene took place in the bathroom of his luxurious suite. Realising, after the Dieppe fiasco, how difficult it would be to capture a major port intact, members of the COSSAC team had been developing an idea to build two giant concrete harbours and tow them across the Channel.[14] Once in position, giant blockships would be sunk around them to protect the artificial harbour from the force of the sea. Churchill did not understand how this would work, so a demonstration was staged in his bath. Little paper boats were launched at one end of the bath and the water splashed about. The paper boats all sank. When a barrier was placed across the bath to represent the breakwater no amount of splashing sank the paper boats. General Hastings Ismay, Churchill's senior military liaison officer, later wrote, 'If a stranger had visited his bathroom he might have seen a stocky figure in a dressing gown of many colours sitting on a stool and surrounded by what our American friends call "Top Brass".' With an admiral flapping water at one end of the bath and a brigadier holding a barrier in the middle, Ismay continued, 'The stranger would have found it hard to believe that this was the British High Command studying the most stupendous and spectacular amphibious operation in the history of war.'[15]

In Quebec the Combined Chiefs of Staff once again argued bitterly over priorities, with the Americans still suspicious of British ambitions in the Mediterranean. But this time the Americans were determined to get their way. On 19 August the Combined Chiefs presented to Roosevelt and Churchill the latest developments in the planning for Overlord. Morgan, Barker and their teams had been busy. They had resolved that although a landing in the Pas de Calais offered the shortest route across the Channel, its beaches were too heavily defended, the excellent road and rail links provided the enemy with an easy way to bring up reinforcements, and the region offered no natural defences for protecting the bridgehead after the landings had been made. So COSSAC concluded that the beaches of Normandy offered better prospects for the landing zone. The Combined Chiefs approved the choice and said that from Normandy they wanted to head across France and 'to strike at the heart of Germany and destroy her military forces'. Wherever there was a choice between allocating scarce resources in the Mediterranean or to Overlord, 'Available resources will be distributed and employed with the main object of ensuring the success of "Overlord".'[16] The target date for the landings was confirmed as 1 May 1944. Churchill still argued that if the German strength in northern France was too great at this time then Overlord should not go ahead and an alternative landing should be planned to take place in northern Norway, Operation Jupiter. No one took this very seriously but general agreement for such a scheme was minuted. The need to keep the Germans guessing as to where and when the invasion would take place was unanimously agreed. More deception planning was needed.

At Quadrant there was also great pleasure expressed not only in the conquest of Sicily, but in the tremendous progress that was being made by the Red Army on the Kharkov front. Plans were mooted for a meeting with Stalin in a three-way summit. The geopolitical situation in late 1943 was changing rapidly. The United States was at last becoming the real 'arsenal of democracy' with its shipyards turning out a new merchant ship every few days, its factories producing warplanes and tanks by the hundred, and jeeps, trucks and other vehicles by the thousand. And the Soviet Union had turned from being a nation on the brink of defeat to a military superpower with the largest army in the world. Britain's war effort, meanwhile, was stretched to the limit. Five million men and women were in uniform of one sort or another. Millions more were in the war factories that were now working at full capacity. In planning for the new manpower demands for 1944, Churchill noted, 'Our manpower is now fully mobilised for the war effort. We cannot add to the total; on the contrary, it is already dwindling.'[17] With the fortunes of war affecting the leading Allied powers in different ways, it now made sense for the three Allied leaders to meet and plan for the final stages of the war. But it would be some months before such a meeting could be organised.

By the time the Allies advanced into Italy the Germans had diverted more troops into that country, increasing their garrison there from 6 to 25 divisions. Allied progress was slow, so Churchill and General Brooke grew increasingly concerned that the Allies were risking a confrontation with the Germans in *both* Italy and northern France in 1944. They feared that by splitting their forces neither would be strong enough to overcome determined German resistance. Landing craft were being diverted from Italy to Britain in anticipation of Overlord. Churchill knew from Ultra transcripts that the Germans had spotted this. He therefore gave instructions 'for an elaborate cover plan' to be made 'to mystify and baffle the enemy.'[18]

In Washington, Marshall saw that exactly what he had predicted and feared was taking place. As the struggle in Italy grew more intense and difficult, so it risked draining Allied resources that were needed to prepare for the invasion of northern France. Churchill continued to plead directly with Roosevelt to sustain the pressure in Italy and to consider other flanking moves by sending troops to Rhodes, Greece and the Dodecanese islands. Roosevelt replied sternly, 'It is my opinion that no diversion of forces or equipment should prejudice Overlord as planned. The American Chiefs of Staff agree.'[19]

Despite this putdown, Churchill continued to be concerned through the autumn of 1943 with the risk that an invasion of northern France might fail. In October he telegraphed

Roosevelt: 'the campaign of 1944 will be far the most dangerous we have undertaken and personally I am more anxious about its success than I was about 1941, 1942 or 1943.'[20] At a Chiefs of Staff meeting in London, Churchill went further and expressed the view that even if the landings were a success, the enemy would fight hard to prevent the Anglo-American armies from moving inland. He argued that if the German Army was able to 'inflict on us a military disaster greater than that of Dunkirk' then 'such a disaster would result in the resuscitation of Hitler and the Nazi regime.'[21]

Plans were finally made for the first three-way summit to be held in Tehran at the end of November. Roosevelt, Churchill and their substantial staffs met in Cairo in advance. This time Roosevelt set the agenda, literally. The presence of the Chinese Nationalist leader, Chiang Kai-shek, ensured that much discussion focused on the Pacific and the East. On 23 November tensions between the British and American chiefs once again erupted when the American Admiral King and General Brooke had a vehement argument about priorities over the supply of landing craft to Europe versus the Pacific. American General Joseph Stilwell was present and wrote, 'Brooke got nasty and King got good and sore. King almost climbed over the table at Brooke. God he was mad! I wish he had socked him.'[22] In his diary, Brooke was a little more restrained, writing that the meeting 'became somewhat heated.'[23]

By the time the Anglo-American parties got to Tehran, the prospects for a successful summit were not looking good. Churchill had a bad cold and had almost lost his voice. His doctor frantically offered him sprays to try to restore his principal weapon. Along with his daughter Sarah, who had accompanied him, the doctor persuaded Churchill to pull out of the first informal meeting and dinner, and so instead, according to Sarah, he 'had dinner in bed like a sulky child.'[24] To make things worse, that evening the President developed a bad stomach ache and there were rumours that he had been poisoned, although this proved not to be the case. By the following afternoon both men had recovered sufficiently for the formal meetings to begin. Churchill told the gathering that they represented 'the greatest concentration of worldly power that had ever been seen in the history of mankind.'[25]

At this first plenary session there was much discussion about Overlord. In debating the timing of the landings, Stalin insisted on May 1944. The British and Americans were considering putting the date back to June. Churchill gave his normal line about not wanting to risk military operations in Italy, where there were now twenty British or British-controlled divisions in combat with the enemy. At the second plenary session, Stalin raised more questions about Overlord and asked who was going to command it. Roosevelt replied that the commander-in-chief had not yet been appointed. Stalin said the operation would 'come to nought' unless one man was put in command of planning and leading the invasion. When Churchill spoke about the need to ensure that the German forces in northern France were not powerful enough to throw the Allies back into the sea, Stalin was horrified. Knowing that there were literally hundreds of divisions battling it out on the Eastern Front, he still feared the British would delay the whole operation. At the end of the session Stalin turned to Churchill and said, 'I wish to pose a very direct question ... Do the British Prime Minister and the British staff really believe in Overlord?' Churchill was much offended and replied by saying that, providing the conditions were met, 'it will be our stern duty to hurl across the Channel against the Germans every sinew of our strength.' At this the meeting ended.[26]

The following day, 30 November, was Churchill's 69th birthday. In the concluding plenary session with the three leaders, the discussion came back once again to Overlord. The President said every attempt would be made for the invasion to take place in May. Stalin agreed that there would be a major offensive on the Eastern Front to coincide with this, to prevent the Germans from transferring troops from east to west. He encouraged the Allies to develop their plans for a second invasion in the south of France, either before or soon after Overlord, to further split German forces in that country. This would be called Operation Anvil. Stalin was clearly against any Allied diversionary attack upon the Balkans, no doubt already thinking about the post-war world and his own plans for the Soviet Union to be master of that area. Churchill then raised the whole question of deception plans. Stalin said he very much approved of them and that on many occasions the Red Army had disguised the moving up of troops at night to mount a surprise attack at dawn. It was agreed that the US, British and Soviet staffs would collaborate in devising joint deception operations. Churchill then came up with the memorable phrase, 'In wartime, truth is so precious that she should always be attended by a bodyguard of lies.' When this was translated Stalin cheered the remark, and on this upbeat note the formal sessions of the first Big Three summit came to an end.[27]

At a dinner that evening to celebrate Churchill's birthday, the Prime Minister sat with Stalin on his left and Roosevelt on his right. In front of him was a large cake with 69 candles. Churchill later described the scene by saying, 'There I sat with the Great Russian bear on one side of me with paws outstretched, and on the other side the great American buffalo, and between the two sat the poor little English donkey.'[28] In the Russian style, toasts were raised throughout the evening, and everyone had to drink what was in their glass. Churchill began by proposing a toast to the King, the President and the Russian leader, whom he called 'Stalin the Great.' As an evening of excellent food and drink passed, the many toasts got merrier. Churchill ended up proposing a toast 'to the proletarian masses' and Stalin responded with a toast 'to the Conservative party'.[29] Cleary it was a good evening.

Despite its inauspicious start and the tensions between the three leaders as Stalin demanded the Allies open the long-promised Second Front in the spring of 1944, the Tehran conference had proved a surprising success. Churchill had been profoundly distressed by what he saw as Roosevelt's cuddling up to Stalin. But the Soviet leader had been supportive to both of the democratic leaders and much important work had been done. Strategies had been agreed and plans made.

In the days following the Tehran conference, Churchill and Roosevelt once again went on to talk in Cairo. Roosevelt proposed that General Eisenhower should be appointed as supreme commander for Overlord. He had initially thought of nominating Marshall for the task but decided he needed him in Washington too badly, in overall command of the US Army. Churchill agreed. As the invasion of Europe was rapidly becoming a majority American operation it was appropriate for an American general to take command. It was later agreed that General Montgomery should be put in command of 21st Army Group, being effectively the commander of land forces. Air Marshal Trafford Leigh Mallory would be in command of the air forces and Admiral Sir Bertram Ramsay in command of naval operations, reflecting the high proportion of British forces in the air squadrons and naval armadas that would support the invasion. The deception plan would now go ahead and, picking up on the word Churchill had used to Stalin, would henceforth be called Operation Bodyguard.

On their last day together in Cairo, Churchill insisted that Roosevelt and he do a little sightseeing. They motored together to the Sphinx, next to the Great Pyramid of Giza. The two men gazed at this ancient wonder for some minutes as the evening shadows fell, in contemplation of all that lay ahead. Churchill later wrote, 'She told us nothing and maintained her inscrutable smile.'[30] Then the President left to depart for the United States. The contemplation was over and the time for action and deception was to begin.

Throughout 1943, in a series of operations, the Allies had tried to deceive the Germans into thinking that they were about to launch an invasion of northern Europe, when they were not. Now they had a new challenge. To find a way to deceive the Germans that they were not going to invade, when in fact they were. Operation Bodyguard would be the difference between success and failure.

Chapter 5

GEHEIMDIENST

The body devoted to the collection of intelligence for the German armed forces was the Abwehr. Set up in the 1920s to defend the country from foreign spies, by 1938 it was the principal intelligence agency reporting to the Oberkommando der Wehrmacht, or OKW, the Supreme Command of the German Armed Forces. The Abwehr's head office was at 47–49 Tirpitz-Ufer, one of the main streets in central Berlin, near the famous Tiergarten and next door to the OKW. The Abwehr was a military organisation run by senior officers and split into three sections. Abwehr I was concerned with collecting secret intelligence abroad and was roughly equivalent to MI6 in Britain. Abwehr II was concerned with dirty tricks and running clandestine operations, roughly equivalent to the Special Operations Executive. And Abwehr III had the responsibility for internal security within Germany and occupied territories, equivalent to MI5. It shared this responsibility with the secret police, the Geheime Staatspolizei (the Gestapo). The Abwehr was a large and rather cumbersome organisation and its officers who served abroad in neutral countries did so under diplomatic cover, as was the case with officials in MI6. The Abwehr offices in Stockholm, Madrid and Lisbon, where Von Karsthoff was chief, were the principal centres that collected information on the United Kingdom.[1] The office in Madrid was enormous, with 87 Abwehr personnel supported by a further 228 other staff, all based at the German Embassy in the city.[2]

The head of the Abwehr from 1935 was Admiral Wilhelm Canaris, a prominent figure in the Nazi state, although, most unusually, not a member of the Nazi Party. Beyond this, Canaris had a dark secret that he had to keep from the regime and all other sections of the German military. His career had been one of smooth and continuous progression up the naval ladder. He had been in the Imperial Navy in the First World War. His ship was one of only two German vessels to survive the Battle of the Falkland Islands in December 1914. He took refuge in Chile and managed to return to Germany via Plymouth; he passed through the British port disguised as a Chilean sailor. He was then sent to Madrid, where he became a prominent spy for the Kaiser. During the 1920s he continued to serve in the German Navy and helped Germany's armed forces evade the restrictions of the Versailles Treaty. Outwardly he led the life of a conventional naval officer who welcomed Hitler's appointment as Chancellor in 1933, hoping for a revival of German strength. In the following year he was made commander of the naval garrison at Swinemünde and was coming up for retirement when his commander-in-chief Admiral Raeder appointed him as head of the Abwehr, as the previous incumbent had left and Raeder wanted to keep the job in the hands of the navy. Thus, rather improbably, did Canaris come to be head of the German Secret Service.

Canaris was a quietly spoken man with a slight lisp who hated violence and loved dogs. He had two dachshunds whom he took almost everywhere with him, often spoke to, and if he travelled abroad and could not take them he would telephone back every day and a member of his office would report on what they had eaten and the state of their health. When in Italy on a wartime visit, his hosts assumed he was talking on the phone in code to Berlin about weighty matters, when in fact he was just catching up on the bodily functions of his dachshunds. He is reported to have said that he preferred dogs to people. Canaris's closest officers showed him tremendous loyalty, but to many outside the Abwehr he remained an enigmatic and curious figure.[3]

From the early rise of Hitler, however, Canaris had a distaste for the brutal and thuggish methods of the Führer's cronies and supporters. Before the war some of his closest associates had become involved with the resistance to the Nazi regime. Canaris moved closer and closer to this group during the second half of the war as it became clear to him that Hitler was driving Germany to certain disaster and defeat. This was the secret he had to keep from the rest of the armed forces, but instead of actively pursuing a line of resistance he fell into a sort of fatalistic melancholy, unable to fully support or actively oppose the evil regime he served. Like many senior figures in Nazi Germany he held muddled views about the country under Hitler's leadership. But he was no democrat, and his spiritual home was probably Franco's Spain, which he visited several times. If he had a hero it was the Spanish fascist leader, whom he met on many occasions, and he even had a signed photo of Franco on the wall of his Berlin office. Yet he was still very much a German patriot and would not directly assist his country's enemies, even if he harboured the hope that one day Hitler's dreadful regime would come to an end before the humiliation of total military defeat.[4]

By 1942, Canaris's Abwehr had begun to provide cover for conspirators against the Nazi regime. If anyone opposing the regime needed to travel in secrecy or to go abroad, the Abwehr provided the facilities and the passes. In the following year the organisation went a step further and began to put feelers out towards the British. On one of his many visits to Madrid, always under a false name, Canaris made secret contact with British intelligence.[5] Bizarrely, and through an intermediary, he offered to meet with Sir Stewart Menzies, the head of MI6. There is no evidence as to exactly what he would have proposed. Maybe he would have reported to MI6 on the growing resistance to Hitler. Anyway, the offer was held up within MI6, where it sat on the desk of the official dealing with Iberian affairs, Kim Philby. But it was not British government policy to neogotiate with German opponents to Hitler, and when Menzies finally heard about the feeler that had been put out he said that he was not interested in a meeting with Canaris.[6] Whether this was a missed opportunity to forge links with the German military resistance or a sensible response to the strange whim of a melancholic intelligence leader will never be known.

What is clear is that Canaris began to walk a dangerous tightrope. On the one hand he commanded Germany's principal military intelligence-gathering operation. On the other he grew to detest the Nazi leadership and looked for ways to undermine the Third Reich. If found out, he would face torture and death. Throughout 1943 he managed to keep up this remarkable balancing act. But as time passed it looked increasingly likely, both to the British and almost certainly to the Admiral himself, that a fall was coming.

If Canaris's position was ambivalent, the deputy head of Section III of the Abwehr, General Hans Oster, had even more direct links to the resistance movement against Hitler and the Nazi regime. He had been involved in a conspiracy of senior officers to overthrow Hitler if he went to war against Czechoslovakia in the autumn of 1938. As it happened Chamberlain effectively gifted the Sudeten region of Czechoslovakia to Germany at Munich and there was no need for war. So the conspiracy faded out. And from 1940 many German military leaders who had initially been opposed to the regime and brutal Nazi tactics became reconciled following Hitler's stunning military successes. But not Oster, who continued to use the Abwehr to assist the anti-Nazi resistance by supporting and hiding leading figures in the movement and by helping small numbers of Jews to escape Germany. This led to his dismissal in 1943, but he was not arrested until after the July Plot against Hitler's life in 1944, with which he had been involved. Oster was a close friend of Canaris, whom he regarded as the spiritual founder of the resistance movement. The risk of this being exposed hung like the sword of Damocles over Canaris's head.

Any organisation like the Abwehr will reflect the personality of its leader. And partly as a consequence of the ambiguous position of its commander, the Abwehr was neither efficient nor run with strict discipline. It did good work in reporting on the Soviet Union and the state of the Red Army. And it co-ordinated all intelligence monitoring of the Royal Navy as its ships passed in and out of the Mediterranean through Gibraltar at night. But its agents were allowed considerable leeway, especially those serving in the havens of the neutral countries abroad. They seemed to be remarkably uncritical of the material they collected from the spies in Britain. That is partly why they never seemed to question even Juan Pujol's wild claims of wine-swilling Glaswegian workers or diplomats fleeing the heat of London in summer. In Berlin they were so delighted with the amount of information their agents were delivering from Britain that they came to believe it all. It was a clear case of being impressed by *quantity* rather than assessing the *quality* of the material collected. Instead, they passed it all on, an avalanche of gossip, rumour and unfiltered claims, which was in reality an overwhelming mass of Allied misinformation sent out to deceive the enemy.[7]

Typical of Hitler's Nazi state, this world of *Geheimdienst* (Intelligence) was divided between different and often warring factions. The fact that many competing voices tried not only to be heard, but also to dismiss their rivals was both an advantage and a disadvantage for any British deception plans that the London Controlling Section and the 'A' Force in the Middle East tried to foist on the enemy.

In its essence, there are two different aspects to the process of intelligence gathering. Firstly, there is the *collection* of information from a variety of sources that might include signals intelligence (Sigint), the interrogation of prisoners, the capture of documents, diplomatic reports, open sources (monitoring newspapers, broadcasts, newsreels, etc.) and finally, of course, reports from agents on the ground, known as Human Intelligence (Humint). This was all covered by the Abwehr. Secondly, there was the need to *interpret* the mass of intelligence that was coming in, to assess it for its value, to judge what can be believed and what cannot, and to draw conclusions from what the many different collection sources might suggest. In the Nazi state during the Second World War there were different agencies concerned with these two different elements.

The agency that was concerned with interpreting the avalanche of intelligence coming in from the Abwehr and elsewhere was the Fremde Heere West (FHW), a department of the Army High Command Foreign Armies West. The in-trays of the FHW were groaning under the weight of material collected by the Abwehr. The FHW consisted of senior and very able staff officers from the General Staff, but they did not stay in post for long. There was tendency within the German military to look down on intelligence work, so officers were rotated in and out of the FHW. Often, just when they had picked up enough experience to be really valuable in their work, they were moved back to the General Staff. The FHW was based in a deep bunker at Zossen, twenty kilometres south of Berlin, covered with what looked like local houses to disguise it from aerial reconnaissance. The FHW produced a daily three-page intelligence report for the OKW and for senior field commanders. It summarised the latest intelligence assessments and provided a round-up of Allied military activities in the last 24 hours. These daily summaries were backed up by fortnightly assessments of the enemy's Order of Battle and occasional long-range predictions of the Allies' strategic intentions. All of these reports also went directly to Hitler and represented the cream of the German intelligence system.

In March 1943 a new commander took control of FHW. Colonel Alexis von Roenne was a Prussian aristocrat whose family had once owned estates along the Baltic. He was straight-backed, totally proper, had a long aquiline nose and wore round gold-framed glasses. But there was a frailty about his demeanour that was distinctly un-Prussian. To some he came across more like a university professor than a professional soldier. And he was ice cool, determined and happy to be out of step with the fawning officers who tended to get to the top in the Nazi Wehrmacht. He had rather surprisingly become Hitler's favourite intelligence analyst after his correct predictions about Allied responses to the German blitzkrieg in 1939 and 1940. Hitler consequently had great faith in his predictions and called him back from the Eastern Front in 1943. But with his aristocratic background, Von Roenne had little genuine sympathy with the Nazis. Supremely professional and reliable to begin with, his anti-Nazi sentiments slowly persuaded him to pretend to be taken in by Allied deceptions that he might well have seen through. He was at the centre of analysis of the Operation Mincemeat deception. The Abwehr officers involved totally accepted as genuine the two letters from General Nye and Admiral Mountbatten that were found in the briefcase attached to the body washed up on the Spanish coast. Their reputations stood to gain considerably from recovering such valuable secret intelligence. However, it has recently been suggested that although he endorsed the message that the Allies were going to attack in Greece and possibly Sardinia, and that the plans to attack Sicily were just a ruse, Von Roenne actually saw through the whole British plot and 'did not believe the Mincemeat deception for an instant.'[8]

The reality was that Von Roenne had a very poor view of the Abwehr and of the quality of the intelligence that the FHW was being fed by Canaris's men. He realised that most of the reports they were forwarding were based on information gathered from agents. And while he had no idea that most of these were double agents simply feeding up misinformation that Allied intelligence wanted them to hear, he had the simple scepticism of a professional military officer for what he looked down upon as the amateur spies working for the Abwehr. But in one regard Von Roenne was happy to accept the misinformation that was coming in from the Abwehr agents. He passed on the details of the Order of Battle that was reported back to the Abwehr as being entirely trustworthy and accurate. We have seen how Dudley Clarke in Cairo was the first to start inventing units that did not exist in order to persuade the enemy that the Middle East Command had at its disposal far more troops than were in fact available. Von Roenne took these figures and presented them as fact. And when the XX Committee told the London Controlling Section to inflate the size of the armies based in England, Von Roenne once again took these numbers as gospel. It has to be asked if he did this because, with his anti-Nazi sympathies, he wanted to make Hitler and OKW nervous of the size of the Allied armies facing them in order to undermine their confidence. But it seems unlikely. It was almost certainly the case that, as he was responsible for the defence of the West, he wanted to ensure the decision makers at the highest level had a sense of the growing size of the Allied armies in order to prevent more German divisions being sent to their destruction on the Eastern Front. Every element of the German war machine was to a degree in competition with all the other elements, and whether Von Roenne believed the Allied Order of Battle details that he was being fed or not, he did not want the western command to lose out in the tug of war with the eastern command. Thus he willingly emphasised the scale of the forces they were up against.[9]

But there was yet another organisation that rivalled the Abwehr and the FSW for supremacy in the world of German intelligence.

This intelligence organisation existed within Heinrich Himmler's SS and was known as the Sicherheitsdienst, or SD. The SD had initially been under the authority of Reinhard Heydrich, who was also in charge of the Gestapo and the Criminal Police. Founded in 1931, the SD became an important feature of the Nazi state after Hitler came to power two years later, collecting information on all the regime's opponents, including trade unionists, communists, journalists and Jews. It helped to run the first camp set up to incarcerate enemies of the regime at Dachau, outside Munich. The SD also played a role in the removal of the leaders of the SA (Brownshirts), who were murdered in what became known as the Night of the Long Knives at the end of June 1934. The killing of so many previously loyal Nazi supporters sent out a clear message of how ruthless the regime would be to anyone who did not offer total obedience to the leader, the party and the state.

In September 1939, the SD became a part of the Reich Security Main Office under Heydrich, who was now effectively Himmler's deputy. Its declared task was to fight all enemies of the Reich, whether inside Germany or abroad. As part of this campaign, the SD helped to organise and run the Einsatzgruppen, the murder squads that operated behind the advancing army units, initially in Poland and then in the occupied Soviet Union. These units murdered anyone who gave even the slightest suspicion of being hostile to the Nazis, including more than a million Jews. Heydrich, with his slicked-back hair, his cool, calculating eyes and his Aryan looks, became one of the most important figures inside Nazi Germany and one of the most brutal and feared leaders in the occupied territories. One of these was Czechoslovakia. His cruel regime there intended to destroy Czech culture, Germanise the nation and terrorise the population. This led to his assassination by a group of Czech and Slovak soldiers who had been trained by the Special Operations Executive. The reprisals that followed included the murder of all the males in the town of Lidice, which it was thought had aided the assassins, the rounding up of the local women, who were sent to concentration camps, and the complete levelling of the town's ruins. These atrocities have become infamous even in the terrible chronicle of Nazi war crimes.

Believing themselves to be the ideological guardians of the Nazi state, the SD and its leaders were deeply distrustful of the Abwehr and felt they should be in charge of all intelligence gathering and interpretation. The SD bugged the offices of the Abwehr and the telephone lines of its senior officials. At times they even put a trail on Canaris. Himmler was continuously looking for evidence that would discredit the Abwehr and provide the case for him to close it down and bring all intelligence gathering under the SS.

The overseas section of the SD was led by Brigadefuehrer Walter Schellenberg. Twenty years younger than Canaris, Schellenberg was bright, energetic and hugely ambitious. He had sophisticated tastes, could talk intelligently about music and the arts, and had a charm that marked him out from many of the thugs who dominated the higher reaches of the Nazi leadership. He was even called by some the 'good' Nazi.[10] Nevertheless, he surrounded himself with upright, black-uniformed guards of the SS and even had a machine gun in his desk aimed at the visitors chair in case an opponent got into his office. Schellenberg came across as very personable but he was utterly ruthless. He kept up a friendly relationship with Canaris, going horse riding with him first thing on most mornings through the tree-lined lanes of the Berlin Tiergarten. Schellenberg appeared to look up to the elderly Abwehr spymaster and admire his achievements. Canaris was impressed by the younger man's deference and his great energy. In reality Schellenberg was keeping up a front while secretly trying to undermine the older intelligence chief. He was constantly trying to gather enough evidence to have Canaris removed and the entire Abwehr operation closed down.

The SD thought that the Abwehr's inefficiency frequently strayed into incompetence, and they had their growing suspicions of the anti-Nazi sympathies of Canaris, Oster and other leading Abwehr officials. They thought that its officers were lazy and lived a good life in the capital cities of neutral countries, well away from the military frontline or the bombing back home in Germany. The SD suspected them of being slow and corrupt, and looked for evidence that they were involved in currency rackets or other scams. The SD called the Abwehr the 'Santa Clauses' because they seemed elderly and avuncular in their approach. The Abwehr called the SD the 'Blacks' because of their SS uniforms and dark, sinister techniques. The rivalry between the different branches of German intelligence was intense, and the antipathy felt by the FHW and the SD towards the Abwehr grew to be extreme.

All intelligence that was gathered by the Abwehr, interpreted by the FHW and reported by the SD was ultimately filtered upwards to the OKW. As Commander-in-Chief and Führer, Hitler was at the centre of this organisation, and his feelings or attitude towards all military matters reigned supreme. His principal assistant was the chief of the OKW, Field Marshal Wilhelm Keitel, who was from a middle-ranking landowning family in Brunswick. In the early years of the twentieth century, he joined the Prussian Army, which was at the core of the Imperial German Army under the Kaiser. But unlike Prussian aristocrats who went into the cavalry, he joined the less prestigious artillery. He was badly wounded while fighting British troops in Flanders in 1914, and after recovering served as a staff officer for the rest of the war. Post-war he remained within the planning staff of the small German army, the Reichswehr, that was permitted under the Versailles Treaty. He played an important part in the secret re-armament of Germany during the 1930s, and when Hitler took command of the Wehrmacht in 1938 and created the OKW he appointed Keitel as its chief. It was a position he would hold until the collapse of the Third Reich. Many senior party and military figures saw Keitel as no more than Hitler's 'yes' man, his lackey, and he acquired the nickname 'Nickgeselle' after a popular toy donkey with a nodding head.

At OKW, the operational commander or chief of staff in the west was Colonel-General Alfred Jodl. He also fought on both the Western and Eastern Fronts in the First World War, was awarded the Iron Cross twice and, like Keitel, remained in the small Reichswehr during the 1920s and '30s. In August 1939, Hitler appointed him chief of staff of the OKW, and the victories that followed in Poland, Norway, France, Holland and Belgium convinced Jodl that Germany's final triumph was just around the corner. He spent much of the rest of the war at the Wolf's Lair, Hitler's command post in a forest in East Prussia. Jodl signed the final surrender document to the Western Allies in May 1945.

The many divisions between the German intelligence organisations played into the hands of the different British intelligence agencies. But there was another enormous advantage enjoyed by the British. In Europe it was relatively easy to smuggle agents across land borders. But getting an agent across the Channel was always far more complicated. The British people during the war years came to believe – entirely wrongly – that spies or fifth columnists were active everywhere and so kept a good look out for anyone behaving suspiciously or even for strangers with an unusual accent. Many a poor refugee from Occupied Europe found themselves being forced to explain to a local police constable what he or she was doing in a locality. Ministry of Information propaganda around the famous theme 'Careless Talk Costs Lives' and the storylines of several feature films fanned the flames of this fear of fifth columnists.[11] And, as we have seen, all the agents that did get to Britain were either rounded up and imprisoned, executed or 'turned' to feed back a mass of deception into the corridors of the Abwehr, and from there into the FHW and ultimately to the OKW. Britain built up an almost impenetrable barrier around its shores, closed off from the continent and Occupied Europe.

From the summer of 1940, Bletchley Park began to intercept the reports from the Abwehr. And within a year the codebreakers were also reading the cyphers sent by the FHW. Their daily reports were intercepted and decoded, and Allied intelligence could see precisely what the FSW was thinking. This gave the Allies an inestimable advantage. The intelligence agencies could clearly assess what misinformation that they had offered up had got through to the FSW and been accepted as genuine.[12] When it came to following the success or failure of Operation Mincemeat, this deciphering proved particularly valuable and enabled the London Controlling Section to see that their deception had been accepted 'rod, line and sinker' (see Chapter 4). It would prove to be just as valuable in the next year of deception games.

In the autumn of 1943, Hitler and the OKW began to consider their priorities for the following year. General Jodl argued that the German forces in the west had been so run down that they were now at a level at which they would no longer be capable of maintaining an effective defence against a major Allied assault. This argument finally got through to Hitler, who for more than two years had been obsessed with the Eastern Front. As a consequence, a major reorientation of strategic thinking was laid down in November 1943 in Führer Directive No. 51. This made it clear that, while the major struggle against Bolshevism would continue in the East, described as 'the hard and costly battle', there was a new and potentially even greater threat, an Anglo-American landing in the west. Hitler wrote, 'I can therefore no longer take responsibility for further weakening the west in favour of other theatres of war. I have consequently decided to reinforce its defences.' This was to consist firstly of a massive building programme to construct a long line of coastal defences from Norway to the Spanish border. And secondly of a plan to reinforce the German army in the west, with new full-strength infantry divisions backed by a set of fully equipped armoured panzer divisions. Together these newly invigorated troops, located behind a vast run of fortifications, would throw the Allies back into the sea at whatever point they chose to land.

The scale of the fortifications that would become known as the Atlantic Wall was awesome: 15,000 bunkers requiring 1.2 million tons of steel and 17 million cubic metres of concrete would go into constructing a vast line of defences covering 2,000 miles from south-western France to northern Norway. Some 600,000 workers, a high proportion of whom were slave labourers, would work on building this vast Atlantic Wall. But with the immense drain on manpower on the Eastern Front, would there be enough troops to man these defences? Decisions would constantly have to be made as to where to concentrate German forces. The Atlantic Wall was simply too long to allow it to be sufficiently well guarded along its entire length.

The principal question that the OKW wanted answered regarding British war plans by late 1943 was: What is the strategy for an invasion of northern Europe? Obviously, only a tiny number of planners and politicians would know the details of where and when an invasion would come. However, there were other indicators that could be looked for. If an invasion of Norway was planned, most probably an army would be gathering in Scotland. If the invasion was planned for Normandy or Brittany, most likely armed forces and landing craft would be assembling somewhere along the Devon or Dorset coast. If, however, the invasion was being planned across the shortest route, to the Pas de Calais, then an army would be forming in the south-east of England around Kent. And however incompetent German intelligence was in penetrating Britain, there were, of course, other means available for the Germans to follow what was going on in England, such as aerial reconnaissance and signals intelligence. The German war machine now reached a critical point. Its intelligence chiefs decided to focus on the south of

England. Was an invasion force assembling in the south-west or the south-east of the country? Hitler ordered that south-eastern England should be the principal area where German radio-operators, photo-reconnaissance aircraft and agents on the ground must concentrate their attention. Kent and the south-east would soon come under the German intelligence spotlight.

Chapter 6

FIRST US ARMY GROUP

On 17 December 1943, Colonel Noel Wild boarded a large flying boat on the Nile in Cairo. Wild was the staff officer recruited by Dudley Clarke at the Shepheard's Hotel in April 1942 as his deputy of 'A' Force. He had been effectively running the Middle East deception operations during Clarke's long absences from Cairo, helping plan the deception campaigns that contributed to victory at El Alamein and the success of the Anglo-American landings in north-west Africa, Operation Torch. The experience Wild had picked up in his eighteen months with 'A' Force made him one of the leading masters of deception in the British intelligence establishment, an expert in inflating the Order of Battle and of disguising tanks and trucks in the desert. He was exhausted by long days of effort without a break for a year and a half and was returning to the UK to see his wife and family after this prolonged spell in Egypt. The usual route to and from Egypt was down the Red Sea and the east coast of Africa, around the Cape and north through the Atlantic. It took several weeks. In certain unusual circumstances, however, a senior officer could be flown out or back by a civilian flying boat service operated by the British Overseas Airways Corporation (BOAC), who had inherited a whole set of routes from the pioneering Imperial Airways at the beginning of the war.

In order to avoid the battle zone in the Mediterranean, the luxury BOAC flying boat flew in a long detour southwards, down the Nile to Khartoum, across central Africa, landing on the Congo river to refuel at Stanleyville (today Kisangani) and Leopoldville (today Kinshasa). Emerging into West Africa at Lagos in Nigeria, the flying boat continued to Bathurst in The Gambia (today Banjul), then north to neutral Lisbon, and after a brief stop at Foynes on the Shannon in the west of Ireland, back to Britain, landing in Poole Harbour on the south coast. Wild stepped off his flying boat on 24 December and managed to get home to his family by Christmas Day.

What Wild did not know was that he was not being sent home simply to see his family. Dudley Clarke and John Bevan had decided that Operation Bodyguard, the newly formed deception operation to accompany the planning for the invasion of Europe, needed a new head and a clear direction in the critical months that were approaching. Wild spent Christmas with his wife and family but, in essence, he had been deceived. He would not be returning to Egypt but had instead been chosen to play a role based in Britain and would soon take on a set of completely new responsibilities.

Deception ideas linked with the rapidly evolving plans to invade northern Europe had been circulating within the intelligence establishment throughout the second half of 1943. The principal objective was to deceive the Germans into thinking that the invasion had been cancelled in September as part of Operation Cockade, and would remain cancelled into 1944. This required convincing the Germans that there would be no D-Day in northern Europe and that Allied ground forces would continue to focus on the Mediterranean. Additionally, the plan was to convince the Germans that the Allied air forces would hope to bomb the Third Reich into submission by an escalation of the bombing offensive. This deception became known as Plan Jael, named after a biblical heroine who lulled her enemy to sleep and then drove a stake through his forehead.

There were a multitude of problems with Plan Jael. First and foremost, it was impossible to hide the growing mass of troops that were assembling in southern England. These included British troops but especially consisted of the rapidly expanding American forces arriving in the UK. Secondly, the public announcement following the Tehran summit that General Eisenhower had been appointed Supreme Commander of an Allied Expeditionary Force based in Britain clearly implied that resources were being gathered for an invasion of some sort. This really put an end to Plan Jael, unless the Germans could be persuaded that Eisenhower's appointment was itself a deception designed to distract attention from military plans elsewhere. But this was getting too far-fetched. General Morgan at COSSAC expressed his dissatisfaction with Plan Jael and the Americans too made it clear that they had no confidence in this particular form of deception. By early December, it was clearly time for a new plan.

John Bevan set to work with his team at the London Controlling Section and a new set of proposals were put before the Chiefs of Staff on 24 December, the very day that Colonel Wild disembarked from his flying boat at Poole Harbour. These new proposals were effectively the first formulation of Operation Bodyguard. The basic objective of this new deception was partly strategic, to 'persuade the enemy to dispose his forces in areas where they can cause least interference with Operations Overlord and Anvil [the invasion of southern France to follow the landings in the north]'. And partly tactical, to 'deceive the enemy as to the strength, timing and objective of Overlord and Anvil.' As part of the deception plan, the Germans were to be led to believe that a joint invasion of northern Norway with the Soviets was planned for the spring. Also, they wanted the Germans to believe that no cross-Channel invasion would be possible until late summer 1944 because of the lack of landing craft. Before then, operations in Italy and against the Balkans would take priority.[1]

As the Germans began to construct the heavy defences of the Atlantic Wall at the end of 1943, with its unprecedented build-up of men and materials, Hitler appointed Field Marshal Rommel to command a new army in the west, Army Group B. He was placed in command of two German armies, the Fifteenth Army defending the Pas de Calais, and the Seventh Army in Normandy, west of the Seine estuary. Rommel threw himself with tremendous energy into supervising the build-up of the coastal defences along the north French coast. He even involved himself in the detailed sighting of artillery and machine-gun posts to maximise their line of fire across potential landing beaches. Coincidentally, Rommel's appointment coincided with Eisenhower leaving the Mediterranean and taking up his new post. At the end of December, COSSAC would cease to exist and a new organisation would take over. The American general formed his new command, known as the Supreme Headquarters of the Allied Expeditionary Force, SHAEF. The Allies had committed at Tehran in November to launch a cross-Channel invasion in May 1944. And, also in November, Hitler had announced his determination to build up German defences in the west. Now, two new commanders were in place to see through these fresh challenges. At the beginning of 1944 they faced each other across the Channel.

While the newly appointed commanders began making their own plans to launch and to repel an invasion, Colonel Wild was concerned with more domestic matters, enjoying Christmas with his family. Soon after he had finished his Christmas dinner, he was told that he would not be returning to the Middle East as he had expected, but that he was to head the section in charge of deception operations at the newly formed SHAEF, a section to be called Ops (B). In January 1944 a fundamental reorganisation of deception planning took place. Ops (B) under Wild was to take overall supervision of deception operations. It was given responsibility for instructing the London Controlling Section, MI5 and MI6 as to what information (or, more precisely, disinformation) was to be passed on to the enemy. Wild had a lot of catching up to do and so was made a member of the XX Committee. Working with him would be Major Roger Fleetwood Hesketh. Another Eton and Christ Church, Oxford, graduate who had gone into law, Hesketh was called to the Bar at the Middle Temple in 1928 and pursued a successful career as a barrister. As the eldest son he devoted much of his time to the grand family home of Meols Hall, near the Lancashire coast in Southport, which had been in his family since the twelfth century. As an amateur architect he developed several plans for rebuilding the country house, which up to the war consisted largely of a mid-seventeenth-century structure.[2] Modest and reticent by nature, Hesketh still enjoyed the good life, and it was rumoured that he had the finest claret cellar in the country.

These two, supported by the small group of men around them, would come up with a dazzling array of deception ideas, and largely shape the Allied deception policy for the next few months. Colonel Wild and Major Hesketh in Ops (B) held the position of final responsibility and were based in Norfolk House in St James's Square. Just around the corner was MI5 and the XX Committee, including Charles Masterman, 'Tar' Robertson and the case officers who were feeding the double agents with information to pass on to their Abwehr controllers. And just a few hundred yards away, in their offices below the Treasury in the War Rooms, was the London Controlling Section with Colonel Bevan and his team. This small group met with each other on a regular basis. They were mostly men of a similar background who would lunch at the same clubs and at times even share offices. United by the values of the old school tie and the college gown, a lot of discussion and planning was done by word of mouth and was never written down in formal memos or minutes. This helped to keep what was being discussed top secret. But it was a way of working which, according to the official historian of strategic deception, made for 'speed and informality' but unfortunately 'left practically no traces for the historian.'[3]

There were, however, other organisations who also contributed to the thinking behind the deception plans. Detailed planning was the responsibility of the operational commands. Below Eisenhower was General Montgomery as Commander-in-Chief 21st Army Group. Montgomery could be a difficult man at times, with immense confidence in the rightness of his own views and he was often tactless in the way he expressed them. Commanding the Eighth Army in North Africa, Montgomery had become a great enthusiast for deception. By mid-1943 the team in charge of deception planning at Monty's HQ was led by Lieutenant-Colonel David Strangeways, who in many ways shared some of the same characteristics as his boss. He was a perfectionist who did not suffer fools gladly and never hesitated to speak his mind, happy to air his forthright views to everyone, including officers well above him in rank. The son of a Cambridge doctor, Strangeways chose not to follow his father's calling but joined the Duke of Wellington's Regiment in 1933 as a regular officer. He led his men from the front and at Dunkirk saved several of his troops by wading out through the surf to an abandoned barge and loading them into it. In the next couple of years he moved into intelligence, but he did not view himself as a deskbound planner and whenever possible got out to the front to see things for himself. When German troops surrendered at Tunis he led a special force to dash into the city in order to capture documents and cipher machines before the Germans had time to destroy them. Dennis Wheatley remembered him as 'a small, good-looking man with a brisk, efficient manner and a very quick mind.' He was an outsider to the small, closed group of Oxford alumni running the deception operations in London. He did not operate on what Wheatley called the 'old boy level.'[4] Christopher Harmer of MI5 wrote, 'Strangeways had a lot of Monty's arrogance and contempt for everyone who fell outside his particular ken.'[5] And with this came a problem. He hated Colonel Wild, whom he regarded as a 'nincompoop' and a 'pain in the neck.' And for Wild the feeling was mutual.[6]

So, when Strangeways returned to London to head up Montgomery's D-Day deception unit he was almost inevitably going to fall out with Wild. When he read the emerging plans for Operation Bodyguard, he did not like them. And it was not long before Strangeways started to make his views absolutely clear. He saw a major weakness in the plans that were initially discussed at SHAEF. If the Germans believed there was an invasion coming in the Pas de Calais region some six or seven weeks after an invasion took place in Normandy, they would have time to respond to the Normandy invasion, possibly even to throw the landing forces back into the sea before returning to do battle with the later assault when it was supposed to take place in the Pas de Calais area. Strangeways argued that in order to get the German High Command to do as the Allies wanted, the Deception plan must build up the number of units assembling in the south of England to something like 50-plus divisions, a total of at least 750,000 men. It must be made clear in the phoney plan that the main attack was coming in the Pas de Calais area and this would consist of six divisions on the first day and six divisions in the follow-up. Six divisions, or 90,000 men, was the maximum number that could be transported with the existing amount of landing craft. After the first few days, the Germans must be led to believe that reinforcements would be arriving at a rate of three divisions per day for about a fortnight. Strangeways argued forcefully that in order to get the German High Command to retain its principal forces in the Pas de Calais region, they must believe that any initial invasion, like the actual landings in Normandy, was only a feint to mislead them away from the major invasion that was still to come in the Pas de Calais. This second event must not be perceived as a subsidiary operation; as far as the enemy were concerned it was to be seen as the main assault.[7]

The strength of Strangeways's argument soon held sway. At a series of meetings in late January the British chiefs of staff and SHAEF both accepted the revised plan. Additionally, the deception planners resolved to keep up the pretence of a further attack against Norway. For this, another six divisions would appear to be held in reserve in the north of Britain. As the full scale of this revised plan sank in, the British chiefs of staff decided that a new codename would be needed. Out of the list of future operations came the name Mespot. Churchill, however, did not like this name and so another was pulled out of the hat, Fortitude. The name of cross-Channel deception would henceforth be Operation Fortitude South, while that of the assault against Scandinavia would be Operation Fortitude North.

In February the deception planners started to invent a new Order of Battle in Britain that could believably sustain the immense scale of planned operations that were being fed to the Germans. Again, Strangeways did not think the ambition of the planning staff was sufficient. Once more there was deadlock. An urgent meeting was called between the intelligence planers of SHAEF and of Monty's 21st Army Group. Christopher Harmer later heard a report of what had happened. 'At this meeting,' Harmer wrote, 'Strangeways had stated that the plan was useless and publicly tore it up in front of everybody, announcing that he proposed to re-write it, and had Monty's authority. It gave maximum offence!'[8] Strangeways carried on making his point regardless of the offence he was creating. He argued that in order to present the realistic possibility *after* the invasion of Normandy had taken place that an even bigger operation was coming against the Pas de Calais, it was necessary months in advance to start to build up the existence of a new army. Four new assault formations would be needed to carry out a large-scale operation north and south of Cap Gris-Nez in the Pas de Calais. But, as Hesketh observed, 'one cannot produce four imaginary assault formations, ready to embark at a moment's notice, by a wave of the hand.'[9] Moreover, if 21st Army Group was seen to be planning from the south-west of England an invasion of the Normandy area, how could it be imagined that it would simultaneously be planning a major cross-Channel assault from the south-east of England? Strangeways's conclusion was clear. A new army group, primarily but not exclusively made up of American troops, needed to be created straight away. Consequently, SHAEF would, as it were, be known to be in charge of two complete Army Groups, the 21st Army Group in the south-west under Monty and another Army Group in the south-east looking to lead the second, shorter cross-Channel invasion. The other planners were both amazed and impressed by his logic. But they now started to ask themselves, 'Could we possibly get away with simulating an entirely fictitious Army Group?'[10]

The answer was that they could and they must. On 23 February, SHAEF finally approved the revised plans Strangeways had insisted on. There was a unit, a planning formation, already in existence that the Germans had got wind of through a radio intercept. This was the First US Army Group, which came to be known from its acronym as FUSAG. It was not in use as an operational combat force but was intended to take over in Normandy once the American troops there had grown to the number that required being placed into a complete Army Group. But now, the First US Army Group provided the skeleton on which could be hung an entirely new and imaginary army. In early 1944, FUSAG really existed on paper only. Now it would become a major pretend formation under the command of SHAEF.

From the end of February, the intelligence staff started to allocate units to this hoax Army Group. For it to be feasible as far as the Germans were concerned, it needed to consist of some actual units as well as some completely fictional ones. The US Third Army was a real force that was located in Cheshire. It was currently part of the 21st Army Group. This US Third Army consisted of two corps, each of three American divisions. These men were training to move into Normandy after the beachhead had been established. Entirely separate to this was the First Canadian Army, consisting of one corps of two divisions. One of the Canadian divisions was based, conveniently for Fortitude, in Dover. The other was based at Aldershot. These two separate armies were now put under the command of the new First US Army Group. Many more imaginary units would be added later.

In the new deception plans that came into being at the end of February 1944, there was to be another crucial element. It was essential that everything that was going on by way of preparation for the real invasion in the south and south-west of England should remain as secret as possible. British troops were assembling in the Southampton and Portsmouth area. American troops were gathering from Poole westwards, along the south Dorset and Devon coasts to Plymouth. Here, hundreds of thousands of men were assembling and training, landing craft were being prepared, the required armoured vehicles were being drawn up in vast depots and all the other vital features of planning for the real invasion of Normandy were taking place. This was *not* meant to be observed by the enemy. But all the dummy activities that were going on under the First US Army Group banner in the south-east of England were intended to be open to observation. So a policy of 'discreet display' was adopted with regard to FUSAG, whereas a policy of 'total concealment' was applied to everything related to the 21st Army Group. For the real army all new installations had to be fully camouflaged, camps had to use smokeless fuel so plumes of smoke did not give away their location. Even the towels had to be khaki rather than white so as to be difficult to spot from the air. But in the FUSAG area camouflage was to be less intense, and in areas like Dover and Folkestone it was far more difficult anyway to hide the existence of large numbers of troops. It was hoped that German aerial reconnaissance would pick up what was happening in the south-east but never discover what was going on in the south-west.[11]

The implementation of Fortitude South would consist of several phases. Firstly, there was the gradual build-up of FUSAG as a credible force to launch a major cross-Channel invasion against the well-defended beaches of the Pas de Calais. Secondly, to make this seem real to the enemy, a vast amount of dummy radio traffic had to be created. At first this had to report the transfer of units who were not already in the south-east into that region. The US Third Army divisions that were in Cheshire did not actually have to move to Kent and the south-east, they just had to report that they *were* moving. A new fictitious command HQ was created at Chelmsford in Essex. According to the radio traffic all the units within the Third Army moved to the region to the east of London, spread from Essex into Suffolk. Beyond this, the new Army Group had to start all the regular chatter that any large force would generate. A complete US Signals unit was dedicated to this, the 3103rd Signals Battalion, who arrived in Britain in February. Signallers began to send the sort of communications that such a vast army would create, with instructions from corps to divisions, from divisions to brigades, from brigades to regiments and then down to battalions. Many of these were very precise, and to add to the reality included the sort of complaints that would frequently come up. One particularly imaginative signaller, for instance, sent messages about the lack of dentists in certain units to attend to the men's teeth. All of this was transmitted in simple codes, knowing that the Germans would intercept the traffic and be able to read the messages.

Meanwhile, the double agents under the control of their case officers in MI5 were all fed information to pass back to their Abwehr controllers. They started to send regular reports about the concentration of Allied forces in the south-east of England. Tricycle made one of his regular visits to Lisbon in March and handed over a mass of documentation about the assembly of troops in the Kent area. When this passed on through the system to the FHW they marked it up as 'particularly valuable.'[12] Brutus, the ex-Polish Intelligence officer, now told his Abwehr controllers that he had been allocated a new position as Polish liaison officer to FUSAG HQ. This would, of course, give him an invaluable opportunity to report on what was going on, and over the next few months MI5 made very good use of this. Tate now appropriately got a job as a farm worker in Kent and was able to pass on reports of troop movements all around him. Once again, Garbo was the jewel that always glittered. From January 1944 his Abwehr bosses were asking for more and more details about forthcoming operations in both the north and the south. No one person could realistically cover all the ground that was needed. But because Garbo was supposedly the centre of a network of notional spies in his employment (at great expense to the Abwehr controllers), he could gather reports from across the country, all sent to him in invisible ink. He could then write them up in his verbose prose and pass the reports on either by letter to Lisbon or by using his new secret radio link.

As more and more invented units came into being, so the case officers telling Garbo, Tricycle, Brutus and the others what to report back had to become increasingly creative. Where a unit was plucked out of thin air, full details had to be passed on. On several occasions the case officers had to invent a divisional crest and motto. Along with new insignia they had to make phoney observations of cap badges and unit flags. Many elements needed to make these hoax units credible had to be created and passed on in a deception that grew increasingly intricate week by week.

Moreover, the existence of such a large group of American troops in one area would have generated considerable social consequences, which would have been the case if FUSAG had been real. The deceivers had this covered, too. Articles were placed in local papers in which people living near the new imaginary camps complained of the disruption caused by the arrival of American soldiers. They wrote to complain of military traffic blocking the narrow country lanes, to bemoan the decline in morals of young British women near the camps, and to record the disgusting sight of finding used prophylactics strewn about the woods near the encampments. All these newspaper stories were passed on by the double agents to the Abwehr.

So began what has been described as 'the largest, most elaborate, most carefully planned … of all the Allied deceptive operations [of the war].'[13] Allied intelligence was able to see how the Germans were being taken in by following the daily German intelligence reports of the FHW, decrypted at Bletchley. At the beginning of 1944 the FHW had estimated that the number of divisions in Britain available for an invasion of the continent was 55. In fact there were 37. By the end of May the FHW assessment had risen to a total of 79 available Allied divisions. In fact there were only 52. It was this misconception, so carefully cultivated over the months, that made the threats to both Norway and the Pas de Calais believable to the Germans.[14]

Every unit allocated to FUSAG and the cross-Channel invasion at the Pas de Calais had to have a commander. And he had to be credible to the Germans to make the units themselves plausible. The FHW had a central register listing the names of all senior Allied commanders that they knew of, including details of previous commands and any other information that was known about them. So the corps and divisions in the mythical First US Army Group all had to have named generals in command, and when their details were passed on or discovered, they had to be recognisable to the FHW. At the top of FUSAG, Lieutenant General Omar Bradley was placed in command. He was a convincing leader of such a major force, having excelled in command in Sicily and having moved to London towards the end of 1943. The Germans would have no difficulty in recognising him as commander of a major American Army Group. However, it was soon spotted that there was a problem. Bradley had a real and active role in the actual invasion of Normandy. He was due, if all went well, to land in Normandy along with his real command headquarters staff four days after D-Day, or D+4. This would be widely reported and could never be kept secret. But how could a man who was known to be in Normandy be in command of the unit that was planning an even bigger landing at the Pas de Calais a few weeks later? This would be impossible and threatened to undermine the total feasibility of the First US Army Group and its intentions.

The Allies needed to find a new commander for the First US Army Group and to get him in place as soon as possible. Such a person had to have credibility to the Germans as the commander of a major amphibious operation. He had to have a track record that was highly regarded by the enemy. He had to be willing to put himself about. He had to enjoy publicity and being seen in the spotlight. He had to be willing to act the part of a commander of an army that never was.

There was only one person available who fitted this bill: General George S. Patton.

Chapter 7
PATTON

General George Smith Patton Junior was a soldier's soldier. He liked to lead from the front, had a naturally aggressive nature and was one of the greatest tacticians and tank commanders of the Second World War. He also had the ability to fire up his men through powerful, emotional speeches that were full of the sort of vulgarities and swear words that would be very familiar to the normal trooper. Additionally, he was an egotist, a poet, a military historian who knew some of the classical accounts of war by heart, and a man who apparently believed in reincarnation. He had a strong conviction that he had fought and died in the wars of the ancient Greeks, in the Roman legions, in Napoleon's army and in the American Civil War. His behaviour towards soldiers whom he regarded as cowards and his outspoken outbursts made him the most controversial general of the war, a leader who was twice removed from his command.

Patton could trace his ancestry back to the Welsh lords of Glamorgan on his mother's side, and to King Edward I of England on his father's side. The first Patton to emigrate to America was Robert Patton, sailing from Ayr in Scotland to

Virginia in about 1770. The Pattons had a long involvement in the military, counting George Washington's great-grandfather as another of his ancestors. During the American Civil War sixteen members of his family fought for the Confederacy, many of them enjoying distinguished military careers and three of them dying in battle.[1]

George Smith Patton was born in 1885 as the eldest son of what by then had become a wealthy Californian family. Although he struggled at first at school, probably suffering from dyslexia, he was very aware of coming from a long line of military men. He believed he had inherited a great tradition of courage, bravery and chivalry, and he never doubted that his destiny would be anything other than becoming a soldier.[2] In 1903, aged eighteen, he enrolled at the Virginia Military Institute, and from there went on to the US Military Academy at West Point. He did well at military drills but poorly in his academic studies and had to retake his first year after failing mathematics. He graduated in 1909 and was commissioned in the US Cavalry.

He also developed as a fine sportsman. After spells at different track and field events he decided to concentrate on the Modern Pentathlon. This was devised for army officers and consisted of five events: fencing, swimming, horse-riding, pistol-shooting and cross-country running. His ambition to excel at sport was nearly as great as his plans to succeed in the military, and he competed in the Modern Pentathlon at the 1912 Stockholm Olympic Games. Patton did well in the first four events, and the climax of the competition was a 4,000-metre run through a muddy, forested swamp. The day of the event came and it was exceptionally hot and humid. Patton set off and just ran as fast as he could, without any attempt at pacing himself. Pacing was for sissies, in his view. He would just run like hell for as long as he could. He entered the stadium in the lead, but the heat and humidity finally got to him and his legs gave way.

He was passed by two Swedes, before he staggered across the finishing line and then collapsed, severely dehydrated. He was unconscious for some time.

In the final reckoning he came fifth, behind four Swedish Army officers. This was perfectly creditable, but Patton was denied the glory he desperately sought. Although he was usually bitterly opposed to anyone who stood in the way of his aspirations, the spirit of the Olympics got to him and he praised the Swedish officers who had beaten him. After the Second World War was over he had a reunion with the members of the Swedish Olympic pentathlon team in which they jokingly re-enacted the pistol-shooting competition. This time Patton came second.[3]

Patton's Olympic performance won him credit with senior army officials and some notoriety in the American press. Based at Fort Myer, just outside Washington DC, he mixed with senior military officials and was selected to ride in President Woodrow Wilson's inauguration parade in 1913. Meanwhile, he had married Beatrice Ayer, the daughter of a wealthy Boston industrialist. Their marriage was happy despite Patton's long absences through his career, and they had three children. Life was looking very promising for the young Patton, but he longed for some military action in which he could prove himself. He would pull strings and use whatever contacts he could to try to position himself where he could at last play the role of the warrior-hero. He soon acquired the reputation as 'a very zealous and ambitious young officer'.[4]

His opportunity came as relations between the United States and Mexico went into a rapid decline. In 1916 the US Army conducted an expedition into Mexico to punish a raid by the revolutionary Pancho Villa on Columbus, New Mexico. Patton talked his way into the role of aide to General John Pershing, the commander of the expedition, and Patton led the first ever American motorised attack against a group of Mexican insurgents. His assault was a success and all the insurgents were killed. It was Patton's glorious baptism of fire. He learned from Pershing an immense amount about the need for order, duty and discipline in a military operation. He wrote that in Pershing's unit 'every man was fit; weaklings had gone … and discipline was perfect.'[5] These were lessons that would stay with him.

When America joined the First World War in April 1917, General Pershing was put in charge of leading an American Expeditionary Force to Europe, and Patton was among the first Americans to travel to France with him. Rapidly promoted, Patton moved from horses to tanks, and from the cavalry to take command of a tank brigade. He quickly realised the immense prospects an armoured vehicle brought to breaking the stalemate of trench warfare and how the tank could be used, like the cavalry of old, to lead a dramatic break-out through enemy lines. He had a clear vision of what mobile tank warfare could be. And he wanted his tank troops to be something of an elite unit, always immaculately turned out, well-drilled, following a strict discipline and with a strong *esprit de corps*.

During spring and summer of 1918, Patton's unit was equipped with French-built Renault light tanks. Colonel Patton prepared his men for the first ever US tank assault. Their chance came at the Battle of Saint-Mihiel in September 1918. He announced in terms that would characterise his later speeches to 'remember you are the first American tanks [into battle]. You must establish the fact that American tanks do not surrender.' He told his men that if their tank was disabled they must go forward with the infantry.[6] Although many of his tanks broke down or ran out of fuel, overall the first American tank engagement was a famous success.

Later that month, the US First Army regrouped further north to take part in a far bigger Allied assault upon the Hindenburg Line. The man responsible for moving half a million American soldiers to their new assembly lines was a staff officer named Colonel George C. Marshall. At dawn on 26 September, in a thick fog, Patton's tanks went into combat for a second time, at the opening of the Battle of Meuse-Argonne. However, by late morning his tanks had become entangled in the German trenches near the town of Cheppy. Patton went forward and found a group of infantry whom he thought were shirking and ordered them to help dig out the sides of the trenches so the tanks could move on. As he began to do this himself as an example to the others, under fire, he hit one hesitant man over the head with a shovel. Again, it would become a character trait that he would show no sympathy to those whom he believed were displaying weakness in battle.

Following this, while still under fire, Patton had a curious vision. He later said that he saw images of his soldier-ancestors from the Civil War looking down at him from the clouds over the German lines, urging him forward. This encouraged him to lead a group of men to assault the German machine guns. Shouting, 'Let's go get them, who's with me?' he led a charge of about 150 men, but as he got to the top of a small hill he realised there were only a handful still with him. Then he was hit and badly wounded in the left leg by a machine-gun bullet. For several hours he lay bleeding in a shell hole before more tanks and infantry reinforcements were able to destroy the German machine-gun posts. Patton was finally evacuated to a dressing station and had to spend the last weeks of the war in hospital. A month after the war was over he was awarded the Distinguished Service Cross 'for extraordinary heroism' on 26 September. The legend of the warrior-hero had been born.[7]

Patton returned to the United States in 1919. He and his now famous tank units were welcomed with several victory parades. He had achieved the warrior fame he had sought, but otherwise he found it difficult to adjust to the post-war world. The US Army quickly shrank in size. Even the future of the Tank Corps and its heroic commander seemed uncertain. Patton spent the next twenty years in a variety of postings, in Hawaii, Washington and Texas. He wrote several papers arguing for the independent existence of a mobile tank force. But no one took much notice and there was no money to support such a project. By 1939 the US Army was down to seventeenth in size in the world.

The war in Europe finally stirred the US into mobilising and re-equipping its armed forces. By the time the US entered the war, Patton was commander of an armoured corps, training his men in the Californian desert. In Operation Torch, in November 1942, Patton led the westernmost landing force at Casablanca. After a successful landing he supervised the occupation of Morocco and the hosting of the Casablanca conference in January 1943.

In the spring of 1943, US forces performed poorly in the North African campaign, suffering a defeat to Rommel's Afrika Korps at the Battle of Kasserine Pass. Patton was sent in to replace the sacked commander of II Corps. He immediately brought in his principles of rigorous discipline, intense training, and strict adherence to military protocols. In a short period of time he turned his corps around and victories followed as the enemy were pushed back into Tunisia and final defeat in North Africa.

Patton then led the US Seventh Army in Operation Husky, the invasion of Sicily. General Omar Bradley was appointed his second-in-command. Patton gave several speeches to his men to fire them up for what were expected to be fiercely resisted landings. In one of these to the 45th Division he warned the men of how the Germans and Italians could be treacherous in pretending to surrender and then opening fire. He told the men to 'watch out for this treachery and to kill the sons of bitches unless they were certain of their real intention to surrender'.[8] Patton's forces were to land in the south-west of the island, and General Montgomery was to land with the British Eighth Army in the south-east. The landings went ahead on 10 July, and the following day the Germans counter-attacked fiercely against American troops at Gela. Patton himself went ashore and once again made the headlines when the US press claimed (wrongly) that he had personally led his troops against the German assault. But the American troops did succeed in fighting off the counter-attack.

Once the main two forces had established a secure beachhead, Montgomery's Eighth Army was to drive north and Patton's American troops were supposed to guard its flank and rear. But Patton had no intention of playing second fiddle to Montgomery, so he turned to the west of the island, capturing the capital Palermo, where he made a grand entrance as the conquering hero and took more than 50,000 Italian prisoners. He then raced along the north coast, determined to reach Messina before Monty. 'This is a horse race in which the prestige of the US Army is at stake. We must take Messina before the British,' Patton informed one of his divisional commanders.[9] His troops entered the town just hours ahead of British forces on 16 August. It was the end of the battle for Sicily, but the beginning of an intense rivalry with Montgomery that would resonate for the next two years.

Patton could have emerged from the capture of Sicily as a great hero, but his military triumphs were marred by a series of incidents. At Biscari, in the heavy fighting following the landings, 73 Italian prisoners were massacred by an officer and a sergeant of the 45th Division. Patton at first seemed to dismiss the story as an exaggeration, but his deputy, General Bradley, had the two men court-martialled. The men argued in their defence that they had only been following orders from Patton in his pre-landing speech, encouraging them not to take prisoners. The claim was thrown out, but Patton became the object of an official investigation by a US Army inspector general.[10] Another incident took place at Comiso airfield when a group of German and Italian prisoners of war were brought in by truck and machine-gunned by men from the same division. Again, Patton's blood-thirsty speeches seem to have got the American soldiers fired up.[11] The second killing remained un-investigated, but the Biscari incident brought the whole issue into the public domain. Not only did it show up Patton in a bad light, but it soured relations with both his deputy, Bradley, and his superior, General Eisenhower, who were both outraged by news of the massacres.

Two further incidents were even more serious for Patton. On the afternoon of 3 August, Patton stopped off at an evacuation hospital outside the village of Nicosia. He talked to several of the wounded men and was moved by their bravery and cheerfulness. Then he encountered a man suffering from what was then called 'battle fatigue' and today would be called post-traumatic stress disorder. The man, Private Charles Kuhl, said he was not wounded but told the General, 'I can't take it.' Patton suddenly erupted. In a rage he slapped the man round his face, lifted him by his collar and kicked the now terrified soldier out of the tent. That evening in his diary, Patton wrote that such men 'if they shirk their duty, they should be tried for cowardice and shot.'[12]

A week later, on 10 August, a second incident occurred, at another field hospital. After meeting and encouraging a group of wounded men he encountered another soldier suffering from trauma who was cowering in a corner, shivering. Patton could see no signs of a wound or bandaging, and when he asked the man what the matter was he said his nerves were shot. His name was Private Paul Bennett. Patton began shouting at Bennett, and according to witness reports screamed, 'You dirty no-good son of a bitch! You cowardly bastard! You are a disgrace to the army … You ought to be lined up against a wall and shot.' At this point Patton got out his pistol and waved it in Bennett's face and then slapped him hard. In the midst of the commotion, the head of the hospital hurriedly arrived. Patton told him to 'get the coward out of here'. As Bennett began to sob Patton grew even more furious, slapped him again and said he didn't want the brave men in the tent to see such 'a yellow bastard being babied'.[13] Those who witnessed the incident were horrified at seeing a soldier who had been fighting for some months but whose nerves had snapped being humiliated. Patton, on the other hand, was proud of what he had done and a few hours later boasted about it to General Bradley.

Word of this incident soon leaked to a group of journalists, who carried out their own investigation. A couple of the them visited the field hospital, interviewed the witnesses and wrote up a detailed account of what had happened. But they were unsure what to do next. Patton was, after all, in the eyes of most newspaper readers a great war hero. How could such a man have displayed such appalling behaviour? They decided not to go public and instead passed the report on to General Eisenhower's headquarters in Algiers. Eisenhower had already heard complaints about the incidents, which had been passed up through the medical service. He was shocked by what he had heard but thought it might have been overblown. When he read the report written by the journalists he realised not only that the story had not been exaggerated, but that it was even worse than he had realised.

Patton's behaviour had shocked those who witnessed it. Hitting an enlisted man was most definitely against army regulations. But it seems most likely that Patton simply could not help himself; his rage overwhelmed him and he lost control. He frequently visited field hospitals near the front, and he would often wind himself up into a highly emotional state when terribly wounded men told him that they were fine and would soon be back with their fighting units. He was in this state when he erupted in what became known as the 'slapping incidents'. More fundamentally, he really did not understand that men had their own individual breaking points. While he developed an act of appearing defiant and apparently fearless under fire, he did not appreciate that other men had a different level of resistance to fear. In the First World War, many senior officers thought that any man who broke under fire was a coward. The concept of 'shell shock' was barely understood and any mental problem was seen as either a form of weakness or an attempt at malingering. In the strict military mind there was a black and white line between being fit and ready for combat, and displaying cowardice in the face of the enemy. Slowly during that war there was a gradual understanding that shell shock or trauma was not a physical state but a nervous condition that required sympathy and understanding, and that it was possible in many cases to treat it. Even so, in the British Army more than 3,000 soldiers were court-martialled and found guilty of cowardice for which the sentence was death, and 343 were actually shot, usually by firing squad at dawn. It is clear from the records that have finally been opened that the majority of these men needed medical attention rather than military discipline.[14]

Although much had been learned about shell shock, war neuroses and the treatment of trauma during the First World War and in the decades following, Patton was of the old school. He could not understand it and simply saw any manifestation of it as weakness and as a sign of cowardice. At one point during the second incident, in a comment that also displayed his nascent anti-Semitism, he was heard to shout out in a fury, 'There's no such thing as shell shock. It's an invention of the Jews.'[15] Without doubt Patton himself was under pressure at the time of the slapping incidents, and one of his biographers has even claimed paradoxically that he might have been suffering from a form of battle fatigue himself without being aware of it.[16]

But none of this can justify or excuse the behaviour of such a senior figure towards men who were clearly undergoing medical treatment for a collapse of their nerves.

Eisenhower was in a quandary. There were grounds for sending Patton home in disgrace. But he admired him as a general, both for his aggressive spirit and for the way in which he threw himself wholeheartedly into combat. These were, of course, the very qualities that had provoked Patton's unforgiveable outbursts. Eisenhower realised that if the stories got out it would be the end of Patton's career as a commanding officer. 'They'll be howling for his scalp,' he wrote. 'I simply cannot let that happen. Patton is *indispensable* to the war effort – one of the guarantors of our victory.'[17]

Eisenhower wrote a powerful letter of reprimand to Patton. At once the General, who was enjoying the spoils of his Sicilian victory, realised he had made a terrible mistake. He later admitted he had been a 'damned fool'.[18] Eisenhower insisted that Patton apologise in person not only to the two soldiers concerned and the doctors and nurses who had witnessed the outbursts, but also to the whole Seventh Army, among whom word had quickly spread about the incidents. His tail between his legs, Patton agreed to carry out the apologies. Kuhl and Bennett willingly shook his hand and were relieved the nightmare of events was over. Bennett in particular was astonished that a three-star general had apologised to a simple private. The doctors and nurses, however, thought his apology was far from genuine and that he was only sorry for having lost face, not for what he had done. At various regimental and divisional gatherings, most men cheered Patton. Only a few booed.

The journalists who had investigated the story agreed to keep it quiet. But in November it was leaked to the American press and made public by Washington columnist Drew Pearson, who told the story of the incident on a radio programme. According to Eisenhower, 'a great public uproar immediately followed.'[19] The lack of a formal reprimand by the Supreme Commander was also publicly questioned. Some congressmen and senators called for Patton's dismissal. But Marshall and Eisenhower stood firm and insisted that their decision to keep him on had been the right one.

Eisenhower wrote to Marshall that Patton's military success 'must be attributed directly to his energy, determination and unflagging aggressiveness', but that he continued 'to exhibit some of those unfortunate personal traits of which you and I have always known.' General Bradley, who had also come out of the Sicilian campaign extremely well and was now marked for even higher command, was far less forgiving. He wrote, 'I would have relieved him instantly.' Bradley was also annoyed not so much by his military decision-making, which he respected, but by his flamboyant self-centred style. Wherever Patton went he drove in a convoy of fast-moving vehicles, his own flying a flag displaying his three stars. The other vehicles contained a personal guard, his closest staff officers and usually another contained a posse of photographers and pressmen who followed him everywhere. 'He was colourful but he was impetuous, full of temper, bluster … He was primarily a showman,' wrote Bradley. 'The show always seemed to come first.'[20] Bradley was spot on in his assessment. And it was this quality that would serve Patton well in his next assignment.

The months following the victory in Sicily were a bad time for Patton. Living in a grand royal palace in Palermo, he spent his days visiting the many Greek, Roman and Norman sites Sicily has to offer. He met many delegations of Sicilian civilians, most of whom bored him stiff. He was entirely cut off from the fighting as the war progressed. At one point a visitor asked him what he did all day, and Patton replied, 'I am studying the history of the Punic Wars.' The astonished visitor reflected that while the war raged in the Mediterranean, an experienced general like Patton was spending his time reading ancient history.[21] In mainland Italy the advance stalled, and Patton was critical of the command decisions made by General Mark Clark, who led the US Fifth Army. His mood swung violently up and down. At times he seemed to accept that the slapping incidents had seriously damaged his professional career. At other times he would lash out and blame others for his enforced idleness, not seeming to accept that he had brought it upon himself. He came to believe that it was the British who had somehow ganged up on him because he had beaten Montgomery into Messina. He watched Montgomery lead the Eighth Army in Italy with growing frustration and rage. 'I know I can outfight the little fart any time,' he confided to his diary.[22]

Eisenhower continued to support Patton, convinced that he would play an important part in the final victory over the Nazis. But he, too, saw him as a potential liability. He told a colleague that Patton 'is one of the best generals I have, but he's just like a time bomb. You can never be sure when he's going to go off. All you can be sure of is that it will probably be at the wrong place at the wrong time.'[23] Patton criticised Eisenhower in private and blamed him for keeping him out of the war, while publicly showing him respect and deference.

When Eisenhower was appointed Supreme Commander of the Allied invasion in December 1943, he moved to England to set up SHAEF. He then appointed Bradley, Patton's deputy in Sicily, as the commander of US land forces for Operation Overlord and Montgomery as commander of 21st Army Group. Patton was frustrated and angry at being passed over in favour of Bradley and his great rival. At the end of January 1944, he was recalled to Britain and Eisenhower gave him both good news and bad news. The good news was that he was to be given another chance and put in charge of the US Third Army. The bad news was that it was still in the United States, and when transferred to Britain it would not take part in the actual invasion and would not be sent to Normandy until about four weeks after D-Day. Eisenhower also made it clear that Patton would have to control his temper and his impulsive behaviour. Patton responded with flattery, saying, 'Ike, as you are now the most powerful man in the world, it is foolish to contest your views.' It was clear that Patton was no longer the top dog but had to become a team player. He decided he had to be nice to all the senior figures at SHAEF. 'After all the ass-licking I have to do,' he wrote in his diary, 'no wonder I have a sore lip.'[24]

The Third Army headquarters were in Knutsford, Cheshire, south-west of Manchester. As the advanced units of the Third Army began to arrive, Patton greeted them but had to tell all the officers he met to pretend they had not seen him. He was supposed to be back in Sicily, not England. It was clear that this subterfuge could not last for long, and so the decision was made to make his presence in England known. On 22 April it was reported in the press that Patton was now in England in charge of troops, although the army he commanded was not named.[25] Three days later he managed to put his foot in it again.

On 25 April he reluctantly and at the last minute accepted an invitation to attend the opening of a Welcome Club in Knutsford. Largely run by members of the Women's Voluntary Services, such places were intended to offer a welcome to newly arriving American servicemen. The chairlady introduced Patton to the sixty or so volunteers present and said he was speaking off the record. By this, Patton assumed it meant there were no reporters present. But there was one journalist there who soon got his notebook out. After various comments about killing Germans, Patton talked about British and Americans as 'two people separated by a common language' and went on to comment that 'since it is the evident destiny of the British and Americans, and of course the Russians, to rule the world, the better we know each other the better we will do.' He then made a series of comments about how attractive the English girls were and that American soldiers should get to know them better.

A brief report of his comments appeared in some British newspapers the following day, and this was quickly picked up and reported in the United States press. Some made no reference to the Russians and reported that Patton had said that the post-war world would be ruled by the British and Americans. Such comments might not have attracted much attention in normal circumstances. But following on from the slapping incidents there were many out to get Patton, and as a consequence there was immediate uproar. In Congress one Republican said that Patton had managed to 'slap the face of every one of the United Nations, except Great Britain.' The *Washington Post* said that Patton risked losing the confidence of the men he led and the public he served, concluding, 'Whatever his merits as a strategist or tactician he has revealed glaring defects as a leader of men.'[26] The Senate refused to confirm his formal promotion to Lieutenant-General, which had been pending for some time.

Once again it fell to Eisenhower to decide how to deal with Patton. This time he was sorely tempted to sack him. He later wrote, 'I began seriously to doubt my ability to hang on to my old friend, in whose fighting capacity I had implicit faith and confidence.'[27] To Bradley he said, 'Valuable as he is, I'm getting sick and tired of trying to protect him.'[28] However, once again he decided to hold on to Patton. He called him in and Patton offered his resignation. Eisenhower told him he was keeping him on, on condition that he made no further public statements or gave no press conferences. Partly this was because Eisenhower needed Patton for a new role.

As the waves were still rippling out from the Knutsford incident, Patton was eased in to a new position key to Operation Fortitude South. Indeed, it was the importance of this new role that helped to save him from being returned to the United States at the end of April. Key to the deception was the belief that the First US Army Group was assembling in the south-east of England, and Patton was very publicly appointed commander of this non-existent Army Group. Command of an imaginary Army Group was clearly not as good as being in command of an actual army preparing for the invasion. But Patton had no choice in the matter. He was lucky still to be in England with a part to play. So, realising he was being offered a lifeline, Patton threw himself into his new role.

To play this new role required every ounce of Patton's showmanship; in fact he needed some of the very qualities that had got him into trouble in Sicily and England. Patton himself admitted to aides that he was a 'goddamned natural-born ham' who enjoyed 'playing Sarah Bernhardt [a leading French actor of the early twentieth century].'[29] Patton and his convoy of vehicles, all displaying the stars and stripes, which had been seen so frequently behind the advancing American troops in Sicily, now started to race around the south-eastern corner of England, everywhere being photographed and always attracting crowds. Splendid in his freshly pressed uniform, often displaying fifteen stars (five sets of three stars emblazoned on his helmet, collar and shoulders), always ramrod straight, Patton easily created a splendid impression. On occasions when there were actual troops present he repeated the sort of stirring speech that he had made his own. 'Why, by God, I actually pity those sons of bitches we are going up against – by God, I do.' Even the dimmest of spies couldn't fail to notice his frequent appearances from Kent to Suffolk. At one point the King even visited him in Dover in what was supposed to be one of his headquarters to inspect his men. A suitable parade of fine-looking Canadian troops turned out for George VI and George Patton, both looking on proudly as the soldiers of the hoax First US Army Group marched by and saluted. Cameras clicked, notes were taken and the German double agents in Britain sent reports to their Abwehr controllers about the splendid occasion.

Patton had mixed feelings about his assignment in Fortitude South. If things had gone differently he would have been planning to leap ashore on the Normandy beaches on the first day of the real invasion. Nothing would have been better, as far as he was concerned. But although still resentful at not being able to take part in D-Day, Patton played his new role to the best of his abilities. At one point in mid-May he bumped into General James Gavin in the lobby of Claridge's Hotel in London. Gavin had led the parachute jump at Gela in the invasion of Sicily and was now training with the 82nd Airborne to drop behind enemy lines on the night before D-Day. After exchanging a few hushed words they parted, and Patton called out in a loud voice that could be heard by everyone in the public lobby, 'See you in the Pas de Calais, Gavin!' Such a security breach, if real, would have resulted in the instant dismissal of the commander concerned. But Patton was playing his part with gusto and enthusiasm. One of the American intelligence officers associated with Fortitude said after the war that Patton 'would do anything you asked him to do in the interest of the overall picture.'[30]

To succeed, a deception plan has to have two core elements. There has to be some basis in fact or reality about it, and it has to play on understandings or beliefs the enemy already has. Patton brought all this together. In German eyes, Operation Fortitude South pretty well became Operation Patton.

To start with, the First US Army Group did include some actual troops. There were the men of Patton's own Third Army who were beginning to arrive in Britain. And added to these were two divisions of the First Canadian Army. The deceivers then needed to build up the size of this force, and they were able to play upon the fact that German intelligence already believed there were far more divisions of fully trained and battle-ready Allied troops available in Britain than there were in reality. So supposedly added to the First Canadian Army with its two genuine divisions was another US formation, VIII Corps, consisting of three divisions who would eventually arrive in Britain but had not yet done so. Later, the Fourteenth US Army would appear to be part of FUSAG, with four infantry divisions, one armoured division and two airborne divisions. In support of these ground troops was supposed to be the US Ninth Air Force. In all, eleven entirely fictitious divisions, approximately 165,000 men, were added to FUSAG.[31] Along with the real troops, the Germans would calculate that Patton was in command of about 300,000 men. This was sufficient to carry out a major cross-Channel operation.

Secondly, the commander of FUSAG had to be believable as the man who would be put in charge of one of the biggest operations of the war. Again, Patton was just the right man. The Germans feared Patton and saw him as probably *the* most able commander the Allies had. Indeed, Hitler had apparently once said that Patton was 'their best general'.[32] It was entirely believable to the FHW that Patton would be put in command of the major cross-Channel invasion force. They knew of the slapping incidents and had almost certainly picked up on the reaction in Washington to Patton's Knutsford speech. But they found it impossible to believe that what in their eyes were extremely minor issues would ever cloud Eisenhower's judgement of Patton when it came to appointing his ablest commander to take on his most challenging task. As more and more disinformation flooded in to Berlin, the FHW began to call the First US Army Group *Armeegruppe Patton*, Patton's Army.

Just as with the real army preparing in south-west England, FUSAG organised a series of training exercises. They had colourful names like 'Jitterbug', 'Filmstar' and 'Honeysuckle'. And just like the real training programmes in Dorset and Devon, they were called off at the last minute if the weather conditions proved difficult. All this was communicated by the 3103rd Signals Battalion, who for months now had been transmitting entirely fictitious messages about the vast assembling forces of the First US Army Group and the difficulties they were facing.

However, to be believable, an army not only had to have a highly visible and impressive commander and make all the noises that hundreds of thousands of men communicating with each other would make, but it needed to have tanks, armoured vehicles, artillery pieces and supply trucks. There needed to be camps, fuel depots and airfields. How were these to be procured in south-east England when every available resource was being allocated to the troops preparing for the real invasion in the south-west?

Chapter 8

SHEPPERTON

Norman Loudon was a successful Scottish businessman who in 1930 founded Flicker Productions, producing flicker books for children. Containing dozens of consecutive photos of sportsmen – say a cricketer bowling or a footballer kicking a ball – the books created a sense of movement when flicked with the thumb or forefinger. This was an early experiment with making pictures move and it made a lot of money. In the following year, Loudon grew far more ambitious and bought a grand mansion in Surrey called Littleton House and 70 acres of grounds. With this he intended to join the booming business of film production.

By the 1930s the movie business had developed into a sophisticated industry employing a large force of trained and creative technicians. At the start of the war, between 20 and 25 million Britons – roughly half the population – were 'going to the pictures' weekly, and visiting the cinema had become a major leisure activity. An evening at the 'flicks' included seeing the main movie, usually American, a shorter B-movie, often British, with a newsreel and sometimes a government or commercially sponsored documentary in between. At the end of an evening, those who had not crept out earlier stood as the national anthem was played. Some city cinemas were giant establishments with a modern streamlined look, adorned with towers or domes and illuminated with bright neon signs. The cinema-goer would enter through a foyer lined with plush carpets, often lit by art deco light fittings, and be ushered into an enormous screening hall to sit in newly sprung comfortable seats. Over 130 grand Odeon cinemas were opened in the 1930s, some of which could seat more than 2,000 people.[1] Other, smaller cinemas were more dingy and less appealing venues to visit, often known as 'fleapits'.

In the late 1920s the vast majority of films shown in the UK had been American. In order to prevent the home industry from being completely overrun the government had passed a Cinematograph Films Act in 1927 that laid down a quota for domestic production. Initially the law said that 5 per cent of all films shown should be British, but this quota was to increase annually to 20 per cent. This gave an enormous boost to domestic film production. The number of feature films made in Britain increased from just 26 in 1927 to 128 the following year. The numbers continued to increase, and investors came forward to put up funds for new studios and original production. In the silent era many films had been shot on location, but with the coming of sound the new technical demands made most film production studio-based.

Norman Loudon was determined to turn the estate he had bought into a major centre of film production. The original seventeenth-century Littleton House had burnt down in the 1870s and been rebuilt in splendid Victorian style over the next couple of decades by Sir Richard Burbidge, the owner of Harrods. In addition to a magnificent conservatory and ballroom, the parklands were beautifully laid out and ran down to a river. Loudon kept the main house for use as offices, a canteen and bar, and in the grounds two sound stages were built with the latest audio technology to mark the now permanent shift from silent to sound films. This gave an immense advantage over many of the other small studios around London that had been built in the silent era and now had to be hastily adapted for sound. Additionally, several support buildings were constructed to house facilities for dressing rooms, make-up, costume, props and all the camera and technical support needed to make films. Loudon advertised the advantage of his site by naming the company he formed Sound City Films, and the studio complex was named after the nearby village, Shepperton. Loudon paid £5,000 for the site and a lot more to build the sound stages.[2]

The studio opened for business in 1932. Loudon was very clear in his objective. He wrote about visiting cinemas and seeing nothing but American movies 'that flashed with brilliance the activities of American everyday life.' But he wrote, 'Subjects of our national life are crying out for filming. There is no lack of material.' And he wanted to make 'vigorous, dramatic' films about 'the everyday life of ordinary British people.'[3] If Loudon's vision was not exactly that of creating a celluloid dream factory, he was certainly determined to project an image of Britain from his new studios.

The first major director to work at Shepperton was Adrian Brunel, a well-known director of comedy shorts in the silent cinema era. But Brunel struggled to make the transition to the sound era and he had dropped out of the top league. He went to Shepperton to direct a crime drama called *Menace*. It was not a happy experience. Brunel thought that Loudon was 'tough, jolly and with undoubted charm,' but he found the whole set-up at the new studios rather amateurish. He wrote that there were several ex-naval men working in the studio supported by a lot of well-heeled, young trainees who had links to the City desperate to learn the ropes of filmmaking. The experienced technicians there apparently called it 'Sound City for the Sons of Gentlemen'. Loudon himself was also very keen to keep costs down. When Brunel suggested a few improvements to the set he found 'they were terrified that anything I suggested would cost money'.[4] However, *Menace* got finished and did perfectly well in Britain and even better in the United States.

From this spartan beginning the young technicians of Shepperton rapidly learned their trade. This was because the studio started to produce a long run of what were called 'quota quickies'. These were B-movies usually of no more than 60 minutes in length, often made at speed and on a low budget but were required in order to fill the legal quota of British films that had to be shown under the government's Film Act. The quota quickies were not known for their quality, but for those working on them they provided an intense and fast learning experience. Directors, cameramen, sound recordists, costume and set designers all had to learn fast on the sets of these quota quickies. Moreover, Loudon realised that to make money he had to keep all his sound stages busy, and the quota quickies were an ideal way of doing this.

One of the first quota quickies made at Shepperton was *Reunion* in 1932. The film was based on a short story in which a retired army major fallen on hard times has to resort to the pawnshop to raise enough money to travel to London to attend his wartime regiment's reunion. But there he meets a corporal who is even more down at heel than he is. The impoverished major gives his last pound to the corporal and concludes that he must act with the same bravery that he and all his men had shown in the war, and 'that a man is never deserted until he deserts himself'.

In the following year came *Doss House*, the first film directed by a new in-house talent, John Baxter. In the film the lives of a group of down-and-outs were shown to be as rich, lively and cheerful as that of any group of counterpart men and women in a wealthy walk of life. Another new director who began his career at Shepperton at the young age of 21 was John Paddy Carstairs. He later went on to direct many of Norman Wisdom's comedies. Often these quota quickies were shot in ten to fifteen days, costing about £1.20 per foot of the final film. This gave the producers of the quota quickies the nickname of 'the pound-a-foot merchants'.[5]

Films about Sir Francis Drake and Captain Blood's attempt to steal the Crown Jewels in the seventeenth century displayed Norman Loudon's desire to explore British history and heritage. For *Captain Blood* a complete reconstruction of the Tower of London was built. The film was a Loudon extravaganza budgeted at the considerable sum of £60,000, intended to break into the American market. It ended up losing him money but added to the prestige of the Sound City studios.

By 1935, Shepperton was busy and Loudon was making sufficient profits to expand the studio complex to seven sound stages, backed up by a dozen editing suites and all the workshops needed to build sets and props for such a considerable output. And with a view to attracting American productions, Littleton House was turned into a hotel and restaurant. The number of technicians needed to crew all these facilities also increased accordingly. This expansion brought the Korda brothers to Shepperton. Alexander and Zoltan Korda were refugees from Hungary who had already built up a formidable body of work, and in 1935 they produced *Sanders of the River* at Shepperton for their company London Films.[6] The film is a jingoistic evocation of the days of Empire and praised the role of a district commissioner in colonial Nigeria (Sanders, played by Leslie Banks). A group of black extras were brought in from Cardiff and an African village was built on the backlot by the river. The black American actor Paul Robeson was persuaded to play the role of a tribal chief.[7]

By the late 1930s, Shepperton was established as one of the biggest and most successful studios in Britain. Although plenty of quota quickies had been made there, the studios had also been hired by many independent production companies who produced some fine British classics. George King, who had connections with Paramount and MGM, produced many films at Shepperton. He first brought Laurence Olivier to the silver screen. Top director Anthony Asquith, designers Paul Sheriff and Carmen Dillon, and a young editor named David Lean all worked at Shepperton in the late 1930s.[8] The last film shot at the studios in 1939 was *Spy for a Day*, a comedy which featured a group of extras dressed in German uniforms. When they went for a walk in Shepperton High Street one lunch hour, still in costume, they inadvertently caused panic in the village. But equally important to all the movies that had been made there, Shepperton had built up a team of experienced and able technicians who worked permanently for the studio.

The coming of war transformed the cinema in Britain. Cinemas were initially closed by government regulations in the fear that a direct hit by a bomb on a crowded cinema would cause carnage and panic. But after a couple of weeks of war, when no bombs had fallen and the men from the Ministry of Information realised that closing them had had a disastrous impact on morale, cinemas were allowed to reopen. But complying with strict blackout regulations meant they opened up without the illuminated signs and lights that had characterised the pre-war cinemas. Nevertheless, the crowds rapidly returned and film-going proved to be a hugely popular form of escape from the drab realities of wartime existence for millions of people. By the end of the war the numbers going to the pictures each week had increased considerably to just over 30 million.

But the war hit the British film production industry hard. About two-thirds of film technicians were called up for military service over the first couple of years of war. There had been 22 studios in active film production in 1939. In two years that number had fallen to nine. One studio, Pinewood, was requisitioned as a base for the newly established Crown Film Unit, a development coming out of the strong socially committed documentary film movement of the 1930s. During the war years the luminaries who worked for the Crown Film Unit included Humphrey Jennings, whose films *Listen to Britain* (1942) and *Fires Were Started* (1943) perfectly captured the mood of a resilient and determined nation at war, and Roy Boulting and Carol Reed, whose wartime compilation documentaries like *Desert Victory* (1943) and *The True Glory* (1945) brilliantly and movingly paid tribute to the ordinary soldier, sailor and airman, and their contribution to victory. Pinewood also became the home of the Army Film and Photographic Unit. Other studios, like Elstree, Nettlefold, Islington and Beaconsfield, stopped production altogether. The huge sound stages, some as big as an aircraft hangar, provided ideal spaces for the government to store essential supplies.

Shepperton had another problem. Only a short distance away was the Vickers-Armstrongs aircraft production centre at Brooklands. Originally Britain's first ever purpose-built banked motor-racing circuit, in the First World War the site had been converted into an airfield and Vickers-Armstrongs opened a factory there in the 1930s. During the first years of the war it concentrated on the production of the Hawker Hurricane, the Battle of Britain fighter, and the Vickers Wellington, the two-engine bomber that proved to be the most popular bomber with the RAF for the first three years of the war. Despite extensive camouflaging of the factory, on 4 September 1940 the Luftwaffe bombed the site in a heavy raid, causing the death of 90 aircraft workers and injuring another 400. Two days later there was another, smaller raid on the Hawker plant. And in the following month, Stage C at Shepperton was hit and two young technicians were killed.

Too close to Vickers-Armstrongs to continue with filmmaking, parts of Shepperton were finally requisitioned by the government. Two of the large sound stages were taken over and very unglamorously converted to store supplies of sugar for Tate & Lyle. Another two sound stages were used to store aircraft parts for the Vickers-Armstrongs factory. But the scene dock and the props workshops remained. The question then became what to do with the large pool of production talent that had grown up in Shepperton in the last ten years since Adrian Brunel had called the studio 'Sound City for the Sons of Gentlemen'.

In late 1939, Colonel John Turner, who had been given responsibility for building decoy airfields to deceive German bombers during the Battle of Britain and the Blitz, started to expand his operation. Having located sites and started the construction of the decoy airfields, he began to look for companies to produce dummy aircraft that were needed to make his airfields appear real to German reconnaissance aircraft from about 15,000 feet. In his first attempt to produce dummy aircraft, Turner naturally enough approached the aircraft manufacturing companies themselves. But they tended to produce models of their own aircraft that were vastly over-engineered, with far too much unnecessary detail. For instance, one company produced a dummy that included a full set of wheels which, of course, would never be seen from above. The cost of some of these dummy aircraft was also far too high, coming in at about £700 per model. However, Turner had the brilliant idea of asking some of the film studios to pitch for the work. After all, they were used to creating something completely unreal that crucially *looked real* on camera. Shepperton and Denham studios were invited to bid for a contract, and Turner was very impressed by the dummy Wellington and Blenheim bombers produced by Shepperton. And the cost was only £225 per model. In November 1939, Sound City at Shepperton was commissioned by Turner's department to build 100 Blenheim and 50 Wellington dummies.[9]

Throughout 1940, Turner grew closer to Norman Loudon. Although he was twenty years older than the movie producer, Turner respected Loudon for his determination and his strong sense of what was practical and possible. Additionally, Turner developed a great admiration for the technicians at Shepperton. The designers, carpenters, painters and set builders were used to working at speed and were accustomed to making staged sets look entirely real. Turner realised that the design talent among the studio technicians was just what was needed for building the dummy aircraft and kit needed to make a decoy airfield look authentic. Indeed, he saw the film technicians as the equivalent to military engineers who could build almost anything more or less instantly. Turner always referred to the craftsmen of Sound City as 'engineers'. Equally important was the fact that Loudon was keen to find alternative work for the studio technicians, who no longer had any films to work on. In November 1940, Turner moved his headquarters to the magnificent mansion house at Shepperton.[10] This began a link between the deception planners and Shepperton that soon blossomed in ways that Norman Loudon could never have imagined even in the wildest of his escapist films. Shepperton was now going to war. And for real, not in celluloid fantasies.

Many of Shepperton's designers had already found a use for their skills in the war. Peter Proud had been an art director at Shepperton, but in 1941 he was in Tobruk, North Africa, now as Captain Proud of the Royal Engineers. He decided to protect the drinking water supply of the besieged garrison by creating the illusion of wreckage all around the water distillery. He dug bomb craters around the site, illuminating them with shadows made from oil and coal dust. On the roof he created the impression of destruction with canvas and paint. The effect was to make German bombers avoid the site because it looked as though it had already been destroyed.[11]

Another illusionist who worked in the desert was Major Jasper Maskelyne. The son of a famous magician, Maskelyne had been one of the most successful conjurors before the war, giving stage shows demonstrating his magic to audiences across Britain. He later wrote, 'War magic and theatrical magic are very similar things.'[12] It took some time for Maskelyne to convince the army high command that there was any purpose in employing a magician, but by succeeding in 'hiding' a machine-gun during an inspection by the Chief of the General Staff, Lord Gort at the time, he persuaded the generals to let him try some of his illusions for real. He was recruited by Lieutenant-Colonel Dudley Clarke, whose uncle had once been president of the Magic Circle, to join his 'A' Force in Cairo. Clarke was always looking for new forms of deception and gave encouragement to Maskelyne, who ended up running a camouflage experimental section. He helped to construct a dummy of Alexandria Harbour, the main eastern Mediterranean base of the Royal Navy, a few miles away at Mariut Bay. When enemy bombers came over heading for Alexandria, the camouflage section ignited explosions at the decoy harbour and the enemy bombers headed for there, believing it to be the real naval base. He came up with the idea of a set of 'dazzle beacons,' using a set of reflecting mirrors alongside searchlights to confuse enemy aircraft looking for the Suez Canal. Clarke encouraged Maskelyne and his team to come up with ever-more imaginative schemes for disguising tanks or trucks, or creating armoured vehicles where there were none. In Maskelyne's own account of his wartime work he greatly exaggerates his contribution, but no doubt he helped persuade some senior commanders to recognise the possibility of decoy construction and made it an area to actively consider.[13]

In Shepperton, Colonel Turner continued to build his rapport with Norman Loudon and Percy Bell, who had been chief electrician for the studios before the war but was now part of the small management team that kept Sound City going. Turner created more decoy airfields, which were lined with canvas aircraft on wooden frames. As in 1940, these were particularly effective at night when lighting could be used to simulate the sense of movement of aircraft around the airfields. From late 1943 several decoy airfields once again sprang up across south-east England, where they would have been needed to provide air support for an attack across the Channel in the Pas de Calais. This was just the beginning of the deception operation in which the cinema industry was called upon to help create the hoax army needed to persuade the Germans that hundreds of thousands of men and all their equipment were gathering in the south-east of England.

There was some debate among the deception planners as to how many German reconnaissance aircraft were able to fly across south-eastern England, as the RAF had won aerial supremacy over the whole area. But SHAEF insisted that it was still possible for German aircraft to nip in and photograph a belt of about fifteen miles inland from the coast, all the way from the Wash to Land's End. SHAEF concluded that if no preparations were made other than those for the actual landings in Normandy, 'the enemy could deduce that no large-scale operation involving a high rate of build-up was contemplated in the Pas de Calais.'[14] So it was clearly necessary for dummy sites and physical objects to be constructed for identification in the south-east, and for those in the south-west to remain heavily camouflaged. Many other dummies were needed to suggest the existence of an army training to invade the beaches at the Pas de Calais. First and foremost was the requirement for dummy landing craft, which would be needed in large numbers. These were built by the Shepperton technicians out of canvas and wood and floated on empty oil drums. The largest of these, resembling large Allied LCTs, Landing Craft Tanks, were known as 'bigbobs'. The smaller landing craft, resembling the infantry assault craft, were known as 'wetbobs'. The term 'wetbob' was an Etonian word to describe a rower (a 'drybob' being a cricketer). The use of these terms clearly indicates the origins of many of those who were laying down the plans for the deception operations.

In the spring of 1944, some 255 of these dummy landing craft were constructed, and towards the end of May they were 'launched' at various ports along the south and east coasts. The bigbobs were substantial items 170 feet long and 30 feet wide, made from heavy canvas stretched across a steel frame and consisted of about a thousand separate components. An entire company of the Worcestershire Regiment was trained to assemble them, and it took thirty men six hours to build one. The craft were difficult to move once assembled, so they were simply put together on beaches and the tide was allowed to come in to float them. The wetbobs and bigbobs appeared at Folkestone and Dover, which had 18 and 46 respectively, along the Essex coast on the rivers Orwell and Deben, where there was a concentration of 122, and in Lowestoft and Yarmouth, where there were 20 and 49 respectively.[15] Assembling the craft was done in complete secrecy, with giant tarpaulins shielding those being put together in Folkestone from prying eyes. Many of them, however, did not have lights on at night, and a local sailing barge ran into one of the dummies one night on the River Orwell and it promptly fell apart. No doubt the crew were astonished at what they had bumped into, but to prevent them from telling anyone what they had discovered they were arrested by the police and held in custody until after D-Day.[16]

Ingenious though the Shepperton designers were, they were not naval engineers, and there were several problems with the dummy landing craft. Being relatively light but with a great surface area, they were liable to be blown about by strong winds. In storms many of them dragged their moorings, which were 1.5-ton concrete blocks, and were blown onto the shore high and dry, often in a battered condition, sometimes upside down. Men from the units overseeing them had to rush out and struggle to turn them the right way up and quickly reposition them in the water.[17] Had an enemy reconnaissance aircraft happened over at one of these moments the whole game would have been given away and the entire Fortitude deception could have been undermined. Fortunately, that did not happen.

Even more ambitious than assembling the landing craft, one of Britain's leading architects, Sir Basil Spence, was asked to produce plans for a complete oil storage facility and docking area near to Dover. The plans were on a vast scale, and the Shepperton set builders were faced with the construction of something far larger than they had ever had to produce for a studio set. The installation ran for several miles along the coastline and consisted of storage tanks, pipelines, pumping stations, jetties, barracks and anti-aircraft defences. This naturally took a while to construct, as it would have done in reality, and when completed, King George VI and General Montgomery visited the site, which was duly reported in the papers. From the air it looked very real, but from the ground it was clearly made of nothing more than canvas, wooden scaffolding, fibre boards and sections of old sewer piping that had been recycled from bomb sites earlier in the war. The intention was to persuade the Germans that this was the terminus of an underwater pipeline to pump oil across the Channel to the Pas de Calais. An actual pipeline project to do exactly the same thing was in construction further west, known as Pluto. For the dummy site one of the construction workers is reported to have said, 'Most of us were film people so naturally we wanted a proper dress rehearsal.' The RAF obliged by sending a low-level reconnaissance aircraft over the 'set.' No doubt the Shepperton design team cheered as the aircraft roared overhead.[18]

As dummy tanks made of canvas were deployed across the Kent countryside, awaiting their pretend marshalling in assembly sites just prior to the phoney invasion, various encounters took place that it was hoped were not observed. At one spot a bull got loose in a field where a squadron of tanks had been constructed, and, angered by something, it charged at one of the tanks. No doubt the mad bull was suitably puzzled when the tank, having been punctured by his horns, slowly deflated.

Areas where hoax facilities were constructed were closed off to the public. On a visit to one of the tank-assembly areas, Churchill was shown the canvas and rubber tanks and was mightily impressed by the deception as a couple of technicians picked up a Sherman tank and carried it away. Churchill is supposed to have asked if these heavy tanks could in reality be taken out by a simple bow and arrow. He was told that they could. He went away smiling.

To check that the dummy sites and the whole range of physical deceptions looked realistic, an RAF photo-reconnaissance squadron was asked to photograph them from the height that Luftwaffe aircraft would do so. The aerial photos were then examined by photo interpreters at RAF Medmenham. They came back to say they were not impressed and that the sites would not fool an experienced photo interpreter. They explained that, although the objects themselves appeared realistic on an aerial photo from about 15,000 feet, the sites looked too 'cold' and lacked the sort of human presence that would inevitably surround such a vast spread of vehicles, landing craft and tanks.[19]

Accordingly, a small army of soldiers and engineers were sent in to 'man' the various sites, to stoke fires in the morning simulating the crews brewing up for breakfast, and to make highly visible demonstrations of human activity by hanging out towels and laundry on washing lines. There was one recorded instance where an airman occupying one of these decoy sites clearly got confused between reality and make-believe. Apparently, he called his superior officer on the field telephone and reported in an agitated tone that the site was coming under air attack. 'Splendid, Sergeant. Good show,' the officer replied. 'But sir,' the airman said, 'they're smashing the place to bits.' 'Yes, excellent, carry on,' responded the officer. 'Sir,' continued the airman, 'we need fighter cover. They're wrecking my best decoys.' No doubt the carpenters and property makers of Shepperton would have been delighted had they been told of the exchange.[20]

Chapter 9

SCOTLAND

On 3 March 1944, Colonel Roderick 'Rory' MacLeod was umpiring a set of war games on the bitterly cold and bleak Yorkshire Moors. The drabness of the setting probably summed up his mood that day, as MacLeod felt the war had passed him by. He had served in the First World War with great distinction, winning a chestful of medals, but had been so badly wounded that part of his skull had been replaced by a silver plate. When war returned some two decades later he had great ambitions that he would play a major and fulfilling role in it. And this war had started with great promise for the 47-year-old Scotsman. In September 1939 he had been an assistant to General Edmund Ironside, Chief of the Imperial General Staff, and was at the centre of the nation's military planning in the War Office. But when Churchill became Prime Minister, Ironside rapidly fell out with the new leader, whom he felt wanted to meddle and interfere with decisions that should be left to the military men. Consequently, two weeks into his new premiership, Churchill sacked Ironside, and with his departure MacLeod's own star seemed to wane.

So MacLeod was delighted when, on that day out on the Yorkshire Moors, he received an urgent message to report to GHQ Home

Forces at the War Office in London. At last, he believed that he was being called up to take part – maybe even to command a division – in the much-anticipated invasion of Europe that everyone knew was being planned in the south. MacLeod rushed to the War Office, where he was told, to his amazement, 'Rory, old boy, you've been selected to run a deception operation for SHAEF from Scottish Command. You will travel to Edinburgh and there you will represent an army which does not in fact exist.' MacLeod was shattered. This was not what he was expecting. He wanted to command real troops in the real war, not what he described as a 'play army.' He was even more surprised when he was told that his job was to 'fool the Germans into believing that an army does exist and, what is more, that it is about to land in Norway.' And he was barely reassured when told, 'The whole scheme is an important part of the coming invasion of France ... It's terrifically important that it should be a success.'[1]

What soon emerged was that MacLeod had been selected to play a leading role in Fortitude North, the parallel deception plan to Fortitude South. This involved creating another hoax army, this time the British Fourth Army in Scotland. As MacLeod had been told, this imaginary grouping was intended to convince the Germans that the Allies were planning an attack upon Norway that would consist of two separate assaults. The first would supposedly be against Stavanger in the south-west of the country. Having established a beachhead there, the invading troops were then to head east, capture Oslo and move on to Denmark. The second notional assault would be against Narvik in the far north, inside the Arctic Circle. The apparent purpose of this assault was to open communications with the Soviets with a view to seizing some of the iron ore mines around Gällivare in northern Sweden, which were supplying Nazi Germany with much of its ore. In the story invented for this deception plan, only when these assaults had succeeded would the cross-Chanel invasion be launched.

Churchill had repeatedly suggested an attack upon Norway. In 1941 he had given personal support to the commando raids on the

Lofoten islands and Vagsoy. In the following year he had pressed his chiefs of staff to actively consider an invasion of Norway. Churchill had a natural instinct to attack the fringes of Nazi Germany, which helps to explain both his interest in the Balkans and Norway as regions to surprise and overwhelm the enemy. The new plans for a phoney invasion were a continuation of Operation Cockade in the previous year, which had played upon Hitler's fears of losing Norway; the Führer regarded Scandinavia as his 'Zone of Destiny'. It was hoped that he would decide to defend Norway vigorously, and indeed had already placed twelve German divisions there to defend the country in addition to the garrison troops needed to maintain the occupation. A force of about 250,000 men was stationed in Scandinavia, which could have been sent to the Eastern Front, the Mediterranean or to reinforce western Europe.

The hoax Fourth Army was to have its headquarters in Edinburgh. It was to consist, like the First US Army Group in the south, of a combination of real troops and imaginary formations. There were to be three corps in this hoax army, each supposedly consisting of three divisions. The US XV Corps did exist but was stationed in Northern Ireland. It consisted of three divisions which had recently landed from the US. Two imaginary British corps were created, VII and II Corps. Each would consist of an actual division that was training in Scotland, the 52nd Lowland Division, based in Dundee, and the 3rd Division, which was training for amphibious landings along the beaches near Nairns on the Moray Firth. The 3rd Division was initially included in the Fourth Army but was sent south to participate in the actual Normandy landings in May. To replace it came an entirely invented unit, the British 58th Division. There was also a group of American Ranger battalions, all of which existed but were in Iceland. And finally there were some Polish and Norwegian units that were drawn into the Fourth Army.

MacLeod had to draw up his deception plan quickly. He decided that British II Corps were to attack in the north; VII Corps in the south; XV Corps were to be held in reserve but almost certainly would be deployed in the southern attack to advance on Oslo and into Denmark. It was to be leaked that the northern attackers were also carrying with them narrow-gauge locomotives and rolling stock that would operate on the railway system around the Gällivare iron ore mines in Sweden. MacLeod was a good choice for planning an invasion of Norway, as he had been assistant to General Ironside when he had been planning the actual invasion of Norway in April 1940, so he knew that country well and could quickly come up with a realistic invasion plan.[2]

As with Patton's role in the south, the Allies needed to find a commander-in-chief for the Fourth Army who had credibility with the Germans. The head of Scottish Command at the time was Lieutenant-General Sir Andrew 'Bulgy' Thorne. It so happened that Thorne had been the military attaché in Berlin in 1934, the year after Hitler had been appointed Chancellor. Thorne had come to the Führer's attention because he had fought in Ypres opposite Hitler's unit in the First World War. They met on several occasions in 1934, and Hitler, along with other senior Wehrmacht officers, had developed a high regard towards Thorne. Indeed, after Hitler's suicide and the fall of Berlin, a translation of a paper written by Thorne about the First World War battle in which they had both taken part was found in the remains of the Führerbunker.[3] Although Thorne did not have the reputation or the notoriety of Patton, he was entirely believable, especially as far as Hitler was concerned, as the commander of a substantial invasion force directed at Norway.

In addition to the army units, the RAF and the Royal Navy both had to play their parts as though they were preparing to assault Norway. The Royal Navy was told to fill the Firth of Forth with as much shipping as was available. The RAF had to assemble bomber squadrons on the east coast of Scotland from where raids could be mounted to soften up sites along the Norwegian coast. Aerial reconnaissance over Norway was stepped up and there was a functioning photo intelligence unit already located at RAF Wick on the cliffs above the Caithness coast. From here long and lonely sorties were mounted to fly up and down the Norwegian coast. These were difficult missions to fly, as weather conditions could rapidly change and become treacherous, and a pilot needed pinpoint navigation skills to return across a grey, featureless sea and get back to Wick before running out of petrol. Difficult though these missions were, earlier in the war a Spitfire pilot flying out of Wick had scored one of the great successes in aerial reconnaissance by spotting the *Bismarck* in Grimstadfjord on 21 May 1941. The sighting of the biggest German battleship just as she was about to begin her journey into the North Atlantic led to one of the most famous pursuits in British naval history, and ultimately the sinking of Hitler's favourite warship. The photo of the *Bismarck* in Grimstadfjord became known as 'the picture that sank a battleship'.[4] It was hoped that by beefing up firstly the reconnaissance missions and then by stepping up the bombing raids over Norway, which were to begin in April, the Germans would be convinced that military action was coming somewhere along the Norwegian coast.

However, the principal difference between the imaginary existence of the First US Army Group in the south and the British Fourth Army in the north was that SHAEF took the view that it was extremely unlikely that German reconnaissance aircraft would fly over Scotland. Once again, the RAF had mastery of the skies, but whereas a quick dash and photograph mission from an airfield in northern France over the south-east of England would be only 30 or 40 miles, it would be hundreds of miles from occupied Denmark or Norway to get to Scotland. This meant there was no need for the sort of physical deception objects that had been produced for the south-east. No bigbobs or wetbobs were needed along the Scottish coast to pretend that fleets of landing craft were being assembled.

This in turn meant that the other forms of deception took a priority. Just as with FUSAG, these new formations had to have a convincing existence through the signals traffic they would have created had they been real. The creation of this signals noise was the top priority for MacLeod, who had to hastily assemble and instruct a team from his headquarters a few miles outside Edinburgh.

Operational messages were to be sent in a simple cipher that the Germans would be able to decode. Training messages were often sent by voice radio. MacLeod was given an allocation of about twenty middle-ranking officers, and each one was 'cast' as a senior commander in one of the phoney divisions. The officers playing the parts of these commanders had to remain the same in case the Germans came to recognise their voices. As MacLeod later wrote, 'A man could not be a corps commander one day, and a brigade major the next.'[5]

All the activities of a real army had to be passed on in this signals traffic. Messages would go from army to corps, from corps to divisions and from divisions to brigades, and vice versa. They would include gossip about upcoming courts martial and new officer appointments, as would have been the case in reality. MacLeod dropped a few 'calculated indiscretions' into the conversations to hint that Norway was their objective. For instance, there was a message to recall all skiers, and a reference to a mountain battery. It was explained to MacLeod that the Germans had listening stations in northern France that, by triangulation, could locate the sources of radio signals to within about five miles. So all the signals had to be sent from the precise locations of where the fake units were supposed to be stationed. MacLeod called all his senior staff together in Edinburgh and explained that they were on a top-secret operation which was to cover a landing in France. He made it clear that no one was 'to breathe a word about it for the success of the landing would depend upon complete secrecy.' They were bound to be asked what they were doing, so they were given a cover story that they were training a new set of signallers.

Transmissions began at the end of March, and soon the airwaves were full of the sorts of messages that would normally travel up and down the command structure. Messages about upcoming exercises suggested that the units were training for amphibious operations and mountain warfare. Messages about staffing problems created an authentic sense of an army building up its strength. And with orders to convey all this as realistically as possible, the teams of signallers came under intense pressure. They were far fewer in number than they would have been had they been genuinely representing real divisions, corps and armies. For days and sometimes weeks there was much frantic activity. Hectic spells were broken by periods of radio silence, as would have been the case in normal military signals traffic. Then, when the messages started up again, the signals officers and the cipher staff went into overdrive, sustained by endless cups of tea and only occasionally emerging for a hasty meal. MacLeod sent some of Fourth Army's pretend units on exercises around Loch Fyne and along the Ayrshire coast, where they supposedly carried out landings on the sandy beaches around Troon. To make all this appear real to the German listening stations the signallers had to be in position in transport vessels in the sea and on the supposed beachheads. Several DUKW amphibious trucks were made available so the signallers could move between ships and the shore. It was a highly elaborate operation and MacLeod made his signallers aware that the slightest error or slip could undermine the whole deception.[6]

General Thorne made a high-profile and very visible visit to Belfast in May. He spent a few days inspecting the US XV Corps and its three divisions, the 2nd, 5th and 8th US infantry divisions, in a manner that clearly made it look as though they were part of his Fourth Army. The American divisional and corps commanders all played along with this. The purpose here was to attract the interest of any German spies working in neutral Eire who could freely cross the border to the north. Such agents would not have been turned by MI5, of course, so Thorne's visit was to make it as clear as possible that the American divisions in Northern Ireland were all training for the planned invasions of Norway.

The RAF simulated the transfer of four bomber squadrons from Suffolk to the east coast of Scotland, spread from Peterhead to Edinburgh. All of this was conveyed by signals traffic without a single bomber actually moving north. The Royal Navy did, however, carry out a real carrier-borne aerial reconnaissance over Narvik on 26 April. Then, over the next three weeks, the Home Fleet assembled 71 real ships, many of them transport vessels, in the Firth of Forth, clearly visible to any Luftwaffe flight over the area. By mid-May it appeared, via visual sources and radio interceptions, that the Fourth Army had trained and prepared for combat in Norway and that a naval fleet had assembled, ready to transport the troops across the North Sea.

Rory MacLeod was told by SHAEF that they could see from intercepting German signals that details of the notional Fourth Army were being picked up. However, it seemed that the Germans weren't listening in quite as assiduously as SHAEF had hoped. So, once again, the double agents controlled by B1A, the division of MI5 handling the supply of disinformation through German agents, had to be relied upon to pass on some of the details about the imaginary army assembling in Scotland. In early March, Juan Pujol, Garbo, was contacted by his Abwehr controllers with an urgent request for information about military preparations in Scotland and northern England. He responded with a vast run of messages, almost one a day, for the next three months, passing on details about the Fourth Army. Garbo, it will be remembered, supposedly had a network of local agents reporting to him, enabling him to amass the information he passed on to his controllers in Madrid. One of these fictitious agents was a Greek sailor on a British ship based on the Clyde who had strong left-wing leanings. The Abwehr was told that the sailor believed he was passing on information to a Soviet intelligence-gathering organisation and so was willing to search out as much detail as he could. He reported to Garbo that he had spotted special davits on the transport ships assembling in the Firth of Forth that were able to launch small infantry-landing assault craft instead of the usual lifeboats. Garbo enthusiastically passed on this misinformation, which was timed to coincide with the assembly of the real fleet in May.[7]

But Tomás Harris, Garbo's principal B1A minder, also wanted a cover for Pujol when events, of course, did not turn out as he was reporting. After another of his sub-agents sent him a report that claimed he had followed an exercise on Loch Fyne in the west of Scotland that clearly pointed to an imminent invasion of Norway, Pujol concluded the report with his own comment that he did not agree with this, but that his agent being in Scotland 'was in a better position than I am to assess this question.' Harris was already planning a way for Garbo to maintain his credibility even when the predictions he had forwarded turned out to be false.[8]

Dusko Popov, Tricycle, also had sub-agents gathering information for him. One was Marquis Frano de Bona, who had been trained in Berlin as a radio operator, and when he arrived in Britain to meet Popov he too was picked up by Tar Robertson of MI5 and turned. He acquired the codename Freak. In April he reported to the Abwehr about a lucky encounter in London with a highly indiscreet American officer from the US XV Corps. He explained that the three divisions in his corps, who were at that point in Northern Ireland, were being transferred to General Thorne's Fourth Army, whose headquarters he was about to join. When Freak passed on details of this conversation he received a message back from the Abwehr saying, 'Your latest wires are very satisfactory. Please continue. Congratulations.' The response went on: 'Please state exact number of divisions etc belonging to Fourth Army under General Thorne. Is anything pointed to intended landings in the German Bight, Denmark and south Sweden?'[9] Clearly the Abwehr were not entirely convinced at this point that the Fourth Army was planning only to assault Norway.

It was lucky that there were Polish troops forming part of the Fourth Army, as this gave an opportunity for Roman Czerniawski, Brutus, to visit Scotland. As we have seen, Czerniawski was the ex-Polish army officer who had reported to his Abwehr controllers that he had been made a liaison officer with the First US Army Group in the south. It was entirely credible that he would be asked to pay a visit to the Polish troops in Scotland, too. On 12 April he made a notional trip to Scotland. His minders prepared a long report after his visit that was passed on to the Abwehr. Brutus identified the Fourth Army headquarters in Edinburgh. He recognised II Corps in Stirling and VII Corps in Dundee from their unit insignias. He also reported on the presence of the completely bogus 58th Division. Supposedly made up of Scottish troops returning from the Mediterranean, Czerniawski's minders had to invent a new insignia for this non-existent unit and came up with an imaginative design of a pair of stag's antlers that seemed entirely appropriate for a Highland division.[10] And a few weeks later Brutus reported that a Soviet military and naval mission had arrived in Edinburgh, presumably to discuss possible collaboration over the joint effort against northern Sweden. Brutus ended this report with his own conclusion that an attack upon Norway was planned for the immediate future.[11]

There was another level of the deception game that was unique to Fortitude North. This had the separate name of Operation Graffham. It came out of the instructions from the London Controlling Section 'to induce the enemy to believe we are enlisting the active co-operation of Sweden in connection with British and Russian contemplated operations against northern Norway.'[12] This particular operation worked through regular diplomatic channels. Sir Victor Mallet was the British ambassador to Sweden. He was told to request from the Swedish government permission to install air navigation equipment on certain airfields in Sweden. The rumour was then spread that after an invasion of Norway, Swedish airfields would be used to fly bombing raids against Germany. In April a further set of requests was passed on in Stockholm to allow British aircraft to refuel, for damaged aircraft to be repaired in Swedish airfields, and for the RAF to fly reconnaissance flights over Swedish territory. There was yet another request for British and Swedish transport experts to meet to discuss the movement of supplies into Sweden in the event of a German withdrawal from Norway. The Swedish government took these requests seriously, and although ministers said no to reconnaissance flights, they agreed for talks between transport specialists. The implication of all this was that the British wanted to bring the Swedes closer into the war, if not to fully join the Allied struggle against the Third Reich then at least to allow the Allies to use Swedish airfields in its war effort. News of this soon leaked to German sources in Stockholm.

The diplomatic game went up a gear when Sir Victor Mallet was rather ostentatiously called back to London. A double agent in London, Wulf Schmidt, codenamed Tate, claimed to have a friend in the Foreign Office. He reported to the Germans that Mallet was having urgent meetings at the Foreign Office and was going to return to Stockholm with extra staff. 'Friend believes that important negotiations with Sweden are being started,' Tate messaged his Abwehr controllers.[13]

While he was in London, Mallet was secretly briefed by Bevan as to the deception plan and agreed to continue to take part in it. He suggested sending a high-level air official to Stockholm to open discussions with the Swedish air minister. He recommended Air Commodore Thornton, who had been air attaché in Stockholm before the war and was highly regarded by the Swedish minister. Thornton was hurriedly promoted to Air Vice Marshal for his supposedly clandestine mission and was rushed around Stockholm in cars with blacked-out windows and smuggled in and out the Swedish air ministry by the back door. All of this aroused the interest of German observers in the city. Thornton explained to the Swedish air minister that if the Allies invaded Norway the Germans would probably withdraw but would most likely massacre the leading Norwegians held in internment camps and blow up Norwegian harbours. This would happen too quickly, it was pointed out, for the Allies to prevent it. But the Swedes could send their army into Norway as a sort of police force to prevent the Germans from committing atrocities. The Swedish air minister was moved by what he was told and promised to pass this message on to other ministers for discussion. Dennis Wheatley later claimed that the office in which the two men met was bugged by the Swedish chief of police, who was sympathetic to the Nazis, and he had a translation of the conversation sent to Berchtesgaden, where a furious Hitler ordered two more divisions to be sent to Norway. Another 30,000 men who could have been stationed in Normandy were added to the Norwegian garrison for no good purpose.[14]

Also, Thornton's visit to Stockholm aroused the interest of the German FHW, who concluded that a small-scale landing in south Norway or Denmark seemed likely. Mallet returned to Sweden and more rumours began spreading about Anglo-Soviet discussions over a joint operation in northern Norway. German sources picked up information that the Russians were reinforcing their bases in Kola Bay in the far north, near its border with Norway. For the first time the Soviets were taking part in an Allied deception plan, at last reaping the benefits of Churchill's discussion with Stalin at Teheran in the previous year.

Additionally, a supposed mole in the British Embassy in Stockholm reported to a German agent in that city that Mallet had given a talk to the staff on his return from London saying that good relations with Sweden might not continue for long. He was reported to have said to his staff that 'deliveries of iron ore and ball bearings benefit Germany and harm us. That must not continue in the future.' The report containing details of Mallet's apparent talk reached Keitel and Jodl, in Germany's military headquarters, and the latter showed it to Hitler.[15] The clear conclusion of the stories reaching the Germans from the diplomatic initiatives was that Britain was attempting to persuade Sweden to abandon its neutrality and join the Allied cause.

Fortitude North did not end when the Normandy invasion took place on 6 June. Three days later, the US, UK and USSR governments formally called upon the Swedish government to make assurances that in the event of a landing in Norway, Stockholm would not allow the Germans to move Finnish troops (Finland being strongly anti-Soviet) across Swedish territory. The Swedish government replied with a satisfactory assurance, but what was even more pleasing for the deceivers was that the Swedish press now made great play of the imminence of an invasion of Norway. The Swedish government did not realise at the time that they were part of a deception plan and no doubt were annoyed when they later discovered how they had been used. But Fortitude North had employed an extensive range of deceptions to get its story across to the Germans. The Norwegian garrison remained far larger than was necessary, and Fortitude North ensured that not a single German soldier was withdrawn from the force stationed in Norway during the spring of 1944.

Chapter 10

MORE TRICKS

General Hans Cramer was a German officer of the upright, Prussian school. When he surrendered on 12 May 1943 in Tunisia to British Lieutenant-General Charles Allfrey, he insisted on wearing his finest dress uniform, despite the fact that his army had disintegrated around him. He and General Hans-Jürgen von Arnim, who surrendered together, were dressed in long-waisted tunics, green breeches and immaculately polished riding boots. When asked to hand over their pistols, Von Arnim pulled his out and contemptuously threw it down at Allfrey's feet. Prussian generals did not take kindly to being forced to surrender.

Hitler had ordered his troops in North Africa to fight to the last bullet. The German generals decided that this meant to the last tank shell, and by the beginning of May even their panzers had run out of ammunition. Outgunned, outperformed in the air and outfought by superior numbers on the ground, the Axis armies were crushed.[1] They had also completely run out of fuel, and no planes had been able to evacuate senior officers, nor ships to take away the men. There was nothing for the German and Italian armies to do but lay down their arms. The mass surrender of approximately 240,000 Axis troops in Tunisia in May 1943 brought to an end nearly three years of fighting in the desert war. The vast capitulation included nine generals, and Cramer was one of the most senior military figures to go into captivity. He had been put in charge of the famed Afrika Korps three months before.

General Cramer was a great catch for the British, who eventually transferred him to Trent Park, a magnificent Georgian mansion to the north-east of London near Cockfosters. The senior Wehrmacht commanders who were incarcerated there lived in some luxury in grand country-house surroundings. They were served good food, were permitted to take walks in the spacious grounds and allowed a ration of whisky every evening. Cramer had his own bedroom, sitting room and a batman to attend to him. The luxury of the surroundings played on the captured generals' sense of self-importance. No wooden huts and barbed wire for them. Moreover, they were encouraged to listen to BBC radio and to talk among themselves. But there was method in the madness. The house was like a large studio set and was full of hidden microphones behind every painting, inside every plant pot and even under the floorboards. The section of the intelligence organisation dealing with the armed forces of the enemy, MI19, listened in to the senior German officers discussing many aspects of the war. Hearing the post-prandial conversation of these men yielded many fascinating gems of intelligence about future military plans and new scientific projects that some of them thought would help rescue the Third Reich. The biggest problem MI19 faced was when the weather was good and the generals spent the day outside in the grounds. One intelligence officer prayed for rain so the generals would stay indoors and chat among themselves, where everything they said could be recorded.[2]

In the spring of 1944, Hans Cramer was mysteriously transferred from Trent Park to a camp in Wales. Then, in May, as he was in failing health it was decided to release Cramer as part of a prisoner exchange. He would be repatriated to the Third Reich via the Swedish Red Cross in Stockholm. On the day of his release a car came for him with a driver, a guard and two British officers as an escort. But the journey from Wales to a port on the south coast was not direct. The two escort officers were extremely friendly and chatted amiably with the Prussian general. Soon they found themselves surrounded by huge numbers of Allied troops, American and British, all clearly preparing for a major event, probably the invasion of Occupied Europe. Cramer was amazed at the scale of activity that he saw out of the car window. The chatty officers were rather indiscreet and let it be known that they were driving through Kent. As all road signs had been removed years before to confuse the Germans in the event of an invasion, Cramer had no reason to doubt what he was being told. In fact, the two officers were part of the double-cross system and the whole event was another element in the Fortitude South deception. Cramer had seen genuine troops preparing for a real invasion. But he had not been in Kent. He had been driven through the south-west of England near to the coast where Allied troops were amassing before D-Day.

The deception did not end there. Before being put on a ship to Stockholm, Cramer was invited to a dinner with General Patton and a group of senior American officers. It was a gesture of chivalry between commanders on two sides of what was often a bitter enmity. Patton was introduced to Cramer as the commanding general of the First US Army Group, and during the course of the dinner various references were made to the Pas de Calais. Patton said that he pitied the Germans, who had planned a cross-Channel invasion of England back in 1940 before the development of all the new amphibious-assault techniques that he was able to make use of. Cramer made a mental note of everything he had seen and was told, and he left with the clear impression that Patton was about to lead the invasion of northern France from south-east England.

On returning to Germany, Cramer was soon telling his old boss, Rommel, that he had seen evidence of a large army in Kent preparing for an invasion across the Channel to the Pas de Calais.

Furthermore, he was rapidly whisked away to Hitler's mountain retreat in Berchtesgaden, where he repeated the story to the Führer of what he had seen and heard on his release. How could Hitler fail to be impressed by the report of what one of his most decorated generals had seen with his own eyes?[3]

Misleading General Cramer was an ingenious piece of play-acting from the inventive minds of the deceivers. But other elements of the deception plan to invent a hoax army in the south-east of England needed to be more scientific. Colonel Turner, who had produced some of the first decoy airfields in 1940 and who had worked closely with Norman Loudon at Shepperton, was given the task of producing a series of lighting displays along the south coast. Some of these were intended to draw attention to the hoax embarkation points in the south-east where the dummy armada was supposedly preparing to sail. And some were intended to protect the real sites in the south-west where the real armada was amassing. It was hoped that German aircraft would pick up the spoof night activity in the south-east and conclude that this was where the principal assault was to come from.

Turner experienced several problems in planning this lighting deception. Firstly, the Admiralty did not reveal its plan for the lighting of the actual sites in the south-west. Not knowing what he had to mimic delayed the work of Turner and his team. When the real lighting rigs were finalised by the Admiralty, Turner thought the lights being used during exercises and night loading were far too intense. He formally complained to Air Marshal Trafford Leigh-Mallory and he, in a fury, 'bit Montgomery'. The army got the message and limited lighting around the yards and harbours where ships were assembling to the use only of hooded lamps and torches. When it came to laying out dummy lighting rigs in the south-east, Turner and his team experienced a variety of other problems. At times they had to work along stretches of coast that were mined, which obviously created its own difficulties. At other times they found it difficult, according to Turner in his report, to combat 'pedigree cows who do not behave like ladies and stamp on all the equipment they cannot eat.'[4]

Finally, by early May, a series of decoy lighting schemes had been established from Cornwall and along the south coast to Newhaven. Some of these were quite elaborate. At Menabilly in Cornwall a valley was dammed and flooded. Lights played on the water to make it appear like the nearby Fowey harbour, where real ships and landing craft were gathering for Overlord. At Cuckmere Haven a replica of Newhaven harbour was constructed, complete with lighting for the nearby railway marshalling yards. A total of eleven separate decoy sites were constructed around the real embarkation points. In the event of bombing raids, fires were to be lit at these decoy sites to divert enemy aircraft in the hope that they would drop their bombs away from the real sites. In the south-east twelve dummy sites were built, from Camber in East Sussex along the Kent coast, and from Tilbury along the East Anglian coast to Lowestoft and Yarmouth. Many of the sites chosen were where dummy landing craft had been assembled. At each of these sites, enemy aircraft would see invasion vessels gathering by day, or lights to suggest a fleet was assembling by night.[5]

A lot of effort went into this deception, but it seems that it had relatively little effect. At the end of May there were a few raids on Portsmouth and Plymouth, known naval bases where real landing vessels were indeed gathering. A few of the raiders were distracted by the decoy sites and wasted their bombs on these. But most of the other protective or display sites attracted little attention. No doubt the displays in Kent and East Anglia added to a general sense that something significant was happening here, but it was overall a marginal result for a substantial effort.[6] A far more effective use of science came in the radar war of spring 1944.

Assessing the enemy's use of radar and radio communications had been, from 1941 onwards, one of the priorities of the Central Photographic Interpretation Unit at RAF Medmenham. Squadron

Leader Claude Wavell was the team leader of the group looking for and analysing every sort of wireless transmitter, radio installation and radar tower in Occupied Europe. Some of these on an aerial photograph taken from 30,000 feet were only a millimetre or two in size, little more than a grain of dust on the image. Measuring the size of these miniscule objects was a key part of his work that helped Wavell distinguish between a radio transmitter base and a radar station, and knowing their exact height was vital. Wavell invented and built his own device for calculating the height of a tower or installation from the shadow it cast on the ground. It was like a small globe made up of concentric circles of wood. The interpreter set the exact latitude of the radar tower and the precise date and time the photo was taken into the device. This information was automatically recorded on every aerial photo. The operator then calculated the angle above the horizon of the sun's rays at the moment the photo was recorded. When the azimuth of the sun was factored in – that is its angle in relation to the equator – along with the exact scale of the photograph, the device was then able to calculate the height of an object from its shadow using the basic principles of spherical trigonometry. The apparatus was much admired and Wavell proudly named it an Altazimeter. Wavell reckoned that, crude though it was, its results, obtained within a few minutes, were within 1 per cent of those obtained from detailed computations that could take up to 30 minutes using a slide-rule, the principal calculating device in the pre-computer era.[7]

Knowing the height of an installation enabled Wavell and his team to distinguish and itemise every radio transmitter and radar tower operated by the enemy. They were all vital pieces of the Atlantic Wall to give the defending troops early warning of an approaching Allied naval invasion force. And the Germans used a variety of sophisticated radar systems, each with its own particular function for detecting aircraft or ships, with names like Freya,

Wasserman, Würzburg and Seetakts. By the end of 1943, Wavell's unit had identified the existence of nearly 200 radar stations within a few miles of the coast, from Skagen at the northern tip of Denmark to Bayonne in south-west France, near the Spanish border. Within these stations they counted about 600 separate radar installations.[8]

Working alongside Wavell was a brilliant 33-year-old scientist at the Air Ministry, Reginald Victor (known as R.V.) Jones. Jones was a classic 'boffin' who was still young enough to be inventive, ingenious and unafraid of authority, but his analytic mind put him way ahead of his youthful years.[9] His work on detecting the beams that the Luftwaffe were using in the Blitz of 1940–41 to guide their aircraft at night with great precision to their targets in Britain brought him to the attention of the senior Air Staff and to Churchill himself. By the end of 1941, as RAF Bomber Command was beginning to hit back, an increasing number of bombers were being shot down as they flew towards Germany. Jones deduced that the Germans had developed a revolutionary new form of short-wave radar that seemed to operate from small, mobile transmitter-receivers and could guide night fighters straight to the bombers. He realised that these radar stations were nothing like the hundred-foot towers developed by the British to transmit radio waves and receive them after they had bounced back from hitting a metal object, known then as Range and Direction Finding.[10]

In late 1941, Wavell spotted on an aerial photograph a small unit consisting of a paraboloid-shaped apparatus, like a bowl on its side, by a villa on the cliffs along the French coast at Bruneval. Jones decided this must be the new form of German radar. He picked up from intercepted radio communications that it was called a Würzburg. He suggested that the only way to discover how this new system operated, and so understand how it could be jammed, was to capture a Würzburg intact. This led to the Bruneval Raid in February 1942, in which a group of paratroopers landed at night on the cliffs near the site of the radar, captured the installation, dismantled the Würzburg, carried it in pieces down the cliff and were picked up off the beaches by the navy, bringing the parts back to Britain for inspection and analysis. The examination of the Würzburg enabled British scientists to come up with the idea of dropping thousands of small strips of aluminium foil that were roughly half the length of the wavelength of the radar. This would amplify the signals bouncing back and deceive the German radar into thinking that a vast bombing force was approaching, spread across a large area of the sky. This form of jamming of the German radar was known as 'Window' in Britain and 'Chaff' in the US.[11]

In the spring of 1944 it became clear to R.V. Jones that some sort of plan was going to be needed to disable most of the German radar sites along the Atlantic Wall and to prepare to jam the surviving radars when the invasion of northern France was launched. He was frustrated to find that no such scheme seemed to be in the minds of the planners. At a chance meeting with Air Marshal Tedder, the young scientist convinced the Deputy Supreme Allied Commander that it was vital to start taking countermeasures against the German radar network. The RAF was galvanised into action and responded with a trial attack on two German radar installations on the coast near Ostend with rocket-firing Typhoons. The sites were surrounded by anti-aircraft guns, but as the Typhoons passed the target at altitude, as though heading inland, they peeled off to strafe and fire their rockets at the Wasserman radar installation below. To the disappointment of the pilots the large antennae on the radars were left standing at the end of the raid, despite what they thought were several direct hits. However, the Belgium underground were asked to assess the damage and reported back that the antennae-operating mechanism had been destroyed and the two radars had been completely put out of action. So, on 10 May, a co-ordinated operation to attack German radar stations along the coast began. For three weeks hundreds of sorties were flown against the German radar installations, many of which, despite being tiny targets, were destroyed. And again, dozens of raids were carried out on radar stations in the Boulogne–Calais region. In one heavy bomber raid the headquarters of the German signals intelligence service in northern France, at Urville-Nacqueville near Cherbourg, was also hit and completely destroyed. This further added to the 'blindness' of the German early warning system as D-Day approached. So as not to give away where the invasion was coming, the air attacks against all the land installations – including airfields, artillery batteries, railway yards, bridges as well as the radar stations – were spread across the whole coast, from Denmark to south-west France. For every bomb dropped or rocket fired within the planned invasion area, two were dropped outside. This greatly increased the work, and the losses, of the Allied air forces but was essential to keep the Germans guessing.[12]

This was excellent as far as it went, but R.V. Jones was soon acquainted with Operation Fortitude and the need to pretend that the major assault was coming from south-east England to the Pas de Calais. Jones had been a great practical joker in his youth and was naturally drawn to deception. He teamed up with another scientist, Robert Cockburn from the Telecommunications Research Establishment (TRE) at Malvern, who was a specialist in jamming German radar. In order to simulate a large seaborne force approaching the French coast east of the Seine, Cockburn came up with a plan for a group of Lancasters to fly in a series of rectangular orbits, eight miles long by two miles wide. They would drop bundles of aluminium strips, Window, every couple of minutes. The centre-point of the orbit had to move in a south-easterly direction at a speed of eight knots, the speed at which an invasion fleet would be moving. This required some precision flying, and Lancasters of the famous 'Dambusters' 617 Squadron, then led by Leonard Cheshire, were selected for the mission. Another squadron following the same technique were to simulate an invasion fleet heading for Boulogne.

The whole procedure had to be picked up by at least one German radar, and although it was assumed that some of those that had been knocked out would be rebuilt, it was decided to leave at least one radar station completely intact. The installation at Fécamp was selected for survival. Additionally, launches were sent out fourteen miles apart, pretending to be at either end of the two supposed invasion fleets. They operated a system called 'Moonshine.' This was another invention from TRE that picked up the pulses from the German radar and sent them back in longer, repeating echoes. Moonshine could be used in aircraft or ships and had the effect of making it appear that a large fleet of ships had been picked up at sea.

Cockburn wanted to try out the system to ensure it worked, and he managed to persuade the Navy and the Air Force to provide him with assets for a trial in the North Sea off a radar station at Flamborough Head on the Yorkshire coast. Aircraft dropped Window and launches approached the coast using Moonshine. The radar operators at Flamborough Head had not been told about the trial and reported in panic that the largest collection of vessels they had ever seen was approaching. The spoof had clearly succeeded, and Cockburn and Jones knew they had developed the right technology to simulate an invasion fleet at sea. However, the reaction of the radar operators at Flamborough Head when they realised they had been duped by a deception trial was not recorded.[13]

On the night of 5 June, as the real invasion fleet was approaching Normandy, the German radar network, shattered as it was, reported back that an invasion force was approaching Fécamp and another at Boulogne, about 150 miles to the east of the actual Normandy landing beaches. Only one German radar station near Caen that had somehow survived the bombing raids correctly picked up the approach of the real invasion armada, but its reports were discounted further up the command chain because they were not verified by other radar stations. The boffins had succeeded triumphantly in bringing the science of radar into the deception game.[14]

But the work of the deceivers went beyond scientific deception. They could still find colourful ways to trick the Germans in the final run-up to the real invasion. At the beginning of January 1944, Colonel Dudley Clarke made a visit to the US Fifth Army headquarters, located at a palace in Caserta, south of Naples. As a keen cinema-goer, he went one evening to see the new Billy Wilder movie *Five Graves to Cairo*, which was being screened for the headquarters staff. The film was set in the North African desert, where a British soldier, the only survivor of a British tank crew after the fall of Tobruk, assumes the identity of a waiter, only to find that the seemingly innocuous waiter had in fact been a German spy. The film features fine performances from Franchot Tone, Anne Baxter and Erich von Stroheim, who rather improbably plays Field Marshal Rommel. Watching the film closely and intrigued by the idea of swapping identities, Clarke spotted a British actor in the movie, Miles Mander, playing a British colonel who looked just like General Montgomery. He began to wonder whether it would be possible to use a Montgomery lookalike on the eve of D-Day to fool the Germans into thinking that Montgomery was not in England planning the invasion, but somewhere else.

Clarke was in London the following month, and with the help of others in the London Controlling Section began to refine his idea. Dennis Wheatley suggested that a good place for Monty to be spotted would be Gibraltar, where the Germans had a villa not far from the airport and were known to record those getting on and off aircraft using a long telescope. And the local press could be encouraged to cover the visit of the distinguished British general. If Monty appeared there on some sort of public visit it might convince the Germans that if one of the most senior figures known to be leading the invasion was not in England but abroad, then surely the invasion could not be imminent.

Unfortunately for Wheatley all sorts of practical difficulties almost scuppered the ingenious plan. Miles Mander turned out to be too short to play Monty. Another actor was quickly found but he broke his leg in a car accident. Finally, someone from the London Controlling Section scoured the pre-war books of a Soho casting agency and found another actor who looked just like Monty and who was the right size and shape. His name was Meyrick Clifton James. It turned out he had given up acting during the war and was currently a lieutenant in the Army Pay Corps in Leicester. In order to persuade him to take part in what would become an elaborate charade, the film star David Niven, who was then part of the Army Kinematography Corps, approached James on the pretext that he was to appear in some films for the army. James was only too pleased to get away from the drudgery of the Pay Corps and back to his original profession. He was consequently called to the War Office and interviewed, or, perhaps more appropriately, auditioned for the role. He seemed to fit the bill and was offered the part by a Colonel Lester from MI5.

Lester now briefed him on the part he was to play in yet another deception. It was decided that, in order to be able to play the role of Montgomery convincingly, James should observe the General closely in order to study his mannerisms and see how he walked and talked. After watching many newsreels of Monty, James was sent to accompany the General for a week or so in the guise of a journalist in the press pack that followed Monty around. Montgomery was told of the deception and gave it his enthusiastic support. It flattered his ego that the Germans could be made to think that the invasion could not happen without him. James watched closely how his principal behaved towards other VIPs and towards the men in his command. He noticed how Monty always walked with his hands clasped behind his back and how he gesticulated with one hand when making a point.

Growing nervous of his upcoming role, James asked for more time to observe Monty and was given it. Then another problem arose. It turned out that James had never flown in an aircraft before. It would not do for the famous general to be seen throwing up on the tarmac at Gibraltar airport. So Dennis Wheatley arranged for James to go up in a Whitley bomber. Fortunately, he took to it straight away and did not suffer from air sickness.

Colonel Lester of MI5 explained to Lieutenant James in detail what was expected of him. Everything was put to him as though he were playing a role in a play. His 'rehearsals' would be his time following Monty, and everything must be ready for 'curtain up.' But endless problems slowed up his rehearsals. James had lost the middle finger of his right hand in an accident in the First World War. A surgical finger was quickly made out of cotton wool and adhesive plaster and stuck to his hand. As long as he did not wave his right hand about it should stay in place. Then someone thought they had better check what the real Montgomery ate, as the lookalike could not be seen eating the wrong sort of food. Lester himself went and asked Montgomery in person if there were any peculiarities in his diet. 'Certainly not,' replied the General. 'I don't eat meat, I don't eat fish, and I don't take milk or sugar with my porridge. That's all.'[15] It was just as well they asked.

On 27 May, nine days before D-Day was scheduled, the plan now known as Operation Copperhead was put into action. James would visit Gibraltar and then fly on to Algiers for a few days, attracting as much attention as he could. Wearing Monty's characteristic battle dress and black beret, James, accompanied by a real brigadier and an aide-de-camp, flew from southern England to Gibraltar. On disembarking early in the morning, James was met by the Governor, Sir Ralph Eastwood, an old friend of the General who had been at Sandhurst with him. 'Hello, Monty, glad to see you,' Eastwood said as he eagerly shook the great General's hand. 'Hello, Rusty, how are you?' replied James. Everyone was playing their part perfectly. It only had to be hoped that the Germans were watching and had picked up who had just walked into their sights.

After breakfast at Government House the Governor accompanied his guest back to his car to return to the airport. But here yet another element in the deception game came into play. The Spanish liaison officer with the British government in Gibraltar had been summoned to a meeting in Government House that morning. He was known to be a German spy. Timed perfectly with Eastwood and Monty's departure, the Spanish diplomat was walking across the courtyard of Government House when he bumped into the Governor and his special guest. They were animatedly discussing something called Plan 303, and the Governor abruptly told the general to be discrete in the presence of the Spaniard. The Spanish diplomat could barely disguise his surprise and amazement at seeing one of the most famous figures in the British Army walking casually by. The Governor feigned embarrassment and confessed that Monty was visiting briefly en route to Algiers. After his short meeting with the Governor, the Spaniard rushed out, hastened to his car and drove quickly over the border to the Spanish town of La Linea. There he put through an urgent trunk call. Within minutes the Abwehr office in Madrid knew about Monty's apparent presence in Gibraltar.[16]

The lookalike's departure from Gibraltar airport was equally showy. An Honour Guard lined the tarmac, stood to attention and presented arms. In full view of a crowd that had gathered, Monty appeared to walk up and down, inspecting the guard with their bayonets glinting in the morning sun. As he went to board his aircraft a flight of Spitfires passed by, dipping their wings in salute. The crowd waved and shouted, 'Good old Monty!' After a short flight to Algiers, James again was very publicly met by the staff of General Maitland 'Jumbo' Wilson, the Allied Commander in the Mediterranean. As he walked through the airport he was spotted by a group of British and American officers who spontaneously cheered. An agent working for the Abwehr at the airport quickly passed on news of the British general's arrival. Then James was driven off in Wilson's motorcade, which, with its motorcycle escort, attracted some attention as it drove at speed through the city. The glamorous American driver had in previous years driven the real Montgomery, but James was playing his part so well by now that she did not apparently spot that it was not the real general that she was driving. Later she even requested permission to ask for his autograph. James was driven to Wilson's headquarters, where he spent several days. He travelled around and very publicly inspected more guards of honour and attended official receptions. Everywhere he went there were cheering crowds and more chants of 'Good old Monty.' The British intelligence network let rumours slip out, as if through negligence, that he was in Algiers to form a new Army Group that was planning to invade France on its Mediterranean coast. The Abwehr were by now receiving dozens of calls reporting the presence of the great general in the city and news of the new army being formed, by French and Arab citizens, all of whom were hoping to earn a decent fee for reporting this remarkable news.

By this point James was really getting into his role and was beginning to enjoy the respect and deference that was paid by everyone, including senior officers, to a famous general. He wrote later, 'I slipped into my part so completely that to all intents and purposes I *was* General Montgomery … Usually when an actor goes off stage he at once drops the part he's playing, but with me it's the other way round. I can't get out of … being Monty.'[17] After several days of being greeted as a great general and high-ranking officer, the lookalike returned to reality and became simply Lieutenant James of the Pay Corps. He was smuggled out of General Wilson's headquarters to a quiet house in Algiers, where he was told to stay put and not to think of going outside. His starring role had come to an end. He came to earth, as it were, with a bump and was so tense that he immediately reached for a flask of whisky, which he quickly downed. It was just as well that nothing more was expected of him in public, as it would have ruined the deception if Monty, who was known not to drink, had been spotted staggering around the back streets of Algiers drunk. After a day or so, James was whisked away to Cairo, where he was kept until 6 June, when it was publicly known and reported that the real Monty had led the 21st Army Group in the D-Day landings.

James had played his part well, but Dennis Wheatley, who had been one of those who created the role for him to play, felt that he was never properly thanked or acknowledged. However, in an act of surprising and unusual generosity, Lieutenant James was given a general's salary for the few days he had been an acting commander. Monty himself insisted this was only right. It seemed a reasonable sign of gratitude, but James probably used up quite a lot of this bonus in the bars of Cairo until he was allowed to go home.[18]

The deceptions had continued up to the very eve of D-Day. But how successful had they been? What had German intelligence made of them and what difference did they make?

Chapter 11

REACTIONS

By the spring of 1944, the Germans had picked up a mass of intelligence from Britain prompting them to assess and interpret what the Allies were supposedly planning. Colonel Alexis von Roenne (the head of intelligence at the FHW) was seriously worried about the scale of the Allied operations. In early March, he put through a telephone call to Colonel von Buttlar-Brandenfels, a member of Hitler's headquarters staff. It was typical of officers of this standing to talk up the prospects of the Third Reich and to diminish the power and capabilities of their enemy. This led to an unreal and inflated sense of optimism about the progress of the war among Hitler's entourage. And the Führer only ever wanted to hear good news about how his forces were doing and how badly the enemy were faring. But Von Roenne wanted to convey a very different message to his colleague in the Führer's headquarters.

A transcript of part of their conversation survives. Von Roenne began by telling Buttlar-Brandenfels that the RAF and the US Army Air Force were about to form a joint command for running missions over France. With the enemy's 'overwhelming superiority in the air,' von Roenne told Buttlar-Brandenfels, 'the operational mobility of our own forces will be reduced to nil.' Buttlar-Brandenfels, probably conscious that most phones in Hitler's headquarters were tapped by the SD, was cautious in his reply, telling Roenne that the Allied air forces had not paralysed German mobility during their landings at Salerno in Italy. And he went on to say, 'If the Anglo-American Air Force attacks us in France we shall reinforce with fighters from the Reich. The Allied bombers will be decimated!' But Von Roenne refused to be put off. He argued in response that the invasion of France would be of a different order to the small-scale Salerno landings and that 'over France the Allied bombers will be escorted by fighters, masses of them, their latest and most up-to-date machines against which ours will not stand a chance.' Von Roenne was no doubt expressing genuine fears he felt about any upcoming invasion of France and felt that he was doing his duty as a patriotic officer to alert his colleagues to the reality of the situation in the west. But he was playing a dangerous game. To be regarded as a defeatist in Hitler's Germany was a sure way of ending a promising career, or of heading straight to a Gestapo interrogation centre or worse.[1]

Von Roenne probably felt confident that, as Hitler's favourite intelligence officer, he was, to a degree, protected and secure. But he also felt that he had to insert a note of reality into the military thinking among the Nazi leadership. That was, after all, his job as an intelligence chief. He had gone along with the high numbers for the Allied Order of Battle that had been reported by the Abwehr, based on misinformation gleaned from their agents. Partly this was to build up the threat to the west in order to argue for sending reinforcements from the mashing ground of the Eastern Front. This had helped the case for Führer Directive 51, as we saw in Chapter 5, that redirected resources to the west and led to Field Marshal Rommel being appointed to take charge of the Atlantic Wall, from Denmark to south-west France. But how would Von Roenne and his colleagues respond to the many deceptions carried out in Fortitude North and South over the next few months after the gloomy call to his colleague at Hitler's headquarters?

The success or failure of Overlord could depend upon how Von Roenne would react.

The Germans were partially taken in by Operation Fortitude North. The FHW repeatedly bemoaned the fact that the Luftwaffe were not flying sufficient reconnaissance missions over Scotland to be able to verify the details they were picking up from Abwehr agents. However, the existence of the fake Fourth Army under General Thorne was accepted, and from the reports of their several 'trusted' agents, the FHW had a pretty clear picture of how many divisions were involved and what each corps consisted of. The British II Corps was identified as being based in Stirling. They knew the US XV Corps were in Northern Ireland but were all part of Thorne's Army. They were unable to trace the location of the British VII Corps, but that was hardly surprising, as it did not exist. But Von Roenne concluded that the size of the Fourth Army in Scotland was not large enough to do more than mount a diversionary attack upon Scandinavia. With some insight he concluded in one of his weekly intelligence summaries that the Allies were trying 'to do everything to tie down the German forces on subsidiary fronts, and indeed divert them from the decisive Atlantic front.'[2] But even though the FHW were aware of this, Hitler's long-term concern with Scandinavia and fear of an assault against Norway and Denmark meant that he was reluctant to reduce the size of the force based in these countries. After the war, Allied intelligence officers interviewed General Jodl about the reaction of the German High Command to the supposed threats to Scandinavia in May and June 1944. He told them that they had believed the threats but they had 'no influence upon the course of the war.' It was not surprising that he would claim this, not wanting to let it appear that the OKW had been deceived. But he did add that the Germans only needed about 100,000 men to garrison Norway and Denmark. Throughout 1944 there had been around 250,000 troops in the two countries, with the surplus being sustained there just in case the Allies did invade.[3] So on the one hand, Fortitude North succeeded because it created a credible threat and prevented the German High Command from moving 150,000 troops out of Scandinavia to other battle fronts. However, in another sense it was not so successful that it persuaded the Wehrmacht to allocate even more troops to idle away their time in this remote and ultimately peaceful northern sector.

The occupying forces who were charged with the defence of northern France consisted of two separate German armies. The Fifteenth Army in the east were stationed along the Pas de Calais coastline. The area they guarded extended from the Seine in the west right up into Belgium. The commander of the Fifteenth Army was General Hans von Salmuth, a tough Prussian who had plenty of experience of fighting on the Eastern Front. The Fifteenth included two battle-hardened panzer divisions who, again, had much experience of combat on the Eastern Front and who had now been rotated out from that front to rest up, train and to prepare to defend north-eastern France. To the west, the Seventh Army held all of France north of the Loire, from Brittany to Normandy and up to Rouen and as far east as the Seine valley. Its commander was General Friedrich Dollmann. He came not from a military family, but from a long line of civil servants. His headquarters was in a comfortable mansion in Le Mans to the south of Normandy. He did not have the charisma of many German generals and was given little respect by his corps and divisional commanders. Overall, he was poorly suited to be in command of an army that would find itself in the front line of one of the most important battles of the war.

These two armies came under Field Marshal Gerd von Rundstedt, Oberbefehlshaber West, or OB West (Commander-in-Chief West). He was the most senior field marshal in the German army, who had retired in 1938 but returned to active service the following year. He had quickly proved his worth as one of the ablest generals in the Wehrmacht, despite his age. He commanded the swift conquest of Poland in September 1939, the blitzkrieg advance to the Channel in May 1940, and it was his Army Group South that surrounded Kiev in one of the biggest battles of the war to date and conquered Ukraine in the summer and autumn of 1941. He was another grim-faced Prussian but was popular with his men, who called him '*der schwarze Ritter*', the black knight. Appointed as commander of OB West in 1942, he lived in considerable luxury at his headquarters at the Hotel George V in Paris, later moving to St-Germain-en-Laye to the west of the French capital. Notionally he was in command of 850,000 German troops. But he never had full control over the defence of the West and his role was quite different to that of a Supreme Commander in the Allied system. Von Rundstedt had no authority over the navy or the air force, nor over SS and Gestapo operations in occupied France. And by 1944, aged 69, Von Rundstedt was tired and depressed about the future of the war. He was sleeping badly, drinking excessively and smoking almost continuously. His son, a lieutenant, had been posted to his Paris headquarters as an aide-de-camp, partly to keep an eye on his father and to report back to Berlin. To Hitler, Jodl and Keitel, it seemed that Von Rundstedt was losing his grip. Although Hitler had respect for Von Rundstedt and his achievements, the defence of the West needed a tougher and more energetic commander.

So, in an action typical of his leadership, instinctively wanting to divide and rule, Hitler kept Von Rundstedt as commander-in-chief but appointed Field Marshal Erwin Rommel, aged 53, to form a new command of Army Group B in northern France in December 1943. Von Rundstedt was an admirer of Rommel's tactical abilities but felt undermined by his appointment and knew he could be difficult to work with. Rommel's first action was to make a whistle-stop tour of the Atlantic Wall. He was not impressed with the scale of the beach defences. He regarded them as only half finished and woefully lacking in artillery to repel an attacking force. And he was even less impressed with the calibre of the soldiers defending the coastline. He thought they were ill-equipped and poorly armed, without sufficient anti-tank weapons. He saw them as lethargic and without enthusiasm for their mission, many having been stationed in France for some time, which in the Wehrmacht was regard as an extremely cushy number.

He believed they had mingled too freely with the local population and had been softened by exchanging goods with local farmers and favours with local French girls. As the commander of the Panzer Lehr Division commented, 'France is a dangerous country with its wine, women and pleasant climate.'[4]

On 31 December 1943, Rommel wrote a report on the state of the Atlantic Wall after his initial inspection. With his experience from North Africa, he argued that defending the coastline of northern France was not going to involve the use of mobile warfare. Up against overwhelming Allied supremacy in the air, mobile units were at the mercy of continuous and devastating aerial attacks by day and night. Rommel concluded that 'an attempt must be made, using every possible expedient, to beat off the enemy landing on the coast' and 'everything must be directed towards destroying the enemy landing force while it is still on the water, or at the latest during the landing itself.' He called for the placing of anti-tank guns and self-propelled weapons along the coast to prevent the Allies from 'creating bridgeheads' and 'achieving a major penetration of our coastal defences.' And he demanded the planting of massive minefields, sometimes of up to five or six miles deep along the stretches of coast where the Allies were most likely to come ashore. Interestingly, his initial instinct was that the Allies were most likely to land in the Pas de Calais, between the towns of Boulogne and Calais. He thought this partly because it would be the shortest sea and air crossing, but also because the Allies would need to capture a major port soon after the invasion. Additionally, this offered the shortest route for an advance towards the Ruhr and the heart of the Nazi war machine. Furthermore, he was sure that the Anglo-Americans would want to destroy the sites where the new missiles would be launched against the UK.[5] These were the V1 cruise-missile-styled jet-powered flying bombs and the V2 ballistic missiles controlled from a vast site to be built just inland from Calais near St Omer, called La Coupole.[6]

General George S. Patton, the warrior General, his three stars displayed on helmet and collar. As commander of the hoax First US Army Group he proved to be a great showman who continually attracted attention. (Alamy Stock Photo)

General Bernard Law Montgomery, the hero of El Alamein, spent months addressing troops he would lead in Normandy. He wanted them to get to know him. (National Archives Catalog)

President Roosevelt and Prime Minister Churchill with their chiefs of staff at the Casablanca Conference, January 1943. All smiles for the camera but there were deep divisions between the British and American military chiefs. (National Archives Catalog)

Soldiers display one of the dummy tanks made of rubber and canvas. Inflated in 20 minutes, they could be lifted and carried around. (National Archives Catalog)

Above left: *Dusan Popov, Yugoslav businessman, playboy and double agent codenamed Tricycle.* (P.D.Enhanced / Alamy Stock Photo)

Above right: *Roman Czerniawski, Polish patriot and double agent codenamed Brutus.* (P.D.Enhanced / Alamy Stock Photo)

Left: *Juan Pujol Garcia, Catalan double agent who tried for eighteen months to spy for Britain, codenamed Garbo. Later called the 'greatest double agent' of the war, here receiving his MBE at Buckingham Palace in 1984.* (Keith Waldegrave/ Mail on Sunday/ Shutterstock)

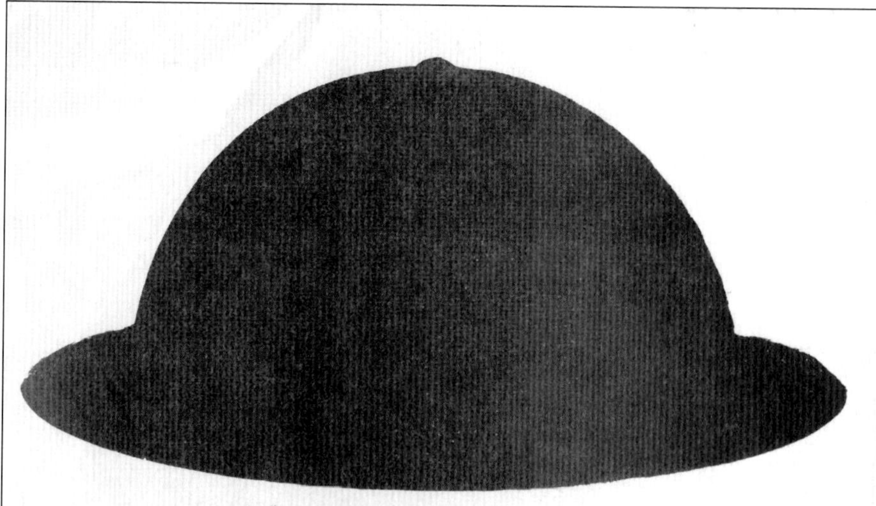

Ministry of Information poster in the 'Careless Talk Costs Lives' campaign. What Britons were not told was that all enemy agents and spies sent to Britain had been captured. (National Archives Catalog)

Lieutenant-Colonel Dudley Clarke, pioneer of deception who laid down the rules for how a good deception operation should work. Clarke was arrested in Madrid in female clothing in October 1941 on some form of mysterious undercover mission. (The National Archives, Kew)

Above left: *Hugh Trevor-Roper, Oxford historian who became the MI6 expert on German military intelligence.* (Pictorial Press Ltd / Alamy Stock Photo)

Above right: *John Masterman, Oxford academic and novelist who chaired the XX Committee for MI5, controlling the double agents.* (© National Portrait Gallery, London)

Below: *Dennis Wheatley, the thriller writer, before the war. Wheatley joined the team of creatives who came up with brilliant ideas for deception.* (Pictorial Press Ltd / Alamy Stock Photo)

The Allied Central Interpretation Unit of aerial photographs, RAF Medmenham, located in a country house outside London. It made a vital contribution to many deception operations. Photo Interpreters, men and women, British and American, pose on the steps at the end of the war. (The Medmenham Collection)

Generals Montgomery and Patton in their very different styles at Palermo, July 1943. They shook hands for the camera but became bitter rivals. (National Archives Catalog)

General Dwight D. Eisenhower, Supreme Commander of Operation Overlord, briefs war correspondents at his Advance Command Post. He was a great supporter of deception operations. (National Archives Catalog)

Field Marshal Gerd von Rundstedt Commander-in-Chief West poses for the camera. One of Germany's most successful commanders, but was he past it by 1944? (Sueddeutsche Zeitung Photo / Alamy Stock Photo)

Field Marshal Erwin Rommel, who was brought in to build up the Atlantic Wall but argued bitterly with colleagues on how best to defend the beaches. (PictureLux / The Hollywood Archive / Alamy Stock Photo)

A mighty concrete and steel fortress in the Atlantic Wall, the mass of defensive fortifications along the coast from Denmark to south-west France. (Sueddeutsche Zeitung Photo / Alamy Stock Photo)

Above left: *Admiral Wilhelm Canaris, the head of the Abwehr, German military intelligence. An enigmatic figure who was no friend of the Nazi Party.* (Granger/Shutterstock)

Above right: *Reinhard Heydrich, SS Intelligence chief and later overseer of Occupied Territories. The SS regarded themselves as guardians of the Nazi faith.* (National Archives Catalog)

Left: *Walter Schellenberg of the SS Intelligence operation, the SD, personable but ruthless and still smiling even though under arrest at the Nuremberg Trials.* (National Archives Catalog)

Lieutenant Clifton James of the Army Pay Corps, Monty's double, who acted the part of the great General in Gibraltar and Algiers. (PA Images / Alamy Stock Photo)

General Sir Alan Brooke, Chief of the Imperial General Staff. He fought with Churchill repeatedly but both men greatly respected each other. (Sueddeutsche Zeitung Photo / Alamy Stock Photo)

Vast arrays of tanks, guns and military vehicles were built up prior to D-Day. In this case Bofors anti-aircraft guns. (piemags/archive/military / Alamy Stock Photo)

General Eisenhower visits paratroopers of 101st Airborne Division at Greenham Common airfield just before they launch D-Day on the night of 5 June 1944. He was terrified at the losses they might face. They were cheerful and confident of victory. (National Archives Catalog)

Field Marshal Günther von Kluge, who was sent by Hitler to tell Rommel he must obey orders. (Sueddeutsche Zeitung Photo / Alamy Stock Photo)

2nd SS Panzer Division, Das Reich, the only division sent from southern France to Normandy after D-Day. Along the way the unit carried out a massacre at Oradour-sur-Glane. (Shawshots / Alamy Stock Photo)

Alexander Korda bought Shepperton Studios after the war and gave it a new lease of life. Here he walks on set with Vivien Leigh during the filming of Anna Karenina *(directed by Julian Duvivier, 1948).* (Masheter Movie Archive / Alamy Stock Photo)

Rommel's conclusions were clear. He believed the first 24 hours after an invasion would be crucial, what he came to call 'the longest day.' A massive reinforcement of the Atlantic Wall with weapons, mines and coastal batteries was essential. And also the rapid training and refocusing of the troops deployed was necessary. With immense energy Rommel started to co-ordinate a vast improvement of the coastal defences. He was everywhere, cajoling and pushing his coastal commanders. New machine-gun posts and artillery positions were constructed from where there was optimum range of fire. Huge new coastal minefields were laid along beaches where a landing might take place. And where the shortages of armaments meant no mines were available, dummy minefields were laid out surrounded by '*Achtung Minen*' (Danger Mines) signs to put off Allied troops.[7] Areas where Allied parachutists might drop or gliders might try to land were staked out with wooden posts, some of which were headed by tripwires or mines. These became known as *Rommelspargel* or 'Rommel's asparagus.' But Rommel also knew that good intelligence was needed to provide the necessary early warning of where and when the invasion was coming. It was good for the Allies that he was confident the Pas de Calais was the location. Much of his energy went into building up the defences there. But would he come to change his mind and refocus his energy and attention elsewhere?

In the early months of 1944, both Von Rundstedt and Rommel agreed that the Allies were most likely to land in the Pas de Calais. Their thinking was initially reinforced by the German Navy, who insisted an invasion force would only ever land at high tide and this would be impossible along the Normandy beaches because the mines being laid there would destroy the Allied landing craft as they tried to come ashore. On the other hand, the Luftwaffe advised that the invasion was most likely to come in Normandy, as the beaches there were further from the airfields from which the Luftwaffe would fly its missions and the Allies would try to exploit this. And indeed, Hitler looking at all the information in March and April began to think that Normandy perhaps was a likely area for an invasion. On 20 March, Hitler announced at a conference with his generals, 'It is evident that an Anglo-American landing in the West will and must come. How and where it will come no one knows.' But he went on to claim that Brittany and Normandy were especially threatened. He began to think that the Cotentin Peninsula would be the likely scene of a landing. Rommel was present and made a note of the Führer's thoughts.[8]

Throughout April, Hitler instructed Jodl in his headquarters to repeatedly press Von Rundstedt and Rommel to improve the defences in Brittany and Normandy. Jodl's deputy telephoned Von Rundstedt's headquarters to pass on a message from the Führer that 'a partial success by the enemy [in Brittany and Normandy] would inevitably at once tie down very strong forces of OB West.'[9] It's clear that there was no agreed view in the OKW as to where the invasion would come, and it's quite possible that Hitler advocated the Pas de Calais at one time and Normandy at another simply so it could be said afterwards that he had been correct in his prediction. At the end of April, as the debate within the German High Command intensified about where and when the Allied invasion would come, Operation Fortitude South began in earnest, using the combination of dummy vehicles, false radio messages and phoney information fed via the double agents. The Great Deception was underway.

However, in early 1944, the Double-Cross Committee, which was controlling the information being sent out by the valuable double agents, received a real shock. The internal disputes within the German intelligence operation had reached a new peak. The poor performance of the Abwehr, its failure to see through the Mincemeat deception and predict the invasion of Sicily, its failure to predict the landings at Anzio, plus a general sense of the lack of loyalty of the senior members and a growing suspicion of Abwehr spymasters abroad, who appeared lazy and were at the least fiddling expenses or in places running currency rackets, all played into the hands of Himmler and the SS. In France the SD were obtaining useful information from having infiltrated parts of the French Resistance movement, in contrast to the Abwehr, who were coming up with nothing of value. And SD agents abroad were observing the Abwehr officials and helping to build up a dossier of incompetence, inefficiency and corruption.[10]

Matters came to a head in February when a senior Abwehr official, the deputy station chief in Istanbul, defected to the Allies, prompting a series of further defections. Himmler decided this was the moment to act against his long-term rival. Admiral Wilhelm Canaris was removed and put under house arrest. The SD overseas section under Walter Schellenberg, the young intelligence chief who had appeared to politely court Canaris for some years, effectively seized control of the Abwehr operation. It was a final victory for Himmler's SS. But it left the Nazi intelligence-gathering system in some chaos at a critical point in the war. The SD officials who took over the work of the Abwehr spymasters might have possessed unquestioning loyalty to the Führer, but they lacked the years of experience of spycraft of their predecessors. For the Double-Cross Committee in London the sudden hardening up of the German intelligence-gathering operation posed a major challenge. Could their double agents continue to peddle their misinformation without arousing suspicion? It was an existential threat to the whole deception operation.

The first to experience the new regime first-hand was Dusko Popov, Tricycle, who in early March flew to Lisbon for one of his regular meetings with German intelligence officials. He took a mass of paperwork with him, including detailed reports of the Order of Battle and of factories, airfields and ports in which preparations had supposedly been sighted for the upcoming invasion. But instead of Albrecht von Auenrode, his regular handler, he found himself reporting to an SD officer, Alois Schreiber, whom he had never met before. Unlike Auenrode, with whom Popov had enjoyed a friendly, jovial relationship, he found

Schreiber cold and unfriendly. The debriefing went on through the night and was gruelling. Popov left the encounter feeling unsure as to where he stood. However, Schreiber passed on his report of the information Popov had brought without expressing any suspicions. Berlin replied saying they were delighted with the information. And to Popov's relief his next meeting with the SD official was much warmer.[11]

The information Popov had passed on, all written by MI5, of course, conveyed details of where many units were across the UK. It represented the opening of the Fortitude South operation. The idea was to inform the FHW of the precise locations of several divisions and corps in Britain, so that over the following weeks, when it was reported that these units had moved to the south-east of England, they could be tracked as they appeared to join the growing invasion force that would be the First US Army Group. On 9 March an FHW weekly report picked up on Popov's information and passed it on, accepting every detail. The FHW report read:

> A V-man [agent's] message which reached the Abteilung on 7 March 1944, brought particularly valuable information about the British formations in Great Britain ... It contained information about three armies, three army corps and twenty-three divisions, among which the displacement of only one formation must be regarded as questionable. The report confirmed our own overall operational picture.[12]

In fact, the claim that the agent had confirmed the FHW's 'overall operational picture' was a complete fabrication. German intelligence had discovered a lot that was new to them in Popov's report. In London, members of the Double-Cross Committee heaved a major sigh of relief when the FHW report was deciphered. The misinformation had been picked up and passed on by the new SD handlers as easily as it had been with the previous

Abwehr officials. And with the FHW now having a clear idea as to where the military units in Britain were located, the real deceptions of Fortitude South could move forward.

Major intelligence began to pour into the SD from the double agents Brutus, Tricycle, Garbo and Freak, all of which added to the massive inflation of the size of the armies in the UK. A few weeks after Tricycle's report had been absorbed into the FHW's Order of Battle in Britain, Von Roenne issued one of his regular intelligence summaries that included estimates of the number of Allied troops assembling in Britain. Taking as fact the misinformation that had come via the Abwehr and now the SD from their agents in the UK, Von Roenne calculated that there were 77 divisions and 19 independent brigades in Britain. This was 50 per cent above the reality. By the end of the month his estimate had risen to 79 divisions, with the independent units adding up to the equivalent of 10 more, whereas there were actually 52 divisions in Britain. And he estimated that there were landing craft available to transport 16 divisions across the Channel. Everything that followed was interpreted and understood against this remarkably over-inflated Order of Battle.

Up until the beginning of May, the FHW had believed there were three groups of forces in Britain: Northern, Central and Southern commands. With the misinformation coming in from Operation Fortitude North, the Northern command was easily redefined in German eyes as the Fourth Army under General Thorne. Under the misinformation coming in from Fortitude South, the Central group became realigned as the 21st Army Group under Montgomery. And the Southern group was reclassified as the First US Army Group, whom the FHW correctly thought at this point was under General Omar Bradley. Aerial reconnaissance flights established the existence of large numbers of landing craft assembling in the south-west of England. On 29 April an FHW review concluded, 'Increased air reconnaissance of the south coast of England has revealed that two concentrations [of landing craft] are showing themselves in this area at the present time namely in the Portsmouth and the Dartmouth/Salcombe areas.'[13] In the first week of May, the various reports sent in from Garbo, Freak and Brutus made the FHW reassess the situation and report a major build-up of Anglo-American forces in the south-east. This was in response to that part of Fortitude South that fed false information about US and British divisions moving from their locations in the north and the Midlands to the south-east and East Anglia, even though, apart from signallers, the units actually moved nowhere. By 15 May the FHW were reporting, 'The main enemy concentration is showing itself ever more clearly to be in the South and the South-East of the island.'[14] By the end of May, the First US Army Group, now under General Patton, had grown in the eyes of the FHW to include a total of twenty-six divisions, not including airborne units. This included four divisions who were actually part of the 21st Army Group, six training divisions who were not yet ready for combat, and six purely imaginary divisions. Although Luftwaffe aerial reconnaissance was limited, the FHW reported 'a considerable increase in landing craft' along the south-east coastline 'as compared with previous results.'[15] The wetbobs and drybobs of the Shepperton studio designers had done their job and were now numbered as the real thing in German intelligence reports.

More evidence of the Pas de Calais as the most likely area for the principal thrust came with the pattern of Allied air attacks during the month of May. Obviously wanting to keep the Germans guessing, the pre-invasion air assault was spread across a wide area. Some air attacks took place along the Norwegian coast and some on the Bordeaux area in the south-west of France. But most were directed at the north French coast. And here a clear focus emerged on the Pas de Calais region. Eleven airfields and nineteen railway junctions in that area were hit by Allied aircraft, against only four airfields and railway junctions in the Normandy area. The bridges over the Seine were bombed, but also attacks were made on bridges over the Meuse, the Oise and the Albert canal, all suggesting the north-east was the principal target. In all, the Allied bombing raids on coastal defences and inland sites were roughly in the proportion of two to one on the Pas de Calais versus the Normandy region. On 29 May, Von Rundstedt reported to Berlin that, having studied enemy bombing patterns in northern France, the principal invasion would be against the Pas de Calais. The RAF and US Army Air Force were playing their parts well in the big deception game.[16]

Gradually through May, alongside the analysis of the air raids, the information from Fortitude South seemed to pile up more and more evidence of an invasion coming from the south-east of England via the shortest Channel crossing. All the means that were being used, from dummy tanks and landing craft to radio signals and the public posing of General Patton as the most aggressive commander in the Allied armies, began to convince Hitler, the OKW, Von Roenne and Von Rundstedt that the major invasion force would now come from the south-east of England. They still believed there might be more than one landing, that the Allies might mount a feint in Normandy, Brittany, in the Bay of Biscay or along the Norwegian coast, but this would be with the intention of drawing troops away from the Pas de Calais area in order to fatally weaken the resistance there. Having accepted the figures for the Allied Order of Battle that Von Roenne was putting out, it seemed entirely feasible that the Allies had enough men and resources to mount more than one invasion over a matter of weeks.

Rommel, on the other hand, having initially believed the principal landing would be between Boulogne and Calais, was now beginning to doubt this. His intelligence chief was Colonel Anton Staubwasser, who had spent three years in the FHW. While there he had started to doubt the figures that Von Roenne was putting out about the size of Allied forces in

Britain. He had no independent sources of intelligence, but his gut feeling told him that the numbers were exaggerated. Imagining this might be the case, Staubwasser and Rommel came to believe there would only be a single invasion rather than multiple landings. Rommel, his chief of staff General Hans Speidel and Staubwasser spent many evenings discussing the invasion prospects in the gardens of his headquarters in the elegant chateau at La Roche-Guyon in a bend of the River Seine, 40 miles north of Paris. After repeatedly assessing and reassessing the situation amid the rose plants that had yet to flower, Rommel came to believe that if there were only to be one invasion then it would have to be on a front wide enough for the Allies to land the large numbers of men and resources needed to establish a secure bridgehead. Because the transport connections were worse in Normandy than in the Pas de Calais, and so would take longer for the Germans to bring up reserves, Rommel came to a new conclusion that the most likely area was going to be in Normandy. He also disagreed with the prevailing view coming from the German Navy that the landings would happen at high tide and at night. He concluded that the Allies would come in at low tide, most probably at dawn or soon after. And that the seaborne landings would be preceded by airborne drops during the night before.

If his hunch was right then controlling the reserves, particularly the panzer reserves, and getting them to Normandy within the critical first 24 hours of a landing now became a leading priority for Rommel. He asked Von Rundstedt to give him control of the armoured units, which he wanted to move near to the coast in the Normandy area. He particularly wanted command of the Panzer Lehr Division and the 12th SS Panzer Division *Hitlerjugend*. Von Rundstedt disagreed with Rommel's verdict that the landings were most likely to come in Normandy and, still believing the principal thrust would be in the Pas de Calais, refused to allow Rommel to have control of the panzer reserves. Von Rundstedt and the commander of the armoured forces, General Geyr von Schweppenburg, both wanted the reserves to be placed well inland, to the north of Paris, giving them maximum manoeuvrability to respond to an invasion wherever it came. Von Schweppenburg took a different view altogether to Rommel, arguing that the Allies should be allowed to land and build up their presence ashore, so they could then be destroyed and thrown back into the sea by a powerful counter-attack led by him and his panzers. Rommel knew that with the Allies having air supremacy the moving up of armoured units over long distances would be difficult, if not impossible. Better that they were near to the scene of the landings in the first place, almost lined up along the beaches.

Rommel had been fighting the British in North Africa for some years and knew that it was essential to concentrate his panzer forces against powerful Allied armoured thrusts. And he thought Von Schweppenburg, who had years of experience of fighting on the Eastern Front, had just not grasped the difference between doing battle with the Soviets and fighting the Anglo-Americans. Rommel and Von Schweppenburg argued violently about the command of the strategic panzer reserve. Rommel decided to appeal above von Rundstedt's head, directly to Jodl in the OKW. He wrote, 'The most decisive battle of the war, and the fate of the German people itself, is at stake.' He argued that if he did not have command of the panzer units 'victory will be in grave doubt. If I am to wait until the enemy landing has actually taken place before I can demand the dispatch of the mobile forces … they will probably arrive too late to intervene successfully in the battle for the coast.'[17] Rommel could not have made himself any clearer.

Hitler now intervened in what was becoming a major row between his generals. He said half the panzer units could be allocated to those defending the beaches. The other half would stay under Von Schweppenburg's command but could only be moved with his own personal and direct approval. It was a compromise that Rommel was sure would be disastrous. He decided there was only one course of action. He must visit the Führer in the Obersalzberg and argue his case in person. Rommel was confident that face to face he could persuade Hitler to change his mind about the command of the panzer reserve. The only problem was that with the weather so favourable in May it was possible that the invasion might come any day, and he could hardly leave his headquarters for a long journey to southern Bavaria. He would have to wait for the right opportunity to present his case.

Hitler was spending all his time in his mountain retreat at the Berghof, which symbolised both his distance from real events and the fact that his head was in the sky when it came to practical matters. After the British and Canadians had sent a raiding force to Dieppe nearly two years before, he was convinced the Allies would try to seize a port and so he ordered that all the major ports from Dunkirk to Bordeaux, including Calais, Boulogne, Le Havre and Cherbourg along the Channel, and Brest and La Rochelle on the Atlantic, should become fortresses where garrisons must fight to the last bullet. No withdrawal would be permitted. This meant that about 120,000 men would never leave these bastions. Moreover, the propaganda about the impregnability of the Atlantic Wall seems to have convinced Hitler that the Allies would never get ashore, and once they were thrown back, he could withdraw his armies from the west, defeat the Red Army in the east and win the war. Self-deception was everywhere in the Führer Headquarters. And this sense of confidence in what lay ahead was only heightened by Joseph Goebbels, whose repeated slogan at this time was, 'They are supposed to be coming. Why don't they come?'

There had been many changes of view among the Nazi military leadership about the location of the now imminent Allied invasion, but by the end of May, Hitler, Jodl and Von

Rundstedt all concluded that even if there was a landing in Normandy, Brittany or Norway, this would only be a ruse designed to draw reserves away from the major event that would take place in the Pas de Calais. By contrast, Rommel believed that there would be a single invasion most likely along the Normandy coast, and that the first 24 hours would be vital in defeating the Allies. Some of the messages between OB West and the OKW had been intercepted and deciphered at Bletchley Park. Allied leaders followed the tug of war with great interest. Hitler's refusal to put the panzer reserve under Rommel's command seemed justification alone for the whole Fortitude South operation. Then a new and even more dramatic intercept came through.

At the end of May, Hitler had a personal meeting at the Berghof with Baron Hiroshi Oshima, the Japanese ambassador to Germany. Short and stocky, Oshima was a regular visitor, and the Führer spoke openly and honestly to the ambassador of the country that was Germany's closest ally. Oshima had been military attaché in Berlin before the war and naturally displayed a lot of interest in military affairs and in the prospects for an Anglo-American landing. He had toured almost the whole Atlantic Wall, from Holland to south-west France, in late 1943. His detailed report to Tokyo on what he saw as the strengths and weaknesses of the beach defences had been deciphered in Washington and presented the Allies with a mass of invaluable details about the units that were stationed along the Atlantic Wall and the fortifications in place at that time. So important were these revelations that General Marshall summoned Eisenhower back from Europe to Washington to discuss them with him face to face.[18]

During Oshima's two-hour meeting with Hitler on 27 May, it was inevitable that the conversation would cover the likelihood of the Allied invasion. An aide from the Japanese embassy took a shorthand note of the discussion. Hitler assured the ambassador that sooner or later the Anglo-Americans would attempt an invasion. He told Oshima, 'I understand that the enemy has already assembled about 80 divisions in the British Isles.' The deception that had dramatically exaggerated the size of the troops in the UK had clearly penetrated the very top of the Nazi regime. Hitler went on that 'judging from relatively ominous portents' he understood that the Allies would first launch 'diversionary actions against Norway, Denmark, the southern part of western France, or the coasts of the French Mediterranean.' Having established a bridgehead there or in Normandy and Brittany, then 'they will come forward with an all-out Second Front in the area of the Straits of Dover.' This meant that he would not be able to strike a single blow against the Allies as he would have wished, but that he would have to defeat the Allied forces at several different points.[19] Oshima listened attentively to what Hitler told him and within hours of their meeting a transcript of the conversation was sent in code from Berlin to Tokyo. It was immediately intercepted and deciphered both at Arlington Hall outside Washington and at Bletchley Park.[20] Not long after it had been received by the Foreign Office in Tokyo, Oshima's message was being read in London, Washington and at SHAEF headquarters. The Allied leaders could barely hold back their excitement at what they read. On the eve of D-Day they had been given an astonishing insight into the state of mind of the Führer. Hitler had absorbed and accepted nearly all the deception details of Operation Fortitude South. The planners could not have hoped for more. It was almost as though the Allied deceivers had written Hitler's script for him.

In the first few days of June the weather in the Channel changed from the dry, balmy conditions that had prevailed for the previous couple of weeks. The prospects for a major landing receded. Rommel decided now was the time to make his visit to the Obersalzberg to argue his case directly to Hitler that the command of the panzer reserve should be transferred to him. He was pleased that en route to Bavaria he could stop by his home at Herrlingen near Ulm and see his wife on what would be her birthday. On the morning of Monday 5 June, Rommel called Hitler's adjutant to request an urgent meeting with the Führer. Then he left La Roche-Guyon by car for the long drive to southern Germany. On the seat beside him was a box of soft suede shoes he had bought in Paris as a birthday present for his wife.

Chapter 12

STANDING BY

In Britain at the end of May, huge resources of manpower and materiel were coming together for the largest amphibious operation in history. Nearly a quarter of a million men in the Allied armies, navies and air forces would be involved on D-Day itself. And hundreds of thousands more from D+1 onwards. But despite the scale of the operation and the encouraging feedback from deciphering German and Japanese messages, many military leaders were still uncertain about the outcome. None other than the Chief of the Imperial General Staff, General Sir Alan Brooke, wrote in his diary on the eve of D-Day, 'I am very uneasy about the whole operation. At the best it will fall to very very far short of the expectation of the bulk of the people, namely those who know nothing of its difficulties. At the worst it may well be the most ghastly disaster of the whole war.'[1]

Except for those living along the south coast, who could see that something big was about to happen, most ordinary citizens living inland still had no idea of what was coming. Meanwhile, life in wartime Britain continued as normal as it could after four and a half years of war. In the cinemas, hundreds of thousands were flocking to see the Technicolor epic *For Whom the Bell Tolls* with Gary Cooper and the glamorous Swedish actress Ingrid Bergman. The film version of Noel Coward's play *This Happy Breed*, directed by David Lean, had just opened and was also proving popular at the box office. The film follows the story of a lower middle-class family in suburban Clapham, the Gibbons, across the two decades between the end of the First World War and the beginning of the Second. The summer cricket season was dominated by fixtures in which what remained of the county sides played teams selected from the military like Aldershot Services or Western Command. But of most interest to cricket lovers, an Australian side was playing at Lords in the beautiful late May sunshine. Music lovers in London had a festival of Russian music to enjoy, including a performance of Shostakovich's latest ballet, and could look forward to the start of the new Proms season at the Albert Hall with Sir Henry Wood conducting.

As May turned into the beginning of June, a general sense of anxious expectation seems to have taken hold. People began to notice that the numbers of servicemen in uniform who had been thronging the streets of London and other cities were shrinking. Every day there seemed to be fewer of them, until hardly anyone in British or American uniforms could be seen. This fact alone began to make people wonder if the long-awaited Second Front was about to be launched. A few hints of imminent action leaked out. The Minister of Production, Oliver Lyttelton, said in a speech in London that no army would ever go into battle as well equipped as the one Britain would be launching on the continent, although, 'We must say nothing as to when or where the attack was coming.' And in Washington, the Secretary of War, Henry Stimson, said that 3.6 million American soldiers were serving overseas and 'the period of decisive action is now at hand.' Both speeches were widely reported in the British press.[2] One journalist based in London reported that in village pubs up and down the country, as well as in the fashionable London clubs, there was one unfailing topic of conversation, 'the invasion' and when it would come.[3]

On 1 June the Supreme Commander of the Allied Expeditionary Force, General Eisenhower, moved from his base at Bushy Park in south-west London to a caravan in the grounds of his advanced headquarters at Southwick House in Portsmouth. From here, a hub of naval communications, he and Montgomery could closely follow the invasion armada as it prepared to cross the Channel. Eisenhower sent a top-secret cable to General Marshall in Washington: 'Everyone is in good heart and barring unsuitable meteorological conditions we will do the trick as scheduled.' That day the long spell of hot weather broke and the morning was overcast with rain, although later in the day the sun came out. A brisk south-westerly wind had started to blow up and thundery black rainclouds appeared in the far south-west. Barometers were showing a sudden drop in pressure.

The whole of southern England had become one vast military camp. Hundreds of thousands of men had gathered in their assembly areas, where they were completely cut off from the outside world and forbidden from leaving their encampments. One after another, commanders were briefed and then, accompanied by intelligence officers, passed on the final briefings to their men. The briefings went from divisional headquarters to every regiment, to each battalion and then to every company. For the first time the men were told exactly where they were going to land. Many were surprised to hear it was in Normandy and not the Pas de Calais, the south-west of France or the Dutch coast. But most were relieved to hear that the beaches were flat and there were no high cliffs to scale. There were five main beaches. From the west, they were codenamed Utah and Omaha, where American troops would land around the Cotentin Peninsula; then Gold, Juno and

Sword, where British and Canadian troops would land to the north of the city of Caen. And each beach was subdivided into dozens of smaller sections, all codenamed and all of which were the specific target of different units.[4] The airborne forces were told where they would jump or where their gliders would come in. The Americans in the west would seize the village of Sainte Mère-Eglise and the British in the east would capture some key bridges and artillery emplacements. This was all intended to prevent the Germans from rushing reinforcements to the beaches during the first hours after the landings. Most men were impressed by the details they were given and felt confident that their commanders had things under control and knew what they were doing. Some of the men were given small amounts of French currency, French phrasebooks and extra rations to cover the 24 hours after landing. A few of the Americans were given condoms. It was not clear if they were for covering the barrel of their rifles to keep them dry in the water, or for other purposes.

Teams of photo interpreters at RAF Medmenham had been analysing the beaches of northern France for a couple of years, observing photos with the tide in and out to assess the sand and the shingle and see how able they would be to support vehicles and armour. They had discovered that mines were attached to the underwater obstacles when a lucky photo was exposed on a low-level run during a bombing raid. The photo revealed fourteen simultaneous explosions from a set of mines ignited by a single bomb at high tide. When they examined the same stretch of beach at low tide they realised that every explosion coincided with the location of one of the underwater obstacles. This information made the planners decide to land at low tide, so the landing craft would not hit the mines as they passed over them. They also looked for potential drop zones and landing grounds for parachutists, seeing exactly where the anti-glider barriers, 'Rommel's asparagus', had been laid and where they had not. As the Atlantic Wall had been expanded, every new machine-gun location and artillery emplacement was spotted and marked on beach maps. At Medmenham they were highly experienced in producing photo maps of a target area. A series of photos taken from the same height on the same scale were carefully attached together in what was called a photo-mosaic. Usually at a scale of about 1:50,000, they were produced for bomber crews before every mission. Sometimes if extra detail was needed, of, say, a factory site or an airfield, the photo-mosaics could be produced at a much larger scale of 1:10,000.

Additionally, for D-Day, the model-making section at Medmenham went into overdrive. Models were made in 3D from aerial photo-mosaics on which hardboard cut-outs were laid to mark out high ground, mounting layer upon layer exactly to replicate contour lines. Then they were covered with a plastic or rubber layer to smooth out the surface. Once the landscape had been laid out, tiny models of buildings, churches, gun emplacements, farms or woods were made and placed precisely in location. The model could then be painted to show up rivers, fields, roads and trees. In the run-up to D-Day some smaller-scale models were made to show a large stretch of coastline and placed on tables about five by five feet. Much larger models on tables about sixteen by sixteen feet could be made of specific beaches. Plaster casts were made of the models and several duplicates produced from these. When the troops who would land on D-Day had been isolated in their camps they were shown the models and could see details of the beach on which they would land. They were able to study the buildings along the shore that they would find as the clambered off the beaches, and also the hinterland beyond. The models showed them what to expect on landing, where the enemy defences were concentrated, what challenges they would face once ashore and where the routes off the beach were located.[5]

Not all aerial photos were taken looking vertically down. Some were taken by low-flying reconnaissance aircraft at an oblique angle. Some of these were taken almost at sea level about 1,500 yards out along every stretch of beach where troops would land to give to the coxswain of the landing craft a clear idea of what their stretch of beach and the defences ahead of them would look like. Thousands more were taken at low level of the beaches and ground features so every platoon commander could see what to expect.[6] In all, hundreds of models were produced and tens of thousands of photos were printed. In the months before D-Day, Medmenham was at its busiest, with the photo interpreters run off their feet. At the peak of the operation there were nearly 80 reconnaissance sorties a day, and on each flight a pilot could take up to 500 separate photos. The teams needed to process, map, interpret, archive and retrieve this number of images every day were huge, and Medmenham grew in size until there were 3,500 men and women from the army, navy and air force, from Britain, America and other Allied nations, working there and making a vital contribution to the top-secret intelligence war.[7]

Once the men had received their orders with details of what their mission would be and where they would land, they were sealed in and told they could not leave. Military police guarded every encampment. Often extra rations were made available and quartermasters supplied extra beer. 'I'm being fattened up for the slaughter and am simply waiting for it to start,' wrote the poet Keith Douglas in one these camps.[8] A major security alert was triggered when it was reported that a British NCO had escaped from his sealed camp in Hampshire. In his pockets were details of the beach he was to land on and the timings of the landings. If they fell into the wrong hands they could have threatened the whole invasion. It was thought the soldier might have been heading for Wales, where his girlfriend and his parents lived. The local police were alerted and their houses were put under surveillance. After several anxious hours for the security services, the soldier was arrested the next day near his parents' home. He revealed he had hitchhiked to Wales in military vehicles and had spent the night in a US Army base, where had had gone drinking with some GIs. The US base, which was not in the security zone, was surrounded, closed off and nobody was allowed out. Every driver who had given the man a lift was rounded up and put into isolation until after D-Day. The soldier was court-martialled and given a ten-year sentence for leaving his camp. It turned out that after receiving the briefing he became convinced that he would never survive D-Day and just wanted to see his parents one final time.[9]

Huge, elongated parks of tanks, vehicles, ammunition, medical supplies, food and every other type of supply that would be needed were piled high behind barbed wire in camps. Again, they were closely guarded and cut off from prying eyes. The government had established zones across the south that no civilian was allowed to enter. Every soldier, every weapon, every tank was entered on a vast schedule and told to arrive at their embarkation point at exactly the right time, to be loaded onto vessels in precisely the right order for their disembarkation on the other side of the Channel. It was a colossal and complex logistics operation. Everything was set. D-Day was scheduled for Monday 5 June. The first ships would sail 48 hours beforehand from the ports along the south coast and right around to Bristol. Eisenhower later wrotc, 'The mighty host was tense as a coiled spring ... a great human spring, coiled for the moment when its energy should be released and it would vault the English Channel in the greatest amphibious assault ever attempted.'[10]

On the afternoon of Saturday 3 June, the weather was still fair and Eisenhower and his principal commanders met in the library at his headquarters at Southwick House. The books had been removed and Ike sat at the front with his chief of staff. The commanders sat facing him in a semi-circle in armchairs, with their chiefs of staff behind them. The reason for such senior figures coming together was the daily meeting with the chief meteorological adviser, Group Captain James Stagg. Aged 44, Stagg was an experienced weather forecaster in the Met Office who had been called up into the RAF and appointed head of Eisenhower's meteorological department. A Lowland Scot with a soft-spoken voice, he was a dour figure who summed up the weather situation as plainly as he could without putting any spin on it. There had been an argument within his team. The American meteorologists were convinced that the weather was set fair. But Stagg had been studying weather reports from the Atlantic for several years and knew how quickly weather conditions could change. The RAF had a series of boats and weather stations reporting back meteorological conditions and Stagg had become an expert at assessing this data and predicting what weather was coming in from the Atlantic. He told Eisenhower that the wind was getting up and was 'full of menace' for the projected D-Day, 5 June. The high pressure over the Azores that had brought the long spell of good weather was giving way to a series of depressions. Having delivered his gloomy report, Stagg left the room. Eisenhower and his chiefs discussed the situation. Delaying the vast operation of men, ships and aircraft would put intense strain on the situation: everything was waiting to go. On the other hand, going ahead in rough seas would risk imperilling the invasion fleet, especially the small landing craft, and could bring disaster. They decided to wait until Stagg's next forecast, at 4.15 the following morning. By then the first vessels of the invasion fleet would have already set sail.

At this meeting, just before dawn, Stagg brought even worse news. He was now predicting high winds, between Force 4 and 6, along the Normandy coast, with low cloud cover at about 500 feet. 'Do you foresee any change?' asked Eisenhower. 'No,' replied Stagg bluntly. Eisenhower asked his commanders what they thought. Air Chief Marshal Sir Arthur Tedder said that with cloud cover that low the air forces would not be able to achieve half of their tasks and attack the enemy gun emplacements on the beaches. Admiral Sir Bertram Ramsay said that rough seas would make the naval task impossible and that the small landing craft would get thrown about mercilessly. Only Montgomery, in charge of land forces, felt confident that once ashore his men could do their job. After a brief conversation, Eisenhower decided there was only one possible conclusion. The invasion would be postponed for 24 hours. Immediately, signals went out to all commands. Ships that had already left port were told to turn around and head back. The hundreds of thousands of men counting down towards D-Day woke up that morning to be told there was a delay. Some were already on their tiny landing vessels and were ordered to stay there, being thrown about by the waves until further notice. Rumours abounded: the plans for D-Day had been discovered by the Germans ... wild storms were lashing the ships in the Channel ... someone at the top had called off the landings for some reason. Everyone feared that the essential element of the invasion, surprise, would be lost. But by midday, Stagg's predictions came true. Strong winds rocked the Channel and turned the sea into a carpet of foaming, angry waves.

Sunday 4 June is primarily remembered for events elsewhere in Europe. The first Allied troops had crossed into Italy in September of the previous year. The long slog up the Italian peninsula had been slow. Skilful, determined German resistance had held up the Allied advance all the way. The delay at Monte Cassino, when the Germans defended the vital valleys heading north from a medieval Benedictine monastery at the top of the nearby mountain, had held up the Allies for four months. But finally the capital had been declared an 'open city', meaning there would be no battle to defend it, and German troops rapidly evacuated. American soldiers of General Mark Clark's Fifth Army entered Rome on 4 June. Crowds came out to cheer as American soldiers passed the ancient sites that fill the city.

With all eyes on Rome, the Germans managed to get away to the north intact, and there would be eleven months of further fighting in Italy. But for now, the capture of the Italian capital was a huge triumph and a great boost to morale.

Back in the library at Southwick House, Eisenhower convened another meeting of his commanders at 9 o'clock that evening. Outside, the wind was howling, the windows were rattling and the rain was coming down in horizontal streaks. Eisenhower later wrote that it seemed impossible 'there was any reason for even discussing the situation.'[11] Once more the grim-faced Stagg joined them. But this time he brought a glimmer of hope. 'Mercifully, almost miraculously,' he reported, 'the almost unbelievable happened at about midday.' He had spotted a lull between two depressions in the Normandy region that would offer a 36-hour window of opportunity, from late Monday through Tuesday. He predicted the wind should slacken, the clouds should lift and the sea calm. A cheer went up around the room. Eisenhower still looked serious and tense. Once again he went around the room asking for opinions. The air chiefs still worried about low cloud cover. But Admiral Ramsay was more confident and pointed out that further delay would put back the invasion by about two weeks, until the tide and moon were next in the right alignment. Everyone knew that it would be virtually impossible to keep the human spring coiled for that long, and that news of the invasion plans would almost inevitably leak out. Finally, Eisenhower asked Monty what he thought. 'I would say, "Go",' the British army commander replied, ever bullish to get at the enemy. All eyes turned to the Supreme Commander. On his shoulders Eisenhower carried one of the most momentous decisions of the war. Thousands of lives and potentially the outcome of the war itself were at stake. Ike stood there, hands clasped behind his back, head bowed. Some described the wait as being as long as two minutes before he said, 'The question is how long can you allow a thing like this to just kind of hang out there on a limb?' Then, after another pause, he went on, 'I'm quite positive we must give the order. I don't like it, but there it is. Let's go.'[12]

Immediately, the headquarters sprang into a frenzy of action. Staff officers sent out the 'Go' codes to all units. Ships were ordered to set sail. The final timetable was set in motion across the whole of the south of Britain. At another pre-dawn meeting the next morning, Stagg repeated that he was confident in his earlier forecast and Eisenhower confirmed his 'Go' order. There was now just over 24 hours before the first troops would hit the beaches. As they left the meeting and the sun was coming up, Montgomery asked Admiral Ramsay what he would do now that the most complex naval action of the war was about to commence. 'The operation has begun,' he replied. 'There is wireless silence and we can expect no signals. I am going to bed.'[13]

While Ramsay slept, Eisenhower spent an anxious day waiting. There was not much else he could do. He watched a few of the last men to embark board their boats in Portsmouth harbour. He returned to his caravan and tried to read a Western for relaxation for an hour or so. That evening he visited Greenham Common airfield, where the 101st Airborne, one of two divisions of American parachute forces, were preparing to embark for their night drop behind enemy lines. Eisenhower had been warned that the airborne drop was so risky there was a possibility of a casualty rate as high as 80 per cent. He had been advised to call off the airborne operation altogether but had made the decision that it should go ahead. Now he felt he had to look into the eyes of the men he was sending to their probable death. He wandered among the men, who were laden with weapons, grenades, ammunition and three days' supply of rations, as they prepared to climb up into the C-47 transport aircraft. He asked to meet anyone who came from his own state of Kansas. A paratrooper named Oyler was brought before him but was so dumbfounded to be addressed by the Supreme Commander in person that when asked his name he couldn't remember it. His mates called out 'Oyler.'

To Eisenhower's astonishment, the men, some with faces blacked up, others with Mohican-style haircuts, were in excellent spirits. 'I've done all I can do, now it's up to you,' Ike told an officer. Clearly they sensed his tension. 'Quit worrying, General' one of the paratroopers called out to him. 'We'll take care of this thing for you,' another called out. 'Leave it to us,' shouted a third. Their gung-ho attitude helped to cheer him up. He saw the men board their aircraft and waited until the last C-47 had taken off before returning to his staff car. His driver remembered that there were tears welling up in his eyes when he climbed in.[14]

As the midnight hour approached, the first Allied troops prepared to launch the invasion of Europe. The first into action were the pathfinder paratroopers who dropped behind enemy lines on the Cotentin Peninsula with electronic beacons to signal the location of the drop zones to the main force that would follow within an hour or so.[15] Their task was to secure the inland flank of Utah beach. But when the squadrons of the main American force, some 800 aircraft, crossed the French coast soon after midnight, the tightly packed formations of C-47s soon broke up in the thick clouds that were left over from the bad weather. As they emerged from the clouds the pilots veered to the right and left to try to identify landmarks below. The anti-aircraft guns soon opened up and the inexperienced pilots in their slow-moving, unarmed transports took evasive action, some slowing down with others speeding up, throwing the aircraft well off course. Tense pilots pressed the signal for the paras to jump, a green light by the aircraft door, far too soon. Men jumped miles off course. Some landed in fields that had been flooded by the Germans and, weighed down with so much kit, drowned in a few feet of water. When the lucky ones were safely on the ground, some of those with maps could not find any names or locations they recognised. Units had got terribly broken up. Plans had to be quickly reformulated. An officer would round up whoever he could find, regardless of their battalion or company. After a confused few hours some order was restored and defensive lines drawn up. A battery of 88mm guns was overpowered and captured at Brécourt, just above the Utah landing zone, where they could have caused devastation on the beach.[16] And after a brief fight, Sainte Mère-Eglise became the first town in occupied France to be liberated.

The process of deception also featured in the airborne landings. Several hundred dummy parachutists had been made that were dropped outside the main drop zones. They were little more than scarecrow-type puppets that on landing exploded, and some of them set off audio recordings of men shouting and firing their weapons, simulating the action of real paratroopers who had opened fire. As part of this operation, small groups of SAS soldiers were also dropped outside the main drop zones. They were to attack troops as they moved across the Normandy countryside through the night and morning, but were instructed to leave enough soldiers alive to sound the alarm as to where Allied forces had landed. All of this was intended to confuse the enemy as to where the parachute drops were coming. They certainly added to the confusion, as reports of their landings were noted in German command centres. But they were less effective than had been hoped, as the real parachute drops had, in error, taken place over such a large area that the Germans had a lot of difficulty in making sense of what was happening even without the deceptions. But the exploding dummies led at least one regiment of the German 352nd Infantry Division to leave its position guarding the beaches and head off on a wild goose chase that took it away from the main action for about twelve hours.

The British airborne troops further east initially had a better time of it than the Americans. In a superb piece of flying, three gliders, each carrying 28 men, landed in complete darkness within yards of their target, a bridge over the Caen Canal known as Pegasus Bridge. Within six minutes of landing they had surprised and overwhelmed the sentries and seized control of the bridge. Another bridge over the Orne River was also captured intact within minutes without a weapon being fired. When the paras started to transmit the code 'Ham and Jam', meaning that both bridges had been captured, the intelligence officer on the ship offshore receiving the message could barely believe the report of success coming in so soon. Other jumps, however, were not so successful, and hundreds of men were dropped in the wrong place because the transports bringing them, as in the west, had got lost in the low clouds and had taken evasive action because of the flak. Some of the pilots mistook one river for another, and some men were dropped sixteen miles from their drop zone and had to awaken a local farmer to ask where they were. Much of the equipment dropped, including Bren guns, ammunition and anti-tank weapons, also went missing or was damaged on landing. As with the Americans, there was much confusion, although again, by the early hours most of the key objectives had been taken. Both the American and British airborne troops were tough, well trained and aggressively minded, and despite being hopelessly jumbled up, without much of the equipment they needed and with detailed plans in tatters, they struggled on through a long night. A BBC correspondent, Chester Wilmot, landed by glider with the divisional commander of the 6th Airborne soon after 3am. On the portable device he carried, which recorded onto a vinyl disc, he reported, 'The landing went just like an exercise and was a most wonderful sight.'[17] Bearing in mind the number of crashed gliders and men dropped over a wide area, this was an extraordinarily upbeat assessment. But despite the challenges, many of the objectives were achieved that night.

The airborne landings were the curtain raiser for the big show to come soon after dawn. A vast armada of vessels coming from east and west, some of them having sailed from Scotland, all assembled to the south of the Isle of Wight in an area that become known as 'Piccadilly Circus'. Having lined up in position, the fleet headed off across the Channel, led by a flotilla of minesweepers. Admiral Ramsay had been fearful of huge losses among these small boats that would lead the way across the Channel clearing lanes for the rest of the naval forces. In a few hours they had reached their positions off the French coast. As they turned back the minesweeper crews signalled 'Good luck' to the rest of the fleet. Ramsay was astonished and delighted to hear there had not been a single casualty among the minesweepers.

Meanwhile, Lancaster bombers of the famous 617 Squadron were dropping aluminium strips, 'Window', along the coast east of the Seine estuary, playing their part in the Operation Fortitude deception. On the few German radar screens that had been allowed to survive the Allied bomber raids, it looked as though a vast armada of vessels was sailing towards Boulogne and the mouth of the Somme. Further north and east up the Channel, a series of motor launches towed reflector balloons, which showed up like large ships gathering off the Pas de Calais coast. The radar operators reported back to their headquarters to sound the alarm at what they were seeing.

The main transport ships pulled up in their allotted places a few miles off the Normandy coast. The infantry on board were given breakfast, lavish on the American ships with steak, chicken, ice cream and candy, and with corned-beef sandwiches on the British ships. Then, from about 3am, in the dark, the infantry started climbing down nets on the side of their ships into the small landing craft that would carry them ashore. The men experienced many emotions as they descended into the landing craft. All of them were aware of the enormity of the task ahead and the huge scale of the operation in which they played a tiny part. Most were quite naturally anxious or scared at what would happen over the next few hours. But as they lined up in their flat-bottomed landing craft they had other things to worry about. The sea was still heaving as a consequence of the storms that had only just passed through. Seasickness became a major issue. Soon the landing craft were swimming in vomit, and some men threw up in their helmets and then emptied them overboard. Many began to regret the large breakfast they had just enjoyed. Lashed by cold sea-water spray and bobbing about in the assault craft, waiting for the dawn light to glow, the night seemed interminable. Rarely in modern times have men gone into battle from such miserable conditions. But they were finely trained, superbly briefed, so spirits were high and morale was good. They just wanted to get on with it.

From some ships the newly styled Duplex Drive (DD) tanks were lowered into the sea. These were specially waterproofed Sherman tanks with giant canvas screens around them to help them float. They had propellers and were to drive ashore at a speed of about 5mph in order to support the infantry in the landings. In the rougher than anticipated sea, many of them sank straight to the bottom. Twenty-nine out of thirty-two tanks sank in one American unit off Utah and Omaha beaches. Mostly their crews managed to get out. The British Shermans further east, where the sea was a little calmer, succeeded in floating and began their agonisingly slow journey towards the shore. Most of them made it to Sword, Juno and Gold beaches.

As this armada of small vessels headed for the five separate beaches and the sun slowly came up, those who could see over the side of their vessels were astonished at the sight. There were ships everywhere filling the sea to the horizon. Then the big guns on the warships opened up. The American battleships fired all their fourteen-inch guns broadside in unison, creating a scene of smoke and explosions so intense that many thought the ships must have been hit. But then the sounds of the shells screaming over their heads almost deafened those below. Salvo followed salvo, cheering the men enormously. Following the battleships came the rocket-firing ships, launching hundreds of three-foot rockets that screamed through the dawn sky.

H-Hour was at 6.30am in the west and 7.45am in the east, the time depending upon the low tides at each of the five beaches. The landing craft approached the shore and, precisely on schedule, the small boats drew up and hit the sand or shingle. The ramps went down and the first wave of assault troops leapt into the water and on to the beaches. The invasion was on.

The first announcement of the invasion came on German radio soon after dawn. It reported that landings were taking place ... along the coast in the Pas de Calais.

Chapter 13

THE DAY

In the early hours of Tuesday 6 June, pilots, navigators and crews of bomber squadrons gathered for their briefings at a hundred airfields across the south and east of England. As the coverings over the maps on the boards in front of them were drawn back to reveal the Normandy coastline, they all heard the same announcement from their briefing officers: 'Gentlemen, today the Allies invade the continent.' In many of the American squadrons there was applause, cheering and whistling. Among the British squadrons the reaction was more muted as the crews took in the scale of the operation that was about to take place. For the British it was a return to continental Europe almost exactly four years after the chaotic evacuation at Dunkirk. By early light about a thousand bombers were lining up off the coast to attack the artillery batteries and other defensive strongholds. RAF Spitfires and American Lightnings were patrolling the coast to make sure no Luftwaffe aircraft were able to get in and attack the landing craft. Further inland, American Thunderbolts and British Typhoons would search the roads leading to the landing beaches, ready to strafe and destroy any reinforcements heading towards the invasion zone. And finally, a squadron of

Spitfire and Mosquito photo-reconnaissance aircraft prepared to patrol above the beaches from one end of the landings to the other, photographing what was going on below every hour throughout the day to come. The thinking was that if the invaders were thrown back into the sea, the planners wanted to see and learn the lessons of exactly where and how things had gone wrong.[1]

The invasion fleet off the Normandy coast that morning was vast. It consisted of nearly 5,000 assault vessels and landing craft. They were supported by 6 battleships, 23 cruisers and 104 destroyers. It was the largest fleet ever assembled to support a single military operation. Men on board this vast armada frequently said that there were so many ships that it looked as though you could step from one vessel to another to reach the horizon.

During the course of that day about 130,000 men were landed on the five beaches. They were primarily American, British and Canadian, but men from French, Dutch, Belgian, Danish, Polish and Norwegian forces also took part in the landings that day, with French commandos landing on Sword beach and Norwegian destroyers assisting the Allied naval force. The coastline that would be attacked spread across nearly 50 miles. But less than half of that coastal stretch was actually to be assaulted on D-Day itself.[2]

In the west, the landing craft bringing American troops from the 4th Division into Utah beach were blown off course by the strong winds and the tide, but the landings went ahead anyway, even if a mile further south than intended. When Brigadier Teddy Roosevelt Jr, son of a former president and cousin of the current president, realised that his brigade had landed on the wrong beach, he told his men it was no problem. 'We'll start the war from here,' he said to them and carried on regardless, successfully leading his men inland. There was very little resistance, many of the defenders being made up of

Russian prisoners who had agreed to fight in the German army, largely to escape starvation and the horrors of life in German prisoner-of-war camps. They were only too happy to surrender at the first opportunity. Six battalions of Americans were ready to move off the beach by 10am. By noon the beach had been cleared. Losses of 200 men in the 4th Division that day were far smaller than anticipated. In fact, they were fewer than at some of the rehearsals that had taken place along the south Devon coast, including a dreadful incident at Slapton Sands in April when 700 Americans had been lost.[3] During the afternoon, the landing force began to meet up with the paratroopers of the 101st Airborne Division who had dropped the night before. Despite the chaos of the night-time drop, the determination of the paratroopers and the success of the landings had brought a quick victory on the western end of the invasion.

On the most western of the British beaches, Gold, the bombers had hit many of their targets just before the landings, which were led by units of the 50th Division. Most of the tanks and armour successfully landed soon after the infantry. There was limited resistance, nothing like on the scale that had been expected, and it was slowly overcome. Sergeant Major Stanley Hollis won the only VC of the day by rushing a German pillbox. He leapt on top of it and fired his Sten gun into it, paused, reloaded and fired again. Finally, he threw a grenade into the gun emplacement. Twenty-six Germans came out with their hands up. Le Hamel and then Arromanches, both seaside towns, were captured during the afternoon. By evening British troops had advanced to the outskirts of the small town of Bayeux, where the famous tapestry recorded the Norman invasion going in the other direction nearly 900 years before.

On Juno beach the Canadian 3rd Division was determined to avenge the fiasco of Dieppe two years before. At 7.45am the first wave hit the beaches, but the tide was rapidly coming in and many of the beach obstacles were soon under water, forcing the next few waves of landing craft to duck and weave between the tips of iron and steel bars. But here, again, the landings were successful, and at 9am the locals in one of the seaside towns opened a bar to celebrate their liberation. Just over an hour later a group of journalists and newsreel cameramen took over a hotel at Bernières, the first base from which reports on progress during the day were sent back. Troops tried to advance to their inland objectives, but this proved slower going. By midday, the principal problem was the traffic jams as the beach masters tried to get the vehicles arriving from landing craft in ever-increasing numbers off the beaches and heading inland. The Canadians advanced seven miles inland, the furthest on D-Day, but never reached the Carpiquet airfield on the outskirts of Caen, which was their objective for the day. It would be a month before the airfield was captured.

On Sword beach in the east, the British 3rd Division also landed at 7.45am. The resort of Colleville Plage was soon in their hands. Forty DD tanks had been launched three miles out. They slowly headed for the shore with only turret and gun showing above the water. A four-foot wave could swamp them. But mostly they made it ashore to support the infantry. Then came flail tanks, Shermans with giant rotating iron flails in front of them, to clear minefields and enable troops and armour to move inland. Lord Lovat's 1st Special Service Brigade, a commando unit, also landed on Sword, with Lovat's personal piper playing 'Highland Laddie' as the men waded ashore. By early afternoon his unit met up with the paratroopers at the bridges they had captured during the night. There was more serious and intense fighting in Ouistreham, where a group of French commandos had landed, the first regular French troops to land in Normandy. But by the end of the day the port town was in their hands. However, as dusk fell, even the troops who advanced the furthest were still four miles from their objectives.

Only on Omaha beach was there a real battle to get ashore. The bombers failed to hit the German beach defences, their bombs instead falling far inland. Men from two divisions of V Corps were due to land at 6.30 that morning. They came under intense machine-gun fire as many landing craft ran aground on sandbars. Hundreds of men were killed or wounded as they leapt out of the landing craft weighed down with 70lbs of heavy equipment. The survivors struggled to get into the water, across the beach and to the shelter of the sea wall.[4] By 9am hardly anyone had got off the beach. As more men gathered by the sea wall they discovered their weapons had been ruined by seawater and their radios were not working. Only the sounds of intense fighting reached the commanders on their headquarter ships offshore. By late morning General Bradley considered abandoning Omaha altogether and rerouting the second wave to Utah and the British beaches.[5]

In the confusion it took the bravery of a small number of commanders to rally the men, most notably Brigadier Norman Cota, the deputy chief of the US 29th Division, and Colonel Charles Canham, commander of the 116th Infantry Regiment of the US 1st Division. Cota and Canham slowly encouraged their soldiers to pass up through steep valleys, or 'draws', to the bluffs beyond. Once sufficient men had reached the bluffs they could pan out and attack the German defenders from the flank and rear. By midday nearly 19,000 American troops had landed on Omaha and as many again were waiting for the orders to land. There were countless examples of heroism under fire, and as the Americans slowly took control there were some examples of Germans who had surrendered being shot. By mid-afternoon the battle was largely won. More troops and vehicles were cleared to come ashore, and finally the commanders of the two divisions landed in the early evening. They surveyed a chaotic situation and began to count the cost of the day. About

1,500 American troops were dead and another 1,000 wounded. The battle for Omaha had been the toughest of the day, but the casualty numbers were still well below those that had been forecast.

By the end of the day about 155,000 men in total were ashore, including the paratroopers who had landed during the previous night. The commander-in-chief of land forces, Montgomery, was offshore. Having consulted his Army commanders he spent the night on a naval destroyer. Most of the divisional commanders were ashore organising the advance inland. The total casualties for the day amounted to approximately 7,600, of which about 4,400 were estimated as dead or missing, less than half the estimated figure for the day of 10,000 men dead.[6]

Part of this was down to the fact that on that day of days all levels of the German command were paralysed. Lacking air reconnaissance and with most of their radar stations out of action, the landings came as a real surprise. The shattering of communications by aerial bombing and by Resistance fighters cutting telephone cables left most local commanders without reliable information as to what was happening where. There are many stories of senior regimental officers, totally bewildered by the unexpected events taking place, travelling up to the coast themselves, or climbing high spots like church towers to try to see what was going on. Many corps and divisional commanders from Normandy were in Rennes for war games because the storms were considered to be too bad to allow an invasion to take place. Without weather stations in the Atlantic, the German meteorologists had failed to predict a break in the weather along the Channel coast. The bad weather and the 24-hour delay had, as it turned out, given a substantial advantage to the Allies.

The deployment of the panzers against troops struggling to establish a beachhead would have proved vital, as Rommel had foreseen. The commander of the principal panzer forces that were available in Normandy, General Edgar Feuchtinger of the 21st Panzer Division, was in Paris on the night of 5 June with his mistress, and took some time to return. Two squadrons of his tanks did move out in the late morning but were ordered not to head for the Orne bridges, where the British paratroopers were grimly holding on, but to attack the 3rd Division at Sword beach to the west of the Orne River. This involved a six-hour diversion around Caen and the units suffered 40 per cent losses from aerial attacks en route. Rommel, thc commander of Army Group B, was at home in Herrlingen to celebrate his wife's birthday. When his chief of staff awoke him during the morning to tell him ships had been sighted off the Normandy coast, Rommel called the Berghof to cancel his meeting with Hitler and immediately headed back to La Roche-Guyon. But as the Luftwaffe had lost control of the skies it was too dangerous for Rommel to fly, so he had to travel by road and it took him most of the day to get back to his headquarters.

Only Von Rundstedt, whom Hitler and the OKW thought was old and past it, acted soundly and decisively. From his headquarters at St-Germain-en-Laye, requests were made to send the panzer reserves towards Normandy. Even before the landings had begun, Von Rundstedt sensed that the parachute drops were too big to be a diversion and so gave the order for the 12th SS Panzer-Division *Hitlerjugend* at Dreux, west of Paris, and the Panzer Lehr Division at Orleans on the Loire, south-west of Paris, to move towards Caen. These were the divisions Rommel had wanted lined up along the coast. But a staff officer at OKW refused to process the request, insisting that, 'The main landing was going to come at an entirely different place.'[7] When pressed, the staff officer pointed out (correctly) that Von Rundstedt did not have the authority to tell the panzer reserve to deploy. Only Hitler could give the order. In the tangled and split command structure that had been created, only the Führer could order the panzer reserves to move forward.

In Hitler's Bavarian mountain hideaway, the Berghof, the staff decided not to wake the Führer until the various reports from Normandy had been confirmed. He had been up talking until at least 2am and had taken a sleeping pill. When he woke at noon and was informed of the invasion, Hitler was initially delighted that at last the Allies had landed in France. He is reputed to have said, 'Now we have them where we can destroy them.'[8] He then went to a reception in Salzburg, and it was not until 4pm that he gave permission for the two panzer divisions to deploy. By then it was impossible for the panzers to travel on the open road, with Allied aircraft ranging over the whole of northern France, attacking anything that moved. They travelled a short distance then had to wait until darkness to continue their journey towards the coast. Most would not arrive until the following day. Several took two days to travel to the battleground, by which time the Allies had landed thousands of tons of ammunition and more armoured brigades.

Only six panzers from Feuchtinger's 21st Panzer Division reached the coast by evening of D-Day. They arrived at a point between Sword and Juno beaches that was still in German hands. Cut off and under fire from the heavy guns of the warships out at sea, they failed to have any impact on the outcome of the fighting. Rommel had predicted the first 24 hours of the invasion would be decisive. By that reckoning the 'longest day' could be classed as a considerable Allied victory.

In London, the BBC had made elaborate and top-secret preparations to announce news of the invasion. John Snagge, who was to make the announcement, was locked in a small studio and, like so many of the soldiers taking part, had not been able to leave for 48 hours, until he was at last given a communique from SHAEF HQ. At precisely 9.30am on the morning of D-Day all BBC radio broadcasts were interrupted, and two minutes later John Snagge read quite slowly the words, 'Under the command of General Eisenhower, Allied naval forces, supported by strong air forces, began landing Allied armies this morning on the coast of northern France.' The news was so momentous that he repeated the announcement in case listeners had not taken it in. Despite the careful planning for the announcement, however, the news editor that morning had picked up from German radio that landings were taking place. Having no knowledge of the secret process that SHAEF had prepared, he put a reference to reports of landings on the 8 o'clock news. The Ministry of Information were furious and accused the BBC of 'having blown the gaff'.[9]

Listeners had to wait patiently until much later in the day, when recordings from the correspondents covering the landings for the BBC were available for broadcast. The BBC had six correspondents in landing craft, on ships, planes and a glider covering the invasion, including Richard Dimbleby, Howard Marshall and Chester Wilmot. They had to record on portable vinyl-disc recording machines what they witnessed, and the discs then had to be transported back to England by the RAF or the Navy, either to Broadcasting House in London or to an outstation at Fareham near Portsmouth, where they could be played down the line to London. Having been checked by the censors, the recordings could then be broadcast. Alternatively, some correspondents returned to England during the day and reported their observations down the line to London. It was a cumbersome process that sounds extraordinary in the age of 24/7 live news reporting, but the long wait to hear these reports did not seem to diminish the power and the drama of their impact. By the end of the day the BBC had also passed on reports to more than 700 radio stations in North America. And its European broadcasts in dozens of different languages were being eagerly followed by tens of millions of French, Belgian and Dutch citizens along with men and women living in all the nations of Occupied Europe. In Britain, after the formal confirmation of landings in the morning, the news rapidly spread through the cities, towns and villages of the country, until every office worker, housewife, factory hand, farmer and school child had heard that the invasion was 'on.'

In a small grocery shop in Dewsbury, West Yorkshire, Kathleen Hey was keeping a diary for Mass Observation. She had picked up in the 8 o'clock news bulletin a report that 'German naval forces were engaged with our landing craft.' She turned to her brother-in-law, who ran the shop, and said, 'It sounds as though they have begun,' but she was doubtful that the report was real. She missed the formal confirmation at 9.30 but wrote that one by one customers started to say to her, 'Well, it's begun,' and, 'It's all been on the wireless,' and 'We should expect a lot of casualties.' Kathleen wrote, 'I heard more talk of the war today and more interest taken in it than at any time since we came here in 1941.' She went to bed that evening having listened on the radio to 'the exciting commentaries by the Correspondents … feeling excited and happy … But above all relieved as if something had been taken off our chests so that we could breathe better.'[10]

That afternoon in the House of Commons, at about 3 o'clock, just after Question Time, in which issues had been raised about the supply of postage stamps to troops in Burma, the export of herring to Russia, the increasing costs of funerals and the theft of ration books, Churchill rose to make an announcement. After talking about the glorious capture of Rome he told the House that landings on the beaches in France 'are proceeding at various points at the present time.' He went on, 'So far, the commanders who are engaged report that everything is proceeding according to plan. And what a plan! This vast operation is undoubtedly the most complicated and difficult that has ever occurred.' He spoke about 'a brotherhood in arms between us and our friends of the United States.' He concluded that, 'Nothing that equipment, science or forethought could do has been neglected, and the whole process of opening this great new Front will be pursued with the utmost resolution.' Members were clearly emotional and, moved by the Prime Minister's words, they repeatedly cheered throughout his short announcement.[11]

Churchill went on to play his part in the continuing deception by saying in the House of Commons that what was taking place was 'the first of a series of landings in force upon the European continent.' He said the landing had been a surprise to the enemy and 'we hope to furnish the enemy with a succession of surprises.'[12] This marked the beginning of the next phase of Operation Fortitude.

Chapter 14

DECEPTION CONTINUES

With the landings in Normandy on such a scale and supported by so vast an invasion armada, it was not easy to see how the deceivers could pretend that this was not the real thing. But the conviction that the Normandy landings were only going to be a feint had penetrated the understanding of German intelligence so deeply that the FHW issued a report on the evening of D-Day which said, 'The enemy landing on the Normandy coast represents a large scale undertaking, but the forces already engaged represent a comparatively small part of the total available.' FHW calculated that of the sixty divisions in the south of England, only ten to twelve were taking part in the landings. They assumed that some of these 'spare' divisions might be used to reinforce Montgomery's 21st Army Group. But then, the FHW report went on:

> The entire group of forces which make up the American First Army Group [FUSAG] comprising about 25 divisions north and south of the Thames, has not yet been employed. The same applies to the ten to twelve active divisions held ready in the Midlands and Scotland. The conclusion therefore is that the enemy command plans a further large scale undertaking in the Channel area which

> may well be directed against a coastal sector in the central Channel area [the Pas de Calais].[1]

When the deceivers in London read this report, after it had been intercepted and deciphered at Bletchley Park, they must have heaved a sigh of relief and said to each other, 'So far, so good.'

Additionally, through the double agents, the deception teams were sending messages to help confirm that FUSAG was still ready and waiting. From his notional observation point with FUSAG HQ, Brutus reported on the morning of D-Day that he was extremely surprised to hear of the landings but that FUSAG 'was ready for an attack which is capable of being released at any moment.'[2] Garbo, by this time supposedly working at the Ministry of Information, informed his minders that a directive had been sent down telling everyone to keep quiet about future Allied intentions, the implication being that the Normandy landings were only the first phase of the invasion of France. Then, on 8 June, Garbo started to send detailed and truthful information as to which Allied units had landed on D-Day, information which the Germans could verify on the ground and which therefore increased their belief in the accuracy of his reports. After supposedly consulting all his sub-agents, on 9 June, Garbo sent what has been called 'the most important report of his career.' It was a long message that effectively summed up all that Operation Fortitude had been trying to achieve. Garbo reported that prior to the Normandy landings there had been 75 Allied divisions in the UK. He confirmed that FUSAG troops had not been involved and that all its divisions and formations were still standing by. Furthermore, well over a hundred large landing craft had assembled in the coastal rivers and ports of the south-east, and if the Luftwaffe sent over aerial reconnaissance this could be verified. He ended with a clear and emphatic message that 'I am of the opinion' that the Normandy landings were 'a large scale diversionary operation' with the purpose of 'drawing the maximum of German reserves to the area of operation in order to make an attack at another place … which may very probably take place in the Pas de Calais area.' He requested that this information should be passed on urgently to the German High Command.[3] We now know that this message went to the FHW and was passed on to German High Command, the OKW, where Jodl saw it and underlined its importance. And it was marked as having been shown to the Führer.[4]

As the different German intelligence agencies sent messages back and forth between themselves, the conclusion was clear. The Fifteenth Army in the Pas de Calais region, with its nineteen infantry divisions and two armoured divisions, would remain in place and on alert, waiting for a second, even bigger invasion from the south-east of England. The German High Command were in no doubt that FUSAG was still ready and waiting and Patton was still in command.

However, the two panzer divisions based in central France, of which Rommel had always wanted control but only Hitler could give orders to deploy, were sent to Normandy. The 12th SS Panzer-Division *Hitlerjugend* arrived in Normandy on 7 June after a 75-mile journey. The Panzer Lehr Division arrived two days later, having been heavily bombed on its 110-mile journey from Orleans. The 2nd Panzer Division based in Amiens was the only unit of the Fifteenth Army that was sent to Normandy, but it took more than a week to get there. However, when it entered the battle its appearance was a surprise to Montgomery and it inflicted a severe reverse on the British armour it came up against.[5] The presence of these panzer units made the Battle of Normandy a long, drawn-out struggle, more intense and difficult than had been anticipated. The Allied bridgehead was 70 miles wide but only 20 miles deep. Deep, sunken roads lined by ancient, thick Norman hedgerows in what was known as the Bocage country, surrounded by dense woods and scattered orchards, were ideal for defence. Allied casualties mounted rapidly. It's beyond the remit of this book to explore the details, but the Americans did not succeed in capturing St Lo until mid-July, six weeks after D-Day. And it took nearly two months to capture Caen. But it shows that had these panzer units been available sooner and had they been nearer to the beaches, as Rommel wanted, it is possible they could have had an even bigger impact on the battle. Whether they could have thrown the Allies back into the sea before a secure bridgehead had been established is one of the big 'What Ifs?' of the war. But they certainly would have made the task of getting hundreds of thousands of men, armoured vehicles, ammunition and supplies ashore a great deal harder.

Predictably, as the battle for Normandy developed, Hitler ordered that no ground should be ceded and that all German units should fight on without retreating. Rommel had got round these orders in North Africa by persuading Hitler that a tactical withdrawal was essential. Sometimes he simply ignored the orders altogether. But in Normandy he grew increasingly frustrated by the Führer's continual interference. Also, he realised that constant harassment from the air, where the Allied air forces enjoyed complete supremacy, and from the big guns of warships off the coast were wearing his men down and slowly destroying his reserves. He wanted to withdraw beyond the Orne River and reassemble his panzer forces out of range of the Allied battleships, for a determined counter-attack. But Hitler would permit no withdrawal. As he had claimed before, victory was to be gained by 'holding fast tenaciously to every square yard of soil.'[6]

Rommel and Von Rundstedt finally got to meet Hitler at a conference at a bunker in Margival near Soissons in north-east France on 17 June. Hitler had flown in from Berchtesgaden with General Jodl and his senior military staff. It was a frosty encounter. Hitler sat fidgeting with pencils, bent over a table, while his two field marshals were left standing. The Führer said he was disappointed by Allied successes in the landings and blamed local commanders for the failures. Rommel declared 'the hopelessness of fighting against tremendous enemy superiority in all three dimensions' and proposed a tactical withdrawal to prepare a counter-attack. Hitler grew angry and announced that the new V-1 flying bomb would soon have a decisive effect on the war against England and that swarms of jet fighters would end Allied supremacy in the air. Rommel became increasingly agitated. He told Hitler that Churchill had recently visited his troops in Normandy and that it would be a great boost to the morale of German troops if the Führer would visit the Caen area. Ironically, at this point an air-raid alarm sounded and the meeting had to move to the basement. Rommel still believed he had the ability to influence Hitler's thinking, and he boldly told his commander-in-chief that the war in the west was as good as lost and he should seek to negotiate with the Allies. This was brave talk and went completely against the grain of telling the Führer only good news about the war's prospects. A furious Hitler ended the meeting by asserting angrily to Rommel, 'Do not concern yourself with the conduct of the war, but concentrate on the invasion front.'[7] Later that day, a V-1 lost control as its gyros malfunctioned and crashed to earth near the bunker. Hitler rushed back to Berchtesgaden and never again left the Reich. There would be no question of a visit to Caen to restore the morale of his fighting troops.

Rommel and Von Rundstedt had completely failed to persuade Hitler to redeploy some of his troops from the Fifteenth Army in the Pas de Calais to the Normandy front. Despite the intensity of the fighting in Normandy, German intelligence grew more certain that an attack was still planned from the south-east of England. FHW had picked up on changes in the plans of the Fourth Army that had been in Scotland threatening Norway. Colonel Rory Macleod, who was running the Fourth Army deception operation, had been told to cease menacing Scandinavia and to become part of the First US Army Group under Patton. This again was done entirely by the use of signallers and the sending of a new set of wireless messages. Macleod quickly devised a new plan for the Fourth Army to land on both flanks of FUSAG. II Corps would land on the beaches to the south of the Pas de Calais around Etaples. To the existing forces in this corps that the Germans already knew of was added another unit, the 35th Tank Brigade, who were based in Dumfries. It was hoped that German intelligence would interpret this as being a complete armoured division. VII Corps, which the Germans also knew to be part of this Scottish army, was now given orders to prepare to land to the north-east of Calais in the direction of Dunkirk, and from there to move inland to capture St Omer. The US XV Corps were to be held in reserve, to be sent in wherever the situation demanded. Again, as before, a large number of enciphered messages were sent from Army HQ to corps HQs and downwards to divisions; and more messages with questions and requests for further information were sent back in the other direction.

On 18 June, the day after Hitler had his stormy meeting with Rommel and Von Rundstedt, the Fourth Army began three days of pretend landing exercises in Scotland. Signals were sent from ships offshore and from wireless stations on the beaches. All of these were closely monitored by the German listening stations with their highly accurate detection finders. In due course, Macleod and his phoney HQ moved south and took up new quarters at Heathfield Park in Sussex. II Corps HQ moved to Three Bridges in West Sussex; VII Corps to Tunbridge Wells in Kent. More dummy exercises were organised along the Dorset coast. Macleod's signallers worked overtime generating the traffic that genuine forces of this size would have created. They soon found that they were running out of signallers to send the messages, so Macleod's deputy was sent out with a recording truck and he got volunteers from a variety of units to record messages that had already been scripted and which were then played out at the appropriate time in the exercises. This stage of the imaginary Fourth Army's bogus existence was carried out as creatively, as elaborately and as convincingly as any of the pre-D-Day deception schemes.[8]

Macleod later wrote about how strange it was living for many weeks in this 'atmosphere of make-believe.' In his unpublished memoirs he recalled, 'As time went on we found it hard to separate the real from the imaginary. The feeling that the Fourth Army really existed and the fact that it was holding German troops immobilised made one almost believe in its reality.' It was probably just as well that the deceivers almost came to believe in their own deceptions, as it gave them the conviction that what was phoney was in fact real.[9]

Deception operations in the Mediterranean, although planned in London, were still run by 'A' Force in Cairo, where Dudley Clarke had begun the whole deception business in 1941. One such operation, codenamed Vendetta, had an impact on the deployment of the German reserves in France. In Operation Vendetta the invented story was that the US Seventh Army under Lieutenant-General Alexander 'Sandy' Patch, based in Algiers, was going to attack the French Mediterranean coast in the region of Narbonne. From there it was going to drive inland to seize the Carcassonne Gap and then move on towards Toulouse and Bordeaux. This was well away from the area between Toulon and Nice, which was genuinely going to be invaded by Allied troops in August in Operation Anvil. But the intention of Vendetta was to keep German forces in the south of France and to prevent them from moving north to reinforce the battlefront in Normandy. In order to do this, a mass of disinformation was put out about the strength of the Seventh Army. In reality, it consisted of one US and three French divisions. But it was rumoured that it consisted of twelve divisions, three American, three British and six French. So, eight of its divisions were entirely fake. Nevertheless, plans were made, dummy landing craft were assembled and photographed from the air, vehicles were waterproofed and a big amphibious exercise was carried out between 9 and 11 June. Sixty naval vessels were involved in the exercise, including two British aircraft carriers, HMS *Victorious* and HMS *Indomitable*. They were actually passing through the Mediterranean, en route to the Far East, when purloined to take part in the bogus exercise. It was also hoped that the visit to Algiers by Lieutenant James masquerading as Montgomery at the end of May would add credibility to the idea of a major operation being launched from North Africa.

Operation Vendetta was only partially successful. Although intended to run on into July, it had to be abandoned in late June. Partly this was because the two aircraft carriers had to withdraw to continue their journey to the Far East, and partly because General Patch and the one US division in Algiers were sent to Italy, where their presence would inevitably soon be picked up. However, it did have the effect of keeping nine out of the ten German divisions based in southern France in that region and out of the battle for Normandy.

The one division that was sent north to Normandy was the 2nd SS Panzer Division *Das Reich*. This unit, hardened in heavy fighting on the Eastern Front, by spring 1944 was based in Montauban. It was ordered north on 7 June and would have gone by railway, but the SOE had managed to sabotage the railcars and they were unusable. Instead, the division moved north on its 500-mile journey much more slowly by road. Along the way it came under attack from several Resistance groups, and in retaliation carried out two appalling atrocities. In Tulle, the SS hanged 99 men and deported 200 to Germany. Then, on 10 June, at a small village called Oradour-sur-Glane, soldiers from one company of *Das Reich* rounded up all the villagers, separated the men from the women, locked all the women and children in the church and took the men to a set of barns. The men were then machine gunned and the church was blown up and set on fire. Anyone who tried to escape was shot. In all, 642 of the villagers were massacred and only six survived to tell the story. Most of those who had committed the atrocity were killed later in fighting after the division finally arrived in Normandy in the last week of June. The French government decided not to rebuild and to leave Oradour-sur-Glane exactly as it was on the day the soldiers arrived, as a permanent memorial to the tragedy. And it still remains, untouched but overgrown, today.[10]

Meanwhile, throughout June, German intelligence continued to fear a second and bigger invasion across the Channel. Garbo, passing on accurate chickenfeed about the actual units in Normandy, was congratulated on his reports. One of these messages read, 'In the name of Fremde Heere West I express appreciation of your previous work in England. The object of further reconnaissance must be to ascertain in good time when embarkation begins and the destination of the group of forces in south-east England.' Brutus also continued to send reports about the growing strength of the First US Army Group and of American troops flooding into Britain. Once more, FHW took the bait and on 28 June reported, 'It is assumed that an attack by Army Group Patton would be timed to coincide with the moment when Montgomery's armies have gained ground [in Normandy].'[11]

The one person who remained sceptical about these intelligence assessments was Rommel. He was convinced that the major assault had already taken place in Normandy, and in this he never faltered. He regarded it as a fatal mistake to keep the Fifteenth Army standing idle near Calais when the decisive battles were being fought 200 miles away in Normandy. On 28 June, both Rommel and Von Rundstedt were summoned to Berchtesgaden to see Hitler once more. It was remarkable to pull the two leading field marshals away from the front at such a critical moment, but on the following day an even stormier meeting than their encounter two weeks before took place. Much of the arguments from the earlier meeting were repeated, with Rommel forcibly explaining that Allied aerial supremacy meant the movement of troops by day was impossible. Von Rundstedt was particularly angry because, having travelled 600 miles to see Hitler, he was kept waiting for seventeen hours. In separate discussions both Rommel and Von Rundstedt asked the Führer how he thought the war in the west could possibly be won. Both men came away from the encounter certain that their careers were at an end.

In a rage Hitler decided to sack Von Rundstedt. Field Marshal Hans Günther von Kluge, an experienced commander from the Eastern Front, was appointed to replace him as commander of Army Group West. Although Rommel was also the subject of Hitler's fury, he was such a famous and respected figure that Hitler decided it would be bad for morale at the front and at home to replace him. Instead, Von Kluge was briefed against him. Jodl and Keitel told him that Rommel was 'independent, defeatist and disobedient.' Von Kluge arrived in France full of the exaggerated optimism that most Eastern Front commanders felt when they surveyed the situation in the west. At La Roche-Guyon, Von Kluge assembled all senior officers and told them that Hitler was dissatisfied with the situation in the west. He then told Rommel to his face and in front of his staff that he displayed an obstinate attitude. 'From now on,' Von Kluge said, 'you too, Field Marshal Rommel, will have to get accustomed to obeying orders without reservation.'[12]

Rommel was deeply wounded by the humiliating remarks. He wrote a long summary for Von Kluge, outlining his litany of complaints at how he had not been able to deploy forces as he had wished because of the belief that Normandy was just a diversion, at how he had been denied control of the panzer forces, at how requests for ammunition and supplies had been refused when they were desperately needed, and at how the Allies had consequently built up overwhelming superiority in numbers and materiel.[13] It was not long before Von Kluge's optimism faded. On the day after rebuking Rommel the new commander went on a tour of the front and met most of the senior field commanders. From them all, he heard the same, unanimous verdict that the battle was being lost. He rapidly concluded that Hitler was completely out of touch with what was happening in the west, just as he had been on the Eastern Front. Von Kluge ended up apologising to Rommel.

Despite the fears of the German commanders, on the ground the German troops were mounting a stiff and determined resistance to Allied forces that were growing in size daily. By early July, a million men had landed in Normandy, along with 170,000 vehicles. But Montgomery's advance was painfully slow, and for weeks at a time non-existent. Partly this was because his strategy was to draw in the principal German forces to attack the British and Canadian troops in the Caen area, hoping to allow the US troops to break out to the west. This was certainly working in that by the end of June, the British VIII Corps faced the greatest concentration of SS panzer divisions that had been seen since the Battle of Kursk, the largest tank battle in history.[14] The fighting and the losses were almost on a First World War scale. By mid-July the British had suffered 30,000 casualties. One by one, major campaigns stalled, like Operation Epsom and then Operation Goodwood. For the British, Canadian and American armies, the longer the forces of the German Fifteenth Army remained hundreds of miles from the battlefront, the better.

In London, the deceivers were facing a new challenge in sustaining the threat from FUSAG. More and more of the real divisions that were making up Patton's imaginary army in the south-east of England were being called to join the escalating Battle of Normandy. Once there, they would soon be identified. Hence the need for the Fourth Army in Scotland to be added to FUSAG to make up its numbers. When the refigured Fourth Army arrived in the south-east it supposedly consisted of eight divisions. But only one of these was real; the other seven were entirely fake. Additionally, a newly created and entirely fictional US Fourteenth Army was also now allocated to FUSAG. Major General John Lucas, who had led the Italian landings at Anzio, was put in charge. Like Fourth Army HQ, the US Fourteenth Army also moved south and began sending signals from bases in East Anglia. The deceivers were now getting braver and more audacious, as this invented Army consisted of entirely fake units supposedly recently arrived from the United States, including the 11th US Infantry Division, the 48th US Infantry Division and the 25th US Armoured Division. The 17th US Infantry Division and the 59th, which was known as the 'Rattlesnake' Division because of its invented insignia of a yellow rattlesnake coiled and ready to strike, had both supposedly been specially trained in amphibious assaults. Not one of these divisions were real.[15]

However, the deceivers faced an even bigger problem when General Patton himself was sent to Normandy in July to take up his position as commander of the newly activated US Third Army that was to participate in the planned breakout. It was known that he would soon be identified by German intelligence as being in France. Wherever Patton went he attracted crowds of soldiers and inevitably correspondents. He announced to one group of men, 'I'm proud to be here to fight beside you. Now let's cut the guts out of those Krauts and get the hell on to Berlin.'[16] Patton was delighted to be back in action again and could never keep quiet.

As the number of American forces in Normandy grew rapidly, so it was always intended that a new Army Group would be created so the Americans would have an Army Group alongside Montgomery's British and Canadian 21st Army Group. This was to be named the First US Army Group, and General Bradley would be put in command of it. The existence of the real First US Army Group in Normandy would clearly end the deceit of its existence in south-east England and the threat to the Pas de Calais. It was David Strangeways who came up with a simple solution. He suggested that Bradley's new Army Group in Normandy should be delineated with another number, and that the First US Army Group should continue to play its role in the deception campaign in England. This was accepted by Eisenhower, and Bradley's new force was renumbered the Twelfth Army Group.

Explaining Patton's disappearance and arrival in Normandy as a general no longer in command of an Army *Group*, but at the lower rank of an Army commander, again taxed the minds of the deceivers. But an ingenious solution was arrived at. The story was put out, largely through the double agents, that Eisenhower was desperately worried about the slow progress in Normandy and called for more and more reinforcements, including those from FUSAG. Patton had been bitterly opposed to the denuding of his forces and had confronted Eisenhower in a brazen act of insubordination. A furious Eisenhower had then apparently demoted Patton on the spot. But he was given a second chance to take up a subordinate position as Third Army commander in Normandy. The story was sent with lots of colourful detail by Garbo in a long message on 20 July. Not only were German intelligence officers now taking as gospel everything Garbo was telling them, but if they had any knowledge of the disputes within the German High Command they would easily have believed this cock and bull story about how an argument between Allied generals had left Patton in France in a more junior role than he had held in England.

Finding a replacement for Patton was not going to be easy. But Eisenhower cabled General Marshall in Washington: 'I cannot overemphasise the importance of maintaining as long as humanly possible the Allied threat to the Pas de Calais area.'[17] Realising the importance of maintaining the FUSAG subterfuge, General Marshall agreed to send Lieutenant-General Lesley McNair, commander of US Land Forces. He had the status to convince the Germans that FUSAG was still a viable force to be feared. However, his appointment had a tragic outcome in that having come to Europe to take up his new and imaginary command, he visited Normandy to get a feel for the fighting there. On 25 July, McNair was killed in a friendly fire incident when an American bombing raid went disastrously wrong and killed or wounded 600 US troops. McNair was the highest-ranking American soldier to be killed in Europe. Marshall promptly dispatched another senior officer to England to replace him, Lieutenant-General John DeWitt. He did not have the prestige of Patton or McNair but was still known to be a tough commander. He arrived in England amid a suitable burst of publicity and took up residence in FUSAG's Dover HQ.

However, with heavy fighting in Normandy and more Allied units being sent in to aid the breakout, by the end of July, different elements of German intelligence were finally beginning to wind down the projected threat of a second invasion. The war diary for Von Kluge's HQ on 27 July noted the possibility 'that the enemy are in fact contenting themselves with the landing in Normandy and are sending the forces still assembled in Great Britain into this area is becoming increasingly probable.' And in the FHW, Von Roenne, who had been the first to accept the wildly exaggerated numbers of Allied troops in Britain, reported in his daily Intelligence analysis on 31 July that 'a second major landing on the Channel coast no longer seems so probable in view of the development of the situation in Normandy.' Accordingly, OKW finally ordered west towards Normandy some of the troops of the Fifteenth Army that had been watching events from Calais. Two divisions were sent in the last days of July and two more at the beginning of August.[18]

But it was all too little, too late. Montgomery's objective of drawing German forces into battle around Caen had succeeded. While furious fighting continued there, the Americans under Bradley began to prepare their breakout in the west. A new operation, codenamed Cobra, began with a massive aerial bombardment at the end of July. For some days, progress was still slow. Finally, on 3 August, the Third Army under General Patton, the *real* Patton that is, leading a *real* army, began its decisive breakthrough. His armour broke out of the Bocage country and started at last to move across the open French countryside at speed. Columns of tanks began advancing twenty miles per day. One by one towns started to fall to the Allies, St Malo, Rennes and further into Brittany. Patton at last achieved his lifelong dream of leading a conquering army into battle.

Hitler ordered four armoured divisions to move south from Caen for a counter-attack. For some days more intense fighting took place. But Eisenhower responded by telling Montgomery to advance south from Caen and Bradley and Patton to turn east towards the Loire and the Seine. By mid-August, the German 7th Army and the 5th Panzer Army were surrounded and the Allied armies were tightening the noose. There was only one road for them to escape along, which passed the small town of Falaise. What remained of nineteen German divisions were cut off and surrounded, and 10,000 German soldiers were killed in the Falaise pocket, about 25,000 wounded and 50,000 captured. When the Allies entered what had been the German pocket at Falaise they found a scene of appalling carnage. Fields were packed with dead soldiers, horses and abandoned vehicles. Having reported on the defeat of his troops and having told Hitler that the war was as good as lost, Field Marshal von Kluge walked into a nearby wood and swallowed a cyanide capsule.

On 25 August, as the Allied armour advanced rapidly up the Seine, the German garrison in Paris surrendered. The commander ignored Hitler's orders to destroy the city first and the magnificent architecture of the French capital survived in all its glory. Nobly, American troops paused and allowed Free French troops to liberate their capital. On the following day, ecstatic Parisians cheered as General Leclerc led his column of Sherman tanks up the Champs-Elysées.

Eisenhower had asked the Fortitude planners to keep the German Fifteenth Army in the Pas de Calais region for at least a week after D-Day. In fact, they remained there for seven weeks. Battle-hardened troops sat twiddling their fingers while 200 miles away the defining battle of the Second World War in the west was being fought and eventually won in Normandy. As Eisenhower later wrote, when the units of the Fifteenth Army finally started to move westwards, 'They were too late. Every additional soldier who came into the Normandy area was merely caught up in the catastrophe of defeat.'[19] The deceivers had done their job.

Chapter 15

EVALUATION

Just after midday on 31 July 1944, SHAEF issued the following communiqué:

> A little after dawn today, units of the First US Army Group, commanded by General John De Witt, landed on three beaches in the Pas de Calais region. Troops from the 17th US Infantry Division and the 59th 'Rattlesnake' Division, both of the US Fourteenth Army, stormed ashore from a variety of large landing craft in the Cap Nez region while British soldiers from the II Corps of Fourth Army landed on beaches to the south of Calais at Etaples and immediately moved inland across the dunes. Further landings were carried out by British troops from VII Corps in the region of Dunkirk, the scene of the withdrawal of British and French troops just over four years ago. Having established a beachhead these forces moved inland in the direction of St Omer. Preceding the landings were major parachute drops and glider landings by three divisions of Anglo-American Airborne troops. General De Witt commented, 'The landings have gone well and bearing in mind the recent

> reduction of German forces in the Pas de Calais region we anticipate good progress in establishing a secure beachhead.' Supreme Commander General Dwight D Eisenhower added that he hoped this long-awaited second wave of landings in northern France would soon lead to the movement of Allied troops towards Antwerp, Brussels and ultimately to the Rhine and the gates of the Third Reich.

Of course, such a communiqué was never released. There never were any landings on the beaches along the Pas de Calais. Nor were any such landings ever realistically planned, other than in the fertile minds of the deceivers, the teams of planners and dreamers in the London Controlling Section, the Double-Cross Committee, MI5 and in the Special Section of the Joint Security Control in Washington. But the fact that, until the very end of July, German intelligence organisations believed that such a report would be a possibility is a great tribute to the skills of the deceivers, who built up a credible belief that a landing like the one just described was not only imaginable, but likely.

To retain their credibility, the double agents had now to convince their German minders why everything they had been predicting for the last few months had not come to pass. Again, Garbo was at the forefront here, and his MI5 minder, Tomás Harris, came up with a fascinating and plausible explanation. *Garbo* reported that intense rivalry had broken out between the British and the Americans, and that although Montgomery had only been leading a diversion in Normandy, he no longer wanted to play second fiddle to the Americans in the First US Army Group. So, Montgomery, whom Garbo added was well known 'for being an astute intriguer', wanted to maintain control over the invasion and 'exploit the fame which he had achieved at Alamein'. By drawing in the German forces against the Canadian and British armies, Montgomery intended to reinforce his own army with units from FUSAG, which had the result firstly of delaying and ultimately of abandoning the prospect of a second major invasion in the Pas de Calais.[1]

Garbo continued by passing on information that the First US Army Group now only consisted of the British Fourth Army that had been brought down from Scotland (and was by now almost entirely phoney) and the US Fourteenth Army based in East Anglia (that was entirely phoney). But on 31 August he reported that this had now been joined by a notional First Allied Airborne Army. This Airborne Army was said to consist of units that were all, in fact, purely fictitious. However, Brutus now entered the fray from his supposed position in FUSAG as a liaison officer. He reported that this Airborne Army was about to be used in a long-range attack against northern Germany, possibly in the region of Bremen or Kiel. This now became a deception cover for Operation Market Garden, Montgomery's plan to drop two American and one British airborne division to seize three crossings over the Rhine at Grave, Nijmegen and Arnhem. The story of an Airborne Army landing in north Germany became focused on keeping German reserves away from the actual drop zones of Montgomery's attempt to get troops over the Rhine and to win the war before Christmas. For reasons beyond the control of the deceivers, Market Garden failed, and the furthest drop at Arnhem proved to be, as it was later called, 'a bridge too far'.[2]

The cover for the Arnhem landings in September 1944 brought the whole strategic deception campaign of Operation Bodyguard to an end. The operation set up after the Tehran conference, adopting the word Churchill had used to Stalin to describe how truth should be shielded from the enemy, had achieved its objectives. Allied armies were now established in strength in northern Europe. Parts of France, Belgium and Holland had by this point been occupied, and Allied forces were moving towards the northern Rhine. The German armies had suffered a series of shattering defeats. So, on 1 October 1944, the Combined Chiefs of Staff ordered the closing down of Bodyguard. They calculated that the German forces in the west no longer had the resources to mount a new threat. In this they were wrong. Ten weeks later, the German Army played its last gamble in the west with a huge counter-attack in the Ardennes, aimed at recapturing Antwerp and splitting the Allied armies in two, in what became known as the Battle of the Bulge. But that is another story.

The end of strategic deception did not bring an end to tactical deception. David Strangeways had formed what was called an 'R Force,' and tactical deception was organised through this unit by deceivers in field commands following D-Day. Strangeways took his orders direct from Montgomery, and his R Force consisted of a team of a dozen majors and captains and four special field companies of Royal Engineers. These companies were equipped with 33-ton trucks, each of which could carry a few full-size deflated tanks and a power inflator. Just like the dummy tanks that had been used in the south-east of England, they were made of tough rubberised fabric with rubber or metal tubing that when inflated took up the shape of the tank. The dummies were erected at night, usually on sites just vacated by Allied armour, taking care to take advantage of existing tank tracks to fool any aerial reconnaissance aircraft that came over. They were then lightly camouflaged with nets to complete the illusion. These sites were also heavily guarded to prevent civilians getting too close and being able to spot the subterfuge.

The creation of dummy vehicles and depots had by the summer of 1944 developed into a highly sophisticated business. There were static dummies, portable dummies that were on wheels and could be shifted around, and there was a popular American dummy version of a Sherman tank constructed around a light steel frame placed over a jeep, which could drive the pretend tank around. It could drive along roads but not up banks or across rivers. By September, 148 inflatable tanks were in use, an indication of the scale of the tactical deceptions. There were also ground mat dummies, which simulated slit trenches, and the Engineers carried rolls of painted canvas with timber and tubular steel to erect replica Bailey bridges or vast ammunition and store dumps – sometimes covering a couple of acres of ground. To make this as convincing as possible, the Engineers had piles of appropriate stencils and paint to apply to the trucks and the many direction signposts needed to lead to the area. Tactical deception had to be more accurate than the strategic deceptions. What an aircraft could see from 15,000 feet was limited. But an enemy observer with field glasses less than a mile away cold pick up far more detail and was less likely to be fooled. What the sappers of R Force required were dummies that could be inflated or laid quickly and be convincing in appearance.[3]

In addition, there was a mobile recording and broadcasting unit. During divisional exercises in Britain they had recorded a mass of radio traffic, which could be broadcast when they were in the field to simulate the existence of fake units. They also recorded the sound of armour moving to the front and the clatter and banging of bridge-building and ammo dumps at night. Scout cars had been adapted to play out sounds at night, broadcast through huge horn-like loudspeakers carried inside the car and raised through a hatchway in the roof when in action. But in daytime the horns were folded away and the vehicle looked just the same as any other scout car.

Rob Olver, a GP before the war, had volunteered for the Royal Army Medical Corps in 1942 and after giving David Strangeways a medical (at which Olver described him as being 'extremely fit and alert') was recruited by Strangeways as the medical officer for one of the Royal Engineers units. With the rest of R Force, Olver had landed on Gold Beach on

D+2 and initially deployed near the Canadian 3rd Divisional headquarters at Colombier-sur-Seulles, about two miles upriver from Montgomery's tactical HQ. Olver stayed with Strangeways's R Force until the unit was stood down in Germany in May 1945. He recorded several amusing incidents caused by the deceptions they had created. While in Normandy, a Canadian soldier strayed into one of their camps of dummy tanks, and before they were able to evict him an air-raid alarm sounded. Everyone took shelter, including the intruder, who hid underneath one of the tanks. The air was soon filled with anti-aircraft shells, and a fragment of one of these shells must have fallen to earth and penetrated this dummy rubber tank. As it began to deflate around him the man gave a scream of terror and, unable to comprehend what was happening, fled, much to the entertainment of the sappers who had just laid out the tank encampment. On another occasion a few months later, the Engineers had built a dummy store dump near the captured Nijmegen bridge and had put up dummy road signs to further fool enemy soldiers who might infiltrate the area. Everything was so realistic that when another sapper officer turned up, he was immensely put out to learn that he was unable to replenish his stores from the fake dump.[4]

There were several risks with tactical deceptions. They were often, of necessity, hurriedly put together to solve an immediate issue on or near the battlefield. But a hurried creation and execution of a deception plan usually brought flaws or inconsistencies that meant it could be seen through and so would be likely to fail. And, more fundamentally, if used too often, these plans could, as it were, devalue the whole technique of deceiving the enemy. There are several occasions recorded where tactical deceptions contributed to gaining an advantage. An operation in mid-June attempted to simulate an attack on the Cotentin Peninsula to take the pressure off the Americans at Omaha, which was partially effective. Another operation was able to draw enemy attention to the east of Caen, before an attack to the west of the city. However, various other small-scale operations were less successful.

The Deceivers were able to continue successfully to inflate the Allied Order of Battle, by convincing the Germans that certain units were still in existence when they were either completely fake, or they were real units that had been withdrawn after weeks or months of heavy fighting. Captured enemy maps showing the layout of Allied units repeatedly suggested that German intelligence had again been fooled into believing the British and Americans had more troops at their disposal than in reality they did. However, from the autumn of 1944 the impact of tactical deception declined markedly. What mattered more in the final six months of war in Europe was the Allied superiority in arms, armour and airpower. What mattered less was the cunning and inventiveness of the deceivers.[5]

How much had the overall strategic deception operation changed the course of events? The Allies had overwhelming aerial supremacy and vast supplies of men, ammunition, armour and fighting vehicles pouring out of the war factories in the United States to draw upon. On the other hand, the Germans simply did not have enough soldiers to fully defend the long Atlantic Wall from Denmark to the Pyrenees. And many of the units they did deploy were second rate and did not shape up well in the first few days of the landings.

However, on Omaha beach the Americans had had real difficulty. In the week following D-Day, the Germans brought up some of their panzer reserves, turning the battle for the breakout from the Normandy beachhead into a long and bloody campaign. How much worse would all this have been if Hitler and Jodl had acted decisively in rushing more reinforcements to Normandy? That they did not was a massive strategic failure on the German side and one of the great Allied success stories of the war.

In retrospect, it is easy to assume that D-Day would probably have succeeded anyway. But that is certainly not how it felt to those planning the most ambitious and risky operation of the war at the time, from Churchill to Eisenhower, or to many of the soldiers in the first waves landing along the Normandy beaches. They knew the risks they were taking during the first few hours and days, and how near they came to failure. Eisenhower had a statement ready if the landings did not succeed and was prepared to accept full responsibility for the disaster. Churchill had been instinctively opposed to the idea of invading northern France for some years, preferring to attack the enemy where it was relatively weak. We have seen how he had consistently opposed the opening of a second front with a cross-Channel invasion since the Casablanca conference. He had pursued the Mediterranean strategy and come up with proposals for action in the Aegean, the Baltic and against Norway instead. The Chiefs of Staff had repeatedly discussed alternatives to the cross-Channel option. On 19 October 1943, Churchill had said he wanted to 'swing round the strategy back to the Mediterranean at the expense of the cross-Channel operation.'[6] Later that month, Churchill and General Smuts gave 'a long discourse' to the Chiefs of Staff on the 'relative merits of [the] Mediterranean theatre as opposed to the cross Channel operation.'[7] And we have seen how even a senior figure like the Chief of the Imperial General Staff, Field Marshal Alan Brooke, had major worries that the whole Overlord operation could end in catastrophe when he confided in his diary on 5 June that 'it may well be the most ghastly disaster of the whole war.'[8]

In this context, the success of Operation Fortitude in persuading Hitler, Jodl, Von Roenne and the chief German intelligence organisation, the FHW, that the real threat was from south-east England against the Pas de Calais was pure genius. Keeping nineteen divisions of the German Fifteenth Army locked up 200 miles from the key battleground was a stunning success. Had these units been moved quickly to the invasion beachhead, had they hit the Allied armies while they were still struggling to get men and supplies ashore, had they prevented the Allies from securing a bridgehead, then the opening of the second front could have been the disaster that many feared. It is doubtful that a repeat invasion would have been mounted in less than a year. By that time, triumphant in the west, the German position might have been completely different. Hitler would have had the support of his generals and, pushed on by the success of his Vengeance Weapons, might have been able to open some sort of negotiations with the Americans and British. The outcome of the war could have been very different.

No one person or organisation can claim total credit for the success of Operation Fortitude. But the deceivers who had started with Dudley Clarke's 'A' Force in Cairo had spread into a complex and sophisticated operation. There were committees in London that were made up of some of the most brilliantly inventive minds of the war. They created an inflated Order of Battle that convinced the enemy that it was possible to mount *two* cross-Channel invasions. There were the double agents and their handlers who created some of the most ingenious cover stories to persuade the Germans that Normandy was only a diversion. And there were the set designers who came up with all the visual deceptions, like dummy landing craft, tanks and fake ammunition depots in the south-east of England. Finally, there were those who created an entirely fictitious Army Group and who maintained its bogus existence for many weeks and months. For a deception to be a success it has to play on the enemy's preconceptions and persuade its intelligence organisations that what they half-believe could be true, *is* the full reality. The Allied deceivers understood that to be successful they had to be credible. Whole teams of disparate and eccentric officers and officials helped to make this happen in the largest, most elaborate and most carefully planned deception operation of the war.

So, it seems totally fair to conclude, as the official historian of strategic deception in the Second World War wrote, that Operation Fortitude was 'the most complex and successful deception operation in the entire history of war'.[9]

EPILOGUE

The stories of what happened after the war to those who had been involved in or were affected by the great deception provides a fascinating tale. It reveals much about the characters of these many remarkable and unusual individuals.

The commander of the army that never was, the indominable General Patton, went on for the rest of the war to play the role of an aggressive commander, justifying Eisenhower's confidence in him by leading his forces with immense drive and ambition. Patton's Third Army advanced at speed across France until the end of August, when its supplies of fuel, ammunition and rations could no longer keep up. Patton was impatient to lead the Allied offensive but did not properly get on the move again until December. During the Battle of the Bulge, Patton offered to disengage three divisions of his army and send them north to relieve the American force at Bastogne, who were struggling to hold the central crossroads in the battle. Eisenhower said it could not be done quickly enough. But Patton got his troops to Bastogne in 72 hours, helping to save the day. As the advance into Germany picked up again in February 1945, Patton's Third Army once again led the drive forwards, capturing Koblenz,

Worms and Mainz. Army Group Commander Bradley was anxious to avoid a major fight to seize Trier, the next city in line, and signalled Patton: 'Bypass Trier.' Patton replied: 'Have [already] taken Trier with two divisions. Do you want me to give it back?'[1] Patton's Third Army fought to the end, capturing at least 600,000 German troops. He was keen to race on to Berlin and was distraught when Eisenhower explained that the Soviets would have the glory of capturing the Third Reich's capital.

After the war's end, Patton was appointed Military Governor of Bavaria. One of his tasks was to carry out the denazification of his region, but instead he attracted great controversy by appointing several Nazi party members to senior positions. He was also tasked with resettling Jews who had survived the Holocaust, but his anti-Semitism soon reappeared and he made many public comments condemning Jews and Jewry, despite the horrors the survivors had lived through. Senior Allied officials in occupied Germany began to fear that Patton had either gone mad or at least had become delusional. Once again, Eisenhower was called upon to act, and once again he relieved Patton of his command. It was the third time in his career.

On 9 December 1945, Patton joined some army colleagues to go pheasant shooting near the Rhine at Speyer. They thought it would help to cheer him up. While driving to the hunting site Patton's Cadillac limousine collided with an American army truck. Patton was severely injured in the accident and taken to hospital, where he was found to have a broken neck and a spinal cord injury. He was paralysed from the neck down. When it was explained to him that there was no hope of recovery he was recorded as saying, 'This is a helluva way to die.'[2] Two weeks later he died of heart failure in his sleep. He was 60 years old. It was a very unsoldierly end for one of the finest Allied commanders of the war and the man who had played his part in Operation Fortitude with tremendous relish and showmanship.

His great rival, General Montgomery, went on to lead a distinguished if disputatious post-war life. Having taken the surrender of German forces in north-western Europe at Luneburg Heath outside Hamburg, he became Commander-in-Chief of the British Army of the Rhine. In 1946 he replaced Lord Alanbrooke as Chief of the Imperial General Staff and served for two years. In 1951 he was appointed deputy military commander of the newly formed North Atlantic Treaty Organisation (NATO), a position he filled until his retirement in 1958. However, in his memoirs he criticised many of his wartime colleagues and spent some years publicly bickering with those with whom he had worked during the war, American and British. It seems he never felt he had received the praise he deserved. These disputes, including arguments with prior friends, somewhat tarnished his reputation, which has never fully recovered. He died at home in 1976, aged 88.

Dwight D. Eisenhower returned to the United States and to his wife Mamie at the end of 1945 to replace General Marshall as the US Army's Chief of Staff. Initially he believed that friendly relations could be maintained with the Soviet Union, but as the Cold War escalated he reluctantly accepted that a rift with his wartime Allies was unavoidable. From 1951 he served as military commander of NATO, before deciding to run for the presidency the following year. Running on the ticket that he would end the war in Korea, he won in a landslide, the first Republican to become President in twenty years. He served two terms as President, years which saw a hardening of the Cold War, the start of the Space Race and a period of unparalleled prosperity at home, partially brought about by increased military spending. When he left the White House in 1961, he offered a warning to his successor to beware of the power of the military-industrial complex. He feared that this powerful group, in which he had once been the starring figure, was beginning to exert excessive influence over American politics. It was a warning that President John F. Kennedy, who had been a junior naval officer in the Pacific, took to heart. Eisenhower died of heart failure in Washington in 1969, aged 78.

On the German side, Erwin Rommel was one of the few senior German commanders who in the end was *not* convinced by Operation Fortitude. But he became more and more angry about the burden the German forces had to fight under in Normandy with the constant threat of attack from the air. And it was clear to him and to his panzer commanders that by mid-July the British were overwhelming them in the Caen sector. The British armoured divisions simply had more tanks, more fuel and more ammunition. The Field Marshal was getting increasingly frustrated with OKW, who refused to accept the situation was as bleak as it was. In an outspoken report addressed to Hitler on 15 July, Rommel wrote that the situation was approaching 'a grave crisis'. His troops had suffered 97,000 casualties but had only received 10,000 reinforcements; 225 tanks had been lost and only 17 replacements had arrived. Only by sending troops from the Pas de Calais and the south of France, he argued, could his exhausted troops be relieved. On the Allied side, he noted that fresh troops and reinforcements were arriving daily. 'The [German] troops are everywhere fighting, heroically,' Rommel concluded, 'but the unequal struggle is approaching its end.'[3] Once again Rommel was sending a message that no one in the Führer Headquarters wanted to hear.

Two days after sending his report to Hitler, on 17 July, Rommel travelled to the headquarters of I SS Panzer Corps, commanded by Sepp Dietrich, for an update. At the end of the afternoon, as he left to return to La Roche-Guyon, Dietrich urged him to avoid the main road. Rommel simply smiled.

An hour later, as he drove along in his armoured Horch staff car, his vehicle was spotted by two Spitfires. The fighters attacked and strafed the car. The driver was wounded and the vehicle veered off the road and hit some trees. Rommel was thrown from the car and suffered severe injuries to his face and fractures to his skull. He was taken to a hospital where his wounds were thought to be mortal. The attack on Rommel's car took place near the village of Sainte-Foy-de-Montgommery. It was noted how ironic it was that he was injured near a village containing the name of his long-time opponent. That evening, Hitler ordered Von Kluge to take over Rommel's command. For Rommel, the war was over.[4]

But that was not the end of the Rommel story. Three days after he was hit and hospitalised, a German staff officer, Claus von Stauffenberg, planted a bomb in a briefcase at a conference Hitler was holding at his Eastern Front headquarters near Rastenburg, known as the Wolf's Lair. Von Stauffenberg left the conference and flew back to Berlin to launch a well-planned and extensive coup to attempt to seize power. However, someone moved the briefcase just before the bomb went off, and although four people at the conference were killed, Hitler was shielded by the heavy oak leg of the conference table and was only slightly wounded.

Von Stauffenberg and the leading conspirators were quickly rounded up by the Gestapo and executed. But following the July bomb plot came a long, intense pursuit of those who were thought to be part of a resistance movement against Hitler. Show trials were held in which 200 conspirators were found guilty of treason and executed, some brutally. Hitler used the bomb plot as an excuse both to hunt down many whom he feared opposed him, and to elevate the role of Himmler and the SS in nearly all aspects of life in Nazi Germany. Some estimates suggest that up to 20,000 were killed or sent to concentration camps as a result.[5] No evidence was ever found to link Rommel directly to the bomb plot, but his anger with Hitler and his arguments with the Führer, whom he had encouraged to end the war in the west, had been observed by many senior officers and he soon fell under suspicion. A Court of Military Honour was set up, including both Keitel and Von Rundstedt, to court-martial senior figures who were thought to be linked to the plot, and Rommel's case was brought before it. The Gestapo presented evidence. No defence was permitted. Enough rumours linking Rommel to the plot emerged to condemn him.

Three months after the bomb plot, Rommel was still recuperating at home from his injuries when he was visited by two generals from Hitler's staff. He was given the choice of either going before the People's Court, a kangaroo court that would have certainly found him guilty, a verdict that would also have implicated his family and many of those in his staff at La Roche-Guyon, or alternatively, he could commit suicide. In that case he would be buried as a war hero and his family would receive a full pension. Rommel chose suicide, explained the decision to his wife and son, and on 14 October took a cyanide capsule. Thus ended the life of one of Germany's finest generals. Whether or not he actively supported the plot against Hitler, he certainly wanted the leadership to negotiate with the Allies to avoid what he saw as the inevitable defeat and destruction of Germany if the war continued. He was 52 years of age.

Field Marshal Gerd von Rundstedt had been one of those convinced that a second cross-Channel invasion would follow the landings in Normandy. He was sacked by Hitler after their angry confrontation at the end of June 1944. Von Rundstedt refused any involvement in the bomb plot against Hitler, but he played a leading role in its bloody aftermath as a prominent figure in the Court of Military Honour that condemned his old colleague Rommel among many others. In September he was recalled as Commander-in-Chief in the west as a propaganda move to boost morale at home and in the army. He held this position until Allied soldiers reached the Rhine, when he was finally dismissed in March 1945. He was captured in May and spent a year in various British prisons, where he was extensively interviewed by the military historian Basil Liddell Hart, with whom he built up a close relationship. Charges of war crimes were prepared against him. His view was that the German Army had behaved properly and honourably throughout the war and had a duty to follow orders from its legitimate government. He was not put on trial due to his age (70) and ill health, suffering as he did from a weak heart. He was released in 1949 but had no money, nowhere to live and was denied a pension in the new West German state. Liddell Hart helped to raise money for him to live in a care home, where he died of heart failure in 1953.

Chief of the OKW, Field Marshal Wilhelm Keitel, known as Hitler's 'yes' man, was tried as a war criminal for approving orders to arrest, torture and murder civilians and for the mass execution of Jews. He was found guilty in the Nuremberg trials and was executed in October 1946. General Alfred Jodl had, like Keitel, been taken in by Operation Fortitude and had become convinced that the Normandy landings were only a diversion and the real landings were still to come in the Pas de Calais. At the end of the war, Jodl was also arrested, charged at Nuremberg with war crimes and crimes against humanity. He was found guilty and executed in 1946.

Of the two intelligence chiefs, Alexis von Roenne had led the FSW and been the one who was taken in by the exaggerated Order of Battle figures that were fed to the Germans in Operation Fortitude. Or at least he had gone along with them in order to build up the case to strengthen the German Army in the west. After the bomb plot he was arrested and interrogated by the Gestapo. Although he knew many of the conspirators, he had not been actively involved in the plot. Nevertheless, he was put through a show trial by the People's Court and found guilty of treason. He was hung by wire from a meat hook on 12 October 1944. Hitler wanted the conspirators to die like slaughtered animals. It was a cruel end for a man who had once been known as Hitler's favourite intelligence analyst.

Admiral Wilhelm Canaris, who had led the Abwehr, had been put under house arrest after his fall in early 1944. But his incarceration was relatively benign to begin with. He took no part in the July plot against Hitler's life, although some within the organisation he had led had certainly contributed to it, including General Hans Oster. And Canaris himself received a telephone call on the afternoon of 20 July to tell him that Hitler was dead. The Gestapo intercepted the call and immediately imprisoned him. There was never a public trial because there was no evidence to link him directly with the plot. For several months he was moved from prison to prison while many of his friends and colleagues were executed. In April 1945, with the war nearing its end, Canaris was tried by a summary SS court and found guilty of treason. On 10 April he was taken from his cell in Flossenbürg concentration camp and was hung by wire from a butcher's hook.

The debate has raged ever since as to whether Canaris was a secret-service head who managed to undermine a Nazi victory by constantly feeding the military with false information, or whether he was an anti-Nazi conspirator who never quite built up the courage or the determination to actively plot against the Führer. It was probably inevitable that he would fall from the tightrope he walked, but the brutality of his death with the Red Army approaching Berlin is testimony to the barbarism of the regime he had agreed to serve.

General Hans Cramer had been freed from a prisoner of war camp in May 1944 and had been allowed to see the preparations for the real D-Day landings but was fooled into believing they were those of the First US Army Group in Kent. Back in Germany, he fell under suspicion of having supported the bomb plot and was imprisoned but never charged. Despite having been released by the British on health grounds, Cramer survived to a ripe old age and died of natural causes in 1968.

After the war was over, many of the deceivers who had run the committees in London slipped back into conventional civilian life, and their friends and families never had any idea of what they had done and how much they had contributed to victory. By the 1960s and '70s, a few of those involved published, or tried but were prevented from publishing, their personal accounts and memoirs.

The true founder of strategic deception had been Dudley Clarke, who at General Wavell's bidding had set up 'A' Force in Cairo at the end of 1940. In late 1944, 'A' Force was disbanded and, according to Clarke himself, the brothel where it had been located was handed back to its former owners and 'the pounding of the typewriters once more gave place to the squeals of illicit pleasure'.[6] Clarke spent some time writing up an official history of 'A' Force to record its successes. But this was never to be published and was only released at the National Archives some 50 years later, well after his death. The British and American chiefs of staff had ruled at the end of the war that little should be revealed about the process of deception, as similar techniques might be employed again if the new Cold War ever went hot. And the story of how the deception operations worked were closely tied in with the code-breaking story, which was also to remain top secret for three decades. Even Winston Churchill, in writing his magisterial history *The Second World War* in the early 1950s, was covered by this prohibition. In describing Operation Fortitude, which he never mentioned by name, he wrote, 'It would not be proper even now to describe all the methods employed to mislead the enemy'.[7] This shroud of secrecy would obscure the deception story for decades to come.

In 1947, Dudley Clarke left the army with the rank of brigadier, and published a history of his early war before being sent to Cairo, called *Seven Assignments*. He then went on to write a memoir of his time in strategic deception, called *A*

Quarter of My Century. When he submitted this to the Cabinet Office in 1953 with a request for publication it was refused, and he was told it was in breach of the Official Secrets Act. It was still too soon after the war for the many secrets to be revealed and Clarke's account remained unpublished. Frustrated, Clarke later wrote a thriller entitled *Golden Arrow* in 1955. Clarke worked for the Conservative Party as head of public opinion research and later became a director of Securicor. No one there knew of his wartime exploits.

Clarke was a real pioneer and almost from scratch in Cairo he had formulated the rules of strategic deception that were soon applied in all other theatres. He declared that the intention of a deception operation was not to make the enemy *think* something – that was not enough. To be successful it had to make them *do* something. He said that all deception must have a clear strategic objective and must be given time to develop; it could not be done in a rush. Finally, he concluded that a strategic deception was most likely to succeed if it confirmed what the enemy already wanted to believe. He was a master of building up the Order of Battle so that in the Mediterranean and the Middle East by mid-1944, the Germans overestimated the size of the Allied armies by a quarter of a million men, resulting in the fact that not a single German division was taken from the area and sent to fight in Normandy.[8] He has been called 'the master' of the game of deception.[9]

Clarke's arrest in Madrid dressed as a woman has raised questions recently about his sexuality.[10] There is no evidence that he was gay, and although he never married he had close relationships with several attractive women whom his friends called 'Dudley's Duchesses'. He died in relative obscurity in 1974. Many of those who had worked with him felt that because of the requirements of official secrecy he had not received the recognition he deserved, and David Mure, an officer in 'A' Force, wrote *Master of Deception* about Clarke and his work in

1980. In more recent years his story has been told and he has started to appear as a colourful and creative character in various semi-fictional accounts of the war.[11] It's fair to say that he has now been restored to his place at the heart of the deception story.

Colonel John Turner had been the pioneer of many of the forms of visual deception, firstly in building decoy airfields in 1940 and then in developing many other decoys and dummies in the run-up to D-Day. At the end of the war, Turner suggested developing a school where visual forms of deception could be studied and taught. This eventually came into existence as the Visual Inter-Service Training and Research Establishment at RAF Netheravon in 1947. But whereas decoys and other visual deceptions had been developed during the war in a matter of weeks or even days, even the most basic concealment planning now took many months and sometimes even years to pull off, as arguments went back and forth between different government departments. The officers who by the 1950s were overseeing forms of concealment to be used in a possible war with the Soviet Union had no knowledge of their wartime precedents, as that story was still covered under the cloak of official secrecy.

John Turner left the military in 1946 and devoted the rest of his life to charitable works, most especially with the Church of England Children's Society, where he was an immensely popular figure. His sudden death in 1958 prompted several obituaries in the press but nowhere could his role in visual deception be acknowledged. Even a specialist publication like the *Royal Engineers Journal* could only write that Colonel Turner had been 'specially employed' by the Air Ministry from 1939–45.[12] Turner was another who died with no one around him knowing of his wartime achievements.

John Cecil Masterman was one of the few who later challenged this wall of secrecy. At the end of the war he was asked to write a secret history of the XX Committee, which he had chaired since 1941. This he did, and when he left the intelligence establishment in late 1945 he took an illicit copy of his history with him. He returned to Oxford and became Provost (head) of Worcester College in the following year. He served as Vice-Chancellor of Oxford University from 1957–58, and to cap his status as an establishment figure he was knighted in the following year.

During the 1960s the world of British intelligence was deeply discredited by the defection of Burgess, Maclean and Philby and the revelation of a Soviet spy ring at the heart of MI6. The morale of those in both MI6 and MI5 plummeted. Masterman decided that he should do something to rehabilitate international confidence in British intelligence operations, so in 1971 he rewrote his original 1945 paper as a book entitled *The Double-Cross System*. Once again, he was prohibited from publishing this by the Cabinet Office for being in breach of the Official Secrets Act. But, not to be deterred, Masterman went to the United States and, through a friend who had himself been part of the XX Committee, was introduced to Yale University Press, who went ahead and published his book in the US in 1972. The book was a considerable success in the United States, where it chimed with contemporary themes of penetration and deceit in the Cold War.

The British intelligence establishment then realised it was pointless trying to prevent the book's publication in the UK and eventually the Cabinet Office finally allowed it to be published as long as several sections were removed. The book provided a set of fascinating accounts of the key double agents, none of whom were identified by name but, like Garbo, were referred to only by their codenames. Also, any reference to the use of the code-breaking intelligence of Ultra was still prohibited, and that particular secret did not come out until a few years later. The decision to allow publication was definitely the right one, as before the end of the decade more garbled versions of the double-agent stories were coming out, and within a few years some of their own accounts were published. Masterman, the quintessential establishment figure, had been the one to confront the establishment rules. He died of old age at 86 in 1977 in Oxford. He had not only led the organisation at the centre of the double-cross system during the war, but had finally broken the taboo about its existence and revealed a few of its secrets to a new generation hungry for such wartime tales.

A similar sequence of events happened to Roger Hesketh, the leading member of Ops 'B', the deception planning staff of SHAEF. At the end of the war he was sent to Germany, where he interviewed several leading German generals to assess how far they had been taken in by Allied deception operations, especially those of Fortitude North and South. His research confirmed how successful they had been by establishing that Hitler had read many of the intelligence predictions that a second invasion was definitely coming in the Pas de Calais. Hesketh was then asked to write up an account of these deception operations. It took him a year and it was a detailed and thorough account, of which he was suitably proud. After he left the intelligence community, he too took up establishment positions, including that of the High Sheriff and later the Deputy Lieutenant of Lancashire, and he was elected as Conservative MP for Southport for most of the 1950s.

In the early 1970s, as the dam was about to burst with revelations of wartime deception, a *Daily Express* journalist named Sefton Delmer, who had led a 'black ops' programme in the war, sending radio signals into Germany purporting to come from dissident Wehrmacht officers, wrote up a detailed and populist account of Fortitude entitled *The Counterfeit Spy*. His two sources were extensive interviews with Colonel Noel Wild and Hesketh's own secret report supplied by Wild, which Delmer copied from considerably. Hesketh was furious, especially when he discovered Wild's involvement, as he had been one of his wartime subordinates. He threatened to sue for plagiarism, which left the Cabinet Office in a quandary, as Hesketh's own report was still secret. Eventually, a second edition of *The Counterfeit Spy* was published with a new introduction that gave due credit to Hesketh. The Cabinet Office gave permission for Hesketh's own account to be published, as it was clear that they could no longer, Canute-like, prevent the revelations from lapping further up the beach. But ironically, Hesketh could not find a publisher. *The Counterfeit Spy* had stolen its thunder and Hesketh's account was thought to be too dry to become a bestseller. Hesketh died in 1987, aged 85, still frustrated by being beaten to the post by Delmer. His book was finally published twelve years after his death, with an introduction by Nigel West.[13]

David Strangeways was the one who had reshaped Operation Fortitude and given it its final direction in early 1944. After the war he remained in the army, initially in the force occupying Germany and then in charge of the Visual Inter-Service Training and Research Establishment set up from John Turner's initiative. He served in Greece and Malaya but, having grown accustomed to being given the freedom of latitude by Montgomery to air his thoughts, he soon became unpopular with his senior officers. He was asked to command the task force responsible for the testing of Britain's new hydrogen bomb on Christmas Island in 1957 but was unhappy with the use of nuclear weapons and so resigned from the military and became a vicar in the Church of England. He ended up as senior canon in the Anglican cathedral in Malta. He retired to Suffolk in 1981 and died in 1998, aged 86.

Johnny Bevan, who had worked long hours under intense pressure running the London Controlling Section, was made a Companion of the Bath (CB) at the end of 1945 and was later awarded the US Legion of Merit. He returned to his successful career as a City broker and later ended up as chairman of the Equitable Life Assurance Society. He offered his services to advise on strategic deception during the Cold War but nothing ever came of this. For many years he hosted an annual dinner at Brooks's Club for his wartime friends and associates, maintaining the 'clubbable' atmosphere of the wartime secret intelligence establishment. He died, aged 84, in 1978 from lung cancer.

Following the cancellation of Fortitude in the autumn of 1944, Bevan's deputy Dennis Wheatley found himself largely unoccupied in the London Controlling Section. He suggested that, with his job done, he should leave the RAF Reserve, but he was well down the list of priorities for demobilisation. He went on wining and dining several prominent figures, and Johnny Bevan suggested that as an accomplished author he should write up an official secret history of the London Controlling Section. He did a draft concentrating on the eccentric personalities involved but Bevan hated it. 'This won't do at all, Dennis,' Bevan wrote to Wheatley. 'No one will want to read all this nonsense about the sort of people we are.'[14] Bevan wanted just a plain, factual outline of the operational history of the LCS. The work was handed over to Ronald Wingate, who wrote it up in the style Bevan required, and the secret history is now held in the National Archives at Kew.[15]

Wheatley returned to his pre-war role as a prolific thriller writer with an interest in the occult. His series of novels set in the Second World War and based around the central character Gregory Sallust include a fascinating insight into some of the workings of the intelligence establishment without giving away any hard information. By the 1960s his publishers were selling a million copies of his books every year, making him one of the top-selling global authors. In 1968, Hammer Films made a movie of his early novel *The Devil Rides Out*, starring Christopher Lee. Towards the end of his life he wrote a few autobiographical pieces about his work in the Second World

War, some of which were published posthumously. In total he published more than 50 novels before he died in 1977, aged 80.

The brilliant young intelligence officer who had built up a tremendous amount of knowledge of how the Nazi government worked, Hugh Trevor-Roper of MI6, was asked at the end of the war to investigate the rumours that Hitler had not committed suicide in the Berlin bunker in April 1945. No body had ever been found, so there were suggestions that he was still alive somewhere, spirited away by one of the Allies for their own strange and nefarious purposes. His investigations led him to conclude that there was no doubt that Hitler had died in the bunker and his body had been burned by the SS guards. It was decided that his internal intelligence report would attract considerable public attention and so it was agreed in this rare instance to publish it. It became a global bestseller as *The Last Days of Hitler*.[16] Although Trevor-Roper tried to return to his pre-war obsession with seventeenth-century history, he could never quite escape from the war years. Although disputatious as a historian, as he had been in MI6, he led a successful academic career and was appointed Regius Professor of History at Oxford, a post he held from 1957 to 1980, when he became Master of Peterhouse, Cambridge. He was also ennobled as Lord Dacre, a rare honour for a historian. His reputation and his credibility, however, were severely damaged when in 1983 he was asked to verify the authenticity of what purported to be a set of diaries kept by Adolf Hitler. After a careful reading of the diaries, Trevor-Roper announced they were genuine. Analysis of the paper and ink used later showed them without doubt to be forgeries. Despite his immense expertise on Nazi Germany, Lord Dacre had been fooled.

Trevor-Roper's colleague in MI6, Kim Philby had spent most of his war years running the Iberian desk of Section V. Despite never severing his contacts with the Soviet Secret Service, he was not in a position to offer much intelligence of interest to Moscow. However, all this changed at the end of 1944 when Philby got himself appointed as head of the anti-communist division of MI6. As the Second World War morphed rapidly into the Cold War, with the Soviet Union as principal enemy of the West, so Philby's position became of prime importance to Moscow. This was the era of the struggle for eastern Europe and the communist coup in Czechoslovakia, tensions in Berlin culminating in the airlift, and of the Korean War. Philby was in a position to pass on high-calibre intelligence about Allied policy and intentions, details of codes, the names of Western agents operating in the Eastern Bloc, and to protect Soviet agents in the West. From 1949–51 he was First Secretary in Washington in one of the most senior MI6 positions, among other things responsible for liaison with the US Intelligence establishment. Many people were convinced he was heading seamlessly to the top and would before long be knighted and appointed head of MI6, the position known as 'C'.[17]

However, when Donald Maclean defected in 1951, soon followed by Guy Burgess, an unpredictable and volatile individual who had been living in Philby's apartment in Washington, the finger of suspicion pointed clearly at Philby. He was removed from MI6, or rather he was allowed to resign, and lived for some years in London reliant upon funds from the Soviet Union until, incredibly, in 1956 he was reinstated by MI6 and sent to Beirut under the guise of a journalist for the *Sunday Times*. Again, internal enquiries failed to name him as the 'Third Man' (after Burgess and Maclean), until an MI6 friend, Nicholas Elliott, interviewed him and obtained a verbal confession of his treachery as a double agent in January 1963. The next night Philby disappeared from Beirut, and it is likely that MI6 enabled him to escape in order to avoid the embarrassment of a public trial in London.[18] A few months later he turned up very publicly in Moscow. His presence in Moscow was lauded by the KGB, for whom he became a sort of cult figure regularly giving lectures to aspiring young KGB officers and offering answers to their questions about the West. In reality, he lived a miserable life in Moscow, entirely cut off from British society, reading *The Times* a day late and longing for the cricket scores. In 1988, the greatest traitor in British twentieth-century history, who had learned his craft in the wartime intelligence establishment, died of a heart attack. He was given a hero's funeral in Moscow and, among several awards, he was posthumously given the Order of Lenin, the highest civilian decoration offered in the Soviet Union.

The double agents who had helped the great deception so successfully also resumed civilian identities, although some of them struggled to live anything like normal lives. Juan Pujol Garcia, Garbo, maintained his apparently enthusiastic support for the Nazi cause to the very end. His final message in early May 1945 included characteristically long-winded sentences like, 'I have absolute confidence in spite of the present crisis which is very hard, that our struggle will not terminate with the present phase and that we are entering into what is developing into a world civil war which will result in the disintegration of our enemies.'[19] Alongside these claims of ongoing support for the Nazi movement were a set of requests for payments to be sent as soon as possible, some in sterling or dollars for his supposed network of supporters in England, and some in pesetas and escudos to be sent to bank accounts for him in Madrid and Lisbon. The Germans loyally continued to send payments to him. In total during the war years, he had received the equivalent of $340,000 from the Germans to pay to his entirely imaginary network of sub-agents. All of this ended up in the coffers of MI5.

When the war was over, MI5 invited Juan Pujol to remain in Britain, thinking he could be useful as a potential double agent working with the Soviets and offered to find him a job in an insurance company. But he was fearful that he would be sought out by neo-Nazis and murdered for having betrayed the regime. So, MI5 helped to fake his death in Angola and spread news of his demise.

After this Pujol said that he would prefer to start a new life in South America, and MI5 gave him a gratuity of £15,000 (equivalent to about three-quarters of a million pounds today) for his war work and to help him get started. He divorced his wife, Aracelli, who back in 1940 had tried to help him get into the world of espionage, married a new lady, Carmen, and settled in Caracas, Venezuela, where he lived a quiet life as a Spanish teacher and bookseller with no one knowing of his wartime work for Britain. 'I wanted to be forgotten, to pass unnoticed and to be untraceable,' he wrote.[20]

When Masterman's book about the double-cross system was published in the early 1970s, Pujol's achievements were listed simply using his codename Garbo. This began a frantic attempt by several writers and journalists to track down this extraordinary figure. Although many people thought he was dead, Rupert Allason, writing under the pen name Nigel West, did not believe this. He tried to track down Tomás Harris to get Garbo's real name, but he had died in a car accident in Majorca in 1964. However, after several years of searching, Allason was the first to track Pujol down in Caracas. Allason persuaded him to make a return visit to London in 1984, to meet some of his wartime colleagues again and to receive an MBE in person from the Duke of Edinburgh at Buckingham Palace. He also persuaded Pujol to collaborate with him on an autobiography published in New York in 1985. Pujol wrote, 'I decided that the time had come for my family to learn about my past.' And he concluded the book by writing, 'My main pride and satisfaction now I look back has been the knowledge that I contributed to the reduction of casualties among the thousands – tens of thousands – of servicemen fighting to hold the Normandy beachheads.'[21] After his brief return to Britain, he went back to Caracas, where he died an anonymous figure, three years later.

By contrast, Dusko Popov, the Yugoslav businessman who had been given the codename Tricycle, continued to live the flamboyant high-life that he had enjoyed during the war funded by his spying activities. He married an eighteen-year-old French girl and lived in a castle near Nice. His business flourished, trading in a variety of items from Peugeot cars to German textiles. In 1947 he came back to Britain briefly and met 'Tar' Robertson at the Ritz, where he was secretly presented with an OBE in a leather box. Having lived at the Savoy for many years at MI5's expense, it seemed entirely appropriate to collect his gong at the Ritz. He continued to live well, and in the mid-1970s Popov wrote a book, *Spy/Counterspy*. It was the heyday of the James Bond movies, and he describes scenes in which naked women appeared in his hotel room and he had hand-to-hand fights with Nazi thugs. Ben Macintyre notes that none of these stories appear in his MI5 files.[22] By then he had probably convinced himself that most of his fabulous stories were true. He finally died in the Bahamas in 1981, aged 69.

Roman Czerniawski, codenamed Brutus, the Pole who had worked for the French Resistance, the Germans and then for the British, had in some ways been the most successful of the double agents. From his notional position as a Polish liaison officer with FUSAG, he had been able to feed the Germans a mass of disinformation that penetrated to the highest levels of the Nazi state and was regularly read by Hitler and Goering. After the war he stayed in Britain, not wanting to return to his homeland, which by then was ruled from Moscow. He was secretly awarded an OBE, settled in west London, became a printer, and collected a menagerie of cats whom he adored. To his neighbours he was known as a charming, elderly east European gentleman who loved his pets. He never sought any fame or recognition for the work he had done in promoting Operation Fortitude. Czerniawski died with nobody knowing of his extraordinary achievements in London in 1985, aged 75.

The studios at Shepperton had been behind many of the great visual deceptions of the war. But in 1945 it was time to move forward. Overall, the British film industry had, as they say, a 'good war'. British films had established themselves in the public's view as being powerful, moving and appealing to audiences at home and abroad.[23] They were at long last seen as being almost on a par with the American movies that had dominated the pre-war cinema screens. On the other hand, the film business had been hit by closedowns and shortages of one sort or another. By 1945, Shepperton, having endured bombing raids, acted as a government warehouse, and after five years of working for the deceivers was only a battered shadow of what it had been before the war. A priority was to reopen some of the studios that had closed during the war years to ensure domestic production continued to flourish and bring much-needed foreign currency into the country.

In 1946, Shepperton Studios slowly came back to life as a hub for film production, but without Norman Loudon, who had founded the studio complex and had run it through his company Sound City since 1932. Loudon moved on from producing celluloid dreams to manufacturing something far more solid and real. He spotted a new boom opportunity in post-war housing construction and set up an engineering company in nearby Chertsey called Bellrock, producing moulds to make plaster panels for new housing. This took him in the 1960s into the production of gypsum plaster, an essential ingredient in plasterboard, which was becoming a major building material of the day. However, Loudon continued to live the grand lifestyle of a movie mogul, often staying at London's Connaught Hotel while also owning a penthouse flat in the West End, and taking weekend shooting parties to his house in Scotland. More than anything Loudon was an entrepreneur, spotting opportunities in moving pictures in the 1930s and in building materials in the 1950s and '60s. He died in London in 1967. His second wife, Alice, his long-term secretary and for many years his mistress, died supposedly of a broken heart only seven months later.

Shepperton studios found a new owner in Alexander Korda, who had first worked at the studios in 1935 to produce *Sanders of the River*. Korda had spent part of the war in Hollywood where, among other films, he produced *That Hamilton Woman* (1941) with Laurence Olivier and Vivien Leigh, a propaganda piece showing Britain standing up to a European tyrant. It was one of Churchill's favourite films. While in the US, Korda allowed his office to be used as an undercover centre for British secret intelligence agents. Korda returned to Britain in 1944 and re-established his company London Films, which also took over British Lion. In a half-hour meeting with Norman Loudon over tea in the Shepperton studio canteen, Korda agreed to buy Shepperton and renamed Sound City as the British Lion Studio Company. Korda loved traditional British surroundings, and with its manor house, baronial staircase and Victorian conservatory he now had these in plenty.

With Korda at the helm, Shepperton was set to leap into the production of some of the most famous and distinctive British films of the post-war era, including *The Third Man*, starring Orson Welles, Joseph Cotten and Trevor Howard, and directed by Carol Reed.[24] All the underground sewer scenes in *The Third Man* that were thought to have been shot in Vienna were actually filmed at Shepperton.

The studios would go on to be at the epicentre of British film production for many decades. Productions that were partially or completely shot there included John Huston's *The African Queen* (1952), Laurence Olivier's *Richard III* (1956) and Fred Zinnemann's *A Man for All Seasons* (1966). In all these films the studio helped to provide a sense of the epic and the grand. At the other end of the movie spectrum, reality dramas like Jack Clayton's *Room at the Top* (1959), John Schlesinger's *A Kind of Loving* (1962) and Joseph Losey's *The Servant* (1963) were all made at Shepperton, bringing not only new voices to the screen but a gritty look and contemporary feel to British cinema. The studio became a favourite for Stanley Kubrick who, exiled from the United States, produced *Dr Strangelove* at Shepperton in 1964. Richard Attenborough, who almost single-handedly tried to revive British cinema from a new doldrum in the 1980s, shot *Gandhi* (1981), *Cry Freedom* (1986) and *Chaplin* (1991) in locations around the world, but all were produced at Shepperton.

In 1984, Lee Electrics acquired the studios. A huge rebuilding programme began and the massive sound stages became a hub for a vibrant production community, with dozens of offices and workshops for a growing legion of film support companies. George Harrison's Handmade Films made all its movies at Shepperton. Contemporary classics like Kenneth Branagh's *Henry V* (1988), *Four Weddings and a Funeral* (1994), the Bridget Jones movies and Christopher Nolan's Batman films were shot there. The list goes on and on, and Shepperton has been at the centre of the huge growth in British film production in the 2010s and '20s. It is known for its lavish sets, superb visual effects and highly skilled technicians.

The technicians, carpenters and designers who had worked in Shepperton in the 1930s and who went on to design and build some of the dummy tanks, landing craft and phoney fuel depots of Operation Fortitude would no doubt be amazed at the scale and ambition of the computer-aided filmmaking at Shepperton today. But for sure they would be proud of their role in starting this high-craft ball rolling more than 80 years ago. In the canvas and wooden dummy tanks and landing craft of Operation Fortitude lay the seeds of the computer-aided filmmaking of today.

The official archives of the intelligence operations were not released when the main Second World War archives were opened up from the mid-1970s onwards. Only since the 2000s has the history of Operation Fortitude been fully revealed. The fact was that a small group of men and women in a few top-secret planning departments, supported by a few hundred model-and-dummy-tank, aircraft-and-landing-craft makers, several hundred signallers, a top American general and his staff, along with a Catalan chicken farmer, a Yugoslav playboy, a Polish army officer and many other colourful characters, managed between them to keep a German army of 140,000 kicking their heels in the Pas de Calais. The Fifteenth Army was ordered to remain there, entirely idle, as the beginning of the end of the Third Reich was being fought out less than 200 miles away in Normandy. It was an astonishing achievement. And only now can the pieces around the hoax be properly put together to tell the full and remarkable story of The Army That Never Was.

Appendix 1

THE ORDER OF BATTLE – ALLIED ARMY STRUCTURE

To understand the scale of the inflation of the Order of Battle of troops in the Middle East, the Mediterranean and in Britain before and after D-Day, it's necessary to have a clear understanding of the organisational and operational structure of the wartime British, US and other Allied armies. Although there were minor differences between the numbers in different national armies, the following system broadly applied.

Regiment: the core unit in the British and Commonwealth armies was the regiment. It usually had a historical link to a region or county, although it was never a requirement that all members of a regiment came from that locality. Most officers and men remained in the same regiment for their entire career, and most soldiers felt the strongest loyalty to their regiment, with its own unique colours and rituals. It usually consisted of three battalions, each about 500 to 1,200 men. So, a regiment usually numbered between 3,500 and 4,000 soldiers.

In the US Army the regiment was more of an administrative sub-section, and the principal unit to which soldiers owed their loyalty was the division.

Brigade: an infantry brigade in the British and Commonwealth armies usually consisted of a couple of regiments, sometimes with an accompanying armoured or artillery regiment, although not always. Brigades were not used in the US Army.

A brigade was commanded by a one-star general, a Brigadier.

Division: an infantry division at full strength usually consisted of 15–16,000 men and included its own reconnaissance, artillery, anti-aircraft, anti-tank, signals, engineers, medical and transport units; everything needed to operate as an independent, self-supporting fighting unit. There were also Airborne divisions consisting of parachute or glider troops, and Armoured divisions consisting principally of tank and armoured units with infantry supporting troops. Both were usually smaller in numbers than infantry divisions.

A division's number was expressed in digits, sometimes with the region from which it was principally raised, although this did not mean that all its men came from that region, e.g. 52nd Lowland Division, or 36th Texas Division.

A wartime division was usually commanded by a two-star general, a Major General.

Corps: a corps would consist of two or three divisions operating tactically alongside one another in a section of the front. A corps, and all units above it during the Second World War, could be multinational, consisting of divisions from different national armies.

A corps' number was expressed in Roman numerals, e.g. XX Corps.

A wartime corps could be commanded by a two-star or sometimes a three-star general, a Lieutenant General.

Army: an army would consist of two or more corps and would always include armoured units as well as infantry. The Eighth Army in North Africa and Italy, or the Third US Army in Normandy are good examples.

An army's number was expressed as a numeral, e.g. Eighth Army.

An army would be commanded by a three-star general, a Lieutenant General.

Army Group: an army group would consist of more than one army and would usually cover a substantial section of the front. In the preparations for D-Day, Montgomery commanded 21st Army Group. Bradley later commanded the Twelfth US Army Group and both included their own intelligence staff planning for the invasion of Normandy and the battle for the breakout.

An army group's number was expressed as a number spelled out up to twenty, and above that in numerals, e.g. Twelfth US Army Group or 21st Army Group.

An army group would usually be commanded by a four-star general, a rank simply known as General, or, sometimes in the British Army, by a Field Marshal.

NOTES

Prologue

1. Patton delivered a similar speech on several occasions in late May and early June 1944. Historians have tended to call it 'the speech.' The quotes here are based on several accounts of the speech. One was written verbatim by a man who had been a court reporter before the war. Others were written down from memory later. See: Carlo D'Este, *Patton: A Genius for War*, pp. 601–5 & Stanley P. Hirshon, *General Patton: A Soldier's Life*, pp. 473–76. A cleaned-up version of this speech opens the movie *Patton* (produced by Frank McCarthy; directed by Franklin Schaffner; with a screenplay by Francis Ford Coppola and Edmund North based on a biography of Patton written by Ladislas Farago; Twentieth Century Fox, 1970). George C. Scott giving one of the greatest performances of his career as General Patton recites parts of the speech in front of a giant Stars and Stripes flag.
2. These caravans can be visited at the Imperial War Museum in Duxford. See: https://www.iwm.org.uk/history/montys-caravans-a-field-marshals-home-from-home
3. Alistair Horne, *The Lonely Leader: Monty 1944–1945*, p. 81

4. Alan Moorehead, *Montgomery*, pp. 187–88
5. IWM: Documents 18974; Rob Olver's personal unpublished memoirs
6. Moorhead, *Montgomery*, p. 188–89
7. Like Patton, Montgomery repeated several versions of this speech in the run-up to D-Day. See Stephen Brooks, *Montgomery and the Battle of Normandy*, pp. 59–61; Moorehead, *Montgomery*, pp. 189–90 & Horne, *The Lonely Leader: Monty 1944–1945*, pp. 82–84
8. Clausewitz *On War* Book 3, Chapter 9
9. J.C. Masterman, *The Double Cross System*, p. 7
10. Michael Howard, *Strategic Deception in the Second World War*, pp. ix–xiii
11. Cabinet papers, 120/88, 14 May 1943, Martin Gilbert, *Road to Victory*, p. 407; see Chapter 4
12. The telling of this remarkable story began with the key figure in the process J.C. Masterman publishing his own account in 1972, *The Double Cross System*, and another central player, Roger Hesketh, having his account published in 1999, *Fortitude*. Among recent publications are two excellent accounts, Joshua Levine *Operation Fortitude* and Ben Macintyre *Double Cross*.
13. Clarke's personal memoir is quoted in David Mure, *Master of Deception*, p. 87

1. Decision

1. Harold Macmillan, *War Diaries: Politics and War in the Mediterranean January 1943 to May 1945*, p. 9
2. Winston Churchill, *The Second World War, Vol III: The Grand Alliance*, p.551
3. Churchill Papers CHAR9/157: Churchill speech, Caxton Hall, 26 March 1942, in Martin Gilbert (ed) *The Churchill Documents, Vol 17*, pp. 444–5
4. Alexander Cadogan, *The Diaries of Sir Alexander Cadogan*, p. 433

5. Churchill, *The Second World War, Vol IV: The Hinge of Fate*, pp. 344
6. Mass Observation Archive: FR 1091 *WAAF Morale*, February 1942, pp. 1–2
7. Mass Observation Archive: FR 1244 *Minister of Defence*, March 1942 p. 2
8. For a full examination of the disasters of 1942 and the collapse of support for Churchill's leadership see Taylor Downing *1942: Britain at the Brink*. The quote about not having a single general who can win a battle comes from Lord Alanbrooke, *Field Marshal Lord Alanbrooke's War Diaries*, Danchev and Todman (eds), p. 226
9. Mass Observation Archive: FR 1522 *Morale in November 1942*, p. 1
10. Robert MacKay, *Half the Battle: Civilian Morale in Britain during the Second World War*, p. 95
11. Sir John Martin, *Downing Street: The War Years*, p. 97
12. John Kennedy, *The Business of War*, p. 208
13. John Keegan (ed), *Churchill's Generals*, p. 90
14. Alanbrooke, *War Diaries*, Danchev and Todman (eds), p. 361
15. Kennedy, *The Business of War*, p. 277
16. The official US history, Gordon Harrison, *United States Army in World War II: The European Theater of Operations, Cross-Channel Attack*, p. 46 says there were 107,801 American troops in Britain at the end of February 1943
17. Richard Overy, *The Bombing War* pp. 303–07
18. Harrison, *United States Army in World War II: The European Theater of Operations, Cross-Channel Attack*, p. 44
19. Sir Frederick Morgan, *Peace and War*, p. 135
20. Alanbrooke, *War Diaries*, Danchev and Todman (eds), p. 395

2. *Deception*

1. Morgan, *Peace and War*, p. 158
2. Harrison, *United States Army in World War II: The European Theater of Operations, Cross-Channel Attack*, p. 51
3. Morgan, *Peace and War*, p. 162
4. See Downing, *1942: Britain at the Brink*, pp. 325-28, and Patrick Bishop *Operation Jubilee: Dieppe, 1942: The Folly and the Sacrifice.*
5. Taylor Downing, *Spies in the Sky*, p. 236ff
6. Harrison, *United States Army in World War II: The European Theater of Operations, Cross-Channel Attack*, p. 60
7. Morgan, *Peace and War*, p. 156; see also L.F. Ellis, *Victory in the West, Vol I*, p. 10
8. Colin Dobinson, *Fields of Deception*, p. 11
9. Dennis Wheatley, *The Deception Planners*, p. 141
10. Dobinson, *Fields of Deception*, pp. 19–21 & 76ff
11. Taylor Downing, *Churchill's War Lab*, pp. 92–94 for an account of how he used his minutes to encourage, instruct, order and cajole. His staff often called them his 'Prayers' because they usually began with the words 'Pray tell me …' or 'Pray explain why we cannot …'
12. Charles Cruikshank, *Deception in World War Two*, pp. 5 & 17
13. Adrian Fort, *Archibald Wavell*, pp. 327-31
14. Mure, *Masters of Deception*, p. 57
15. Fort, *Archibald Wavell*, pp. 83–84
16. Tom Clarke, always credited as T.E.B. Clarke, became a central member of Michael Balcon's Ealing Studios from 1944 onwards, dedicated to projecting an image of Britishness. He wrote scripts for many of Ealing's most famous post-war comedies, including *Passport to Pimlico* (1949), *The Lavender Hill Mob* (1951) and *The Titfield Thunderbolt* (1953), all of which extoll the virtues of local community over big business interests, in some way representing the struggle

between the wartime spirit of togetherness and the post-war corporatist world. But he also wrote dramas like *Hue and Cry* (1947) and *The Blue Lamp* (1950), which celebrate the victory of the small guy over criminal gangs. *The Blue Lamp* starring Jack Warner went on to inspire an early BBC Television classic series *Dixon of Dock Green* (1955–76), also starring Warner, as Sergeant Dixon. See Charles Barr, *Ealing Studios*, pp. 80–106. Clearly Dudley Clarke shared the same sense of humour and ability to invent a story as his script-writing brother, Tom.

17. Wheatley, *The Deception Planners,* pp. 20 & 97
18. Mure, *Masters of Deception*, pp. 81–82
19. William Breuer, *Hoodwinking Hitler*, p. 82
20. Thaddeus Holt, *The Deceivers*, pp. 40–44
21. Howard, *Strategic Deception in the Second World War*, pp. 43–44
22. Cruikshank, *Deception in World War Two,* p. 33
23. https://api.parliament.uk/historic-hansard/commons/1942/nov/11/debate-on-the-address p. 37
24. Mure, *Masters of Deception*, pp. 90–91. The General who fumed at Wild for leaving the central role as his Staff Officer, General Richard McCreery, did later apologise to Wild and accepted that 'A' Force was not a dead-end job but was playing a vital role in the war in the Western Desert.

3. *XX: Double Cross*

1. J.C. Masterman, *An Oxford Tragedy*
2. Ben Macintyre, *Double Cross*, p. 43
3. John P. Campbell, 'Sir John Cecil Masterman', *Oxford Dictionary of National Biography*
4. The camp, known as Camp 020, was the principal interrogation centre for newly arrested agents in Britain and was run by MI5. The principal interrogation officer was an Indian Army

veteran, Lt Col Robin Stephens, known as 'Tin Eye' because he always wore a monocle. Stephens was happy to use every trick in the book in interrogating enemy spies, except physical violence. Known as Latchmere House, the large Victorian house had been a respite centre for officers suffering from shell shock in the First World War, and after the Second World War became a prison and a deportees detention centre. In 2015 it was sold and converted into a set of luxury homes.

5. In the case of the request to Tate about Coventry, the authorities hesitated for some time before allowing him to report that he had made a visit to Coventry, but that the police had much of the city cordoned off and he was unable to report accurately about the state of the factories that had been bombed. He did, however, pass on rumours he had supposedly picked up that many of the factories were being dispersed into the countryside. By this ruse the authorities hoped the Germans would decide against re-bombing the city. See Howard, *Strategic Deception in the Second World War*, pp. 10–11
6. Joshua Levine, *Operation Fortitude*, p. 24 – the quote is from the personal papers of Christopher Harmer
7. Macintyre, *Double Cross*, p. 38
8. Howard, *Strategic Deception in the Second World War*, p. 8
9. Masterman, *The Double Cross System*, p. 64
10. Ibid., p. 65
11. Wheatley, *The Deception Planners*, p. 59
12. CAB 80/63, 21 June 1942 reproduced in Howard, *Strategic Deception in the Second World War*, p. 243
13. The War Rooms are today open to the public as the Churchill War Rooms, an outpost of the Imperial War Museum, see: https://www.iwm.org.uk/visits/churchill-war-rooms
14. This was his first published novel, *The Forbidden Territory*
15. Wheatley, *The Deception Planners*, pp. 128–37
16. Hugh Trevor-Roper, *The Secret World*, pp. 1–35

17. Ibid., p. 85
18. Ibid., p. 7
19. A classic example of this is the film *School for Secrets*, directed and written by Peter Ustinov just after the war in 1946. It features a group of five boffins played by Ralph Richardson, John Laurie, Raymond Huntley, Ernest Jay and David Tomlinson who are sent off to a remote seaside guest house to do secret work on developing different forms of radar for the RAF. Their landlady is very suspicious of her guests, all of whom have eccentric habits, and much comedy is generated by their strange behaviour. When her son, an RAF pilot played by Richard Attenborough, discovers they are five of the most brilliant scientists in the country the landlady retorts, 'Oh, if I had known I'd have treated you all much better!'
20. The central argument of Downing, *Churchill's War Lab*, is how Churchill chose to encourage the boffins who frequently came up with new ideas, because, even if he did not understand them, he realised they could be the ideas and technologies that could help to win the war.
21. Holt, *The Deceivers*, p. 280
22. Masterman, *The Double Cross System*, pp. 55–56 & 73
23. Ibid., p. 140
24. Macintyre, *Double Cross*, p. 110
25. Juan Pujol Garcia followed the Spanish custom of using his father's surname followed by his mother's maiden name. However, while in England during the war he only used his mother's maiden name and so was known as Juan Garcia.
26. Many of his reports are reproduced in Public Record Office, *Garbo*, and demonstrate his verbosity. At one point he said he developed this style deliberately because it lengthened everything he sent to his Abwehr controllers, making it all look more substantial.

27. Public Record Office, *Garbo*, p. 58
28. Juan Pujol and Nigel West, *Garbo*, p. 49
29. Public Record Office, *Garbo*, p. 1
30. Masterman, *The Double Cross System*, p. 2

4. *Bodyguard*

1. Churchill Papers, 20/111, Personal Telegram to Harry Hopkins, 2 May 1943, *The Churchill Documents, Vol 18*, p. 1173
2. Daniel Todman, *Britain's War, A New World 1942–1947*, p. 343. The U-boat pack had attacked two convoys, one going east and the other west, crossing in mid-Atlantic, and 21 of the 87 ships in the two convoys had been sunk for the loss of 1 U-boat. However, the fact that by the end of March Bletchley Park were once again able to decipher German naval signals after a long period of being in the dark, along with big improvements in the tactics of naval escorts and long-range air protection that was able to use centimetric radar to track down U-boats when on the surface, meant that the spring of 1943 saw a turning of the war in the Atlantic. In May alone the Germans lost 41 U-boats and would never pose the same scale of threat again. Victory in the Battle of the Atlantic was every bit as significant as the battles of Alamein or Stalingrad. Of course, at the time when Churchill and company crossed in the *Queen Mary* no one knew this and the threat was still significant.
3. Averell Harriman and Elie Abel, *Special Envoy to Churchill and Stalin, 1941–1946*, p.205
4. Alanbrooke, *War Diaries*, Danchev and Todman (eds), pp. 398–99
5. Trident Minutes, Cabinet Papers 99/22, Meeting held in the White House, 12 May 1943, *The Churchill Documents, Vol 18*, p. 1271
6. Downing, *Spies in the Sky*, p. 244
7. Cabinet papers, 120/88, 14 May 1943, Gilbert, *Road to Victory*, p. 407

8. The initial story of the Mincemeat deception was told by Ewen Montagu in his book *The Man who Never Was*, published in 1953 and turned into a lavish Cinemascope film by 20th Century Fox in 1956, directed by Ronald Neame and featuring Clifton Webb as Montagu. But several aspects of the story were kept secret in the 1950s, including the role played by Charles Cholmondeley. Two recent books have retold the story, Ben Macintyre in *Operation Mincemeat: The True Spy Story that Changed the Course of World War II* (2010) and Denis Smyth in *Deathly Deception: The Real Story of Operation Mincemeat* (2010). Macintyre's gripping account concentrates more on the interplay between the personalities involved and the incredible twists of the operation as it unfolded. Smyth looks more at how the framework of the Allied and German intelligence systems worked. Macintyre's book was a bestseller and Warner Brothers turned it into a very successful film, *Operation Mincemeat* directed by John Madden and starring Colin Firth, Mathew Macfayden and Kelly Macdonald.
9. The best recent account of Operation Husky and the conquest of Sicily is James Holland, *Sicily '43*. Historians have generally been critical of the campaign in Sicily, accusing the Allies of poor planning and of over-caution. Holland makes the capture of the island one of the great turning-point battles of the war, involving all three armed services and for the first time putting Anglo-American combined operations to the test.
10. CAB 121/105: PM's Personal Minute to Chiefs of Staff, 18 April 1943, *The Churchill Documents, Vol 18*, p. 1034
11. Howard, *Strategic Deception in the Second World War*, pp. 75–76
12. Ibid., p. 80
13. Holt, *The Deceivers*, p. 492

14. The concept of taking your own harbours to support an invasion in order to allow thousands of tons of supplies to be landed had been suggested initially by Churchill himself in a memo in May 1942. In the memo Churchill had gone through some of the difficulties of ensuring the artificial harbours would float up and down with the tide, and had used the words, 'Let me have the best solutions worked out. Don't argue the matter. The difficulties will argue for themselves.' The Minute with Churchill's handwritten comments on it is reproduced opposite p. 78 of Churchill, *The Second World War Vol V.*
15. Hastings Ismay, *Memoirs*, p. 309
16. Churchill Papers 23/12: Progress Report to the President and the Prime Minister's Combined Chiefs of Staff, 19 August 1943, *The Churchill Documents, Vol 18*, p. 2288
17. Churchill Papers 23/11: Churchill to War Cabinet, 1 November 1943, Memo on Manpower, *The Churchill Documents, Vol 19*, p. 744
18. Churchill Papers 20/122: PM's Personal Telegram to General Marshall, 24 October 1943, *The Churchill Documents, Vol 19*, p. 635
19. Churchill Papers 20/120: President to Prime Minister, 8 October 1943, 'Personal and Most Secret,' *The Churchill Documents, Vol 19*, p. 422
20. Churchill Papers 20/121: Prime Minister to President, 17 October 1943, 'Personal and Most Secret,' *The Churchill Documents, Vol 19*, p. 551
21. Cabinet Papers 79/66: Minutes of the Chiefs of Staff Committee, held at 10.30pm on 19 October 1943; statement by the Prime Minister, *The Churchill Documents, Vol 19*, p. 578
22. Ronald Lewin, *Churchill as Warlord*, p.228
23. Alanbrooke, *War Diaries*, Danchev and Todman (eds), p. 478
24. Sarah Churchill, *Keep on Dancing*, p. 70

25. 'Eureka' Minutes, Plenary Meeting No. 1, 28 November 19943, Soviet Embassy, Teheran, *The Churchill Documents, Vol 19*, p. 985
26. Churchill, *The Second World War, Vol V, Closing the Ring*, p. 329
27. Churchill, *The Second World War, Vol V*, p. 338 & 'Eureka' Minutes, Plenary Meeting No. 3, 30 November 1943, Soviet Embassy Teheran, *The Churchill Documents, Vol 19*, p. 1032
28. Ronald Lewin, *Churchill as Warlord*, p. 231
29. Lord Moran, *Churchill at War 1940–1945*, p. 174–75 & Harriman, *Special Envoy to Churchill and Stalin*, pp. 276–78
30. Churchill, *The Second World War, Vol V*, p. 371

5. Geheimdienst

1. Howard, *Strategic Deception in the Second World War*, pp. 46–47
2. Pujol and West, *Garbo*, p. 71. The numbers working in Intelligence in the Madrid embassy totalled 315, greatly outnumbering the genuine diplomats who totalled only 171.
3. Breuer, *Hoodwinking Hitler*, p. 22
4. Max Hastings, *The Secret War*, pp. 60–65
5. Howard, *Strategic Deception in the Second World War*, pp. 47–48
6. Trevor-Roper, *The Secret World*, pp. 106–7
7. Denis Smyth, *Deadly Deception*, p. 231
8. Macintyre, *Operation Mincemeat*, p. 239
9. Howard, *Strategic Deception in the Second World War*, pp. 51–52 & Levine, *Operation Fortitude*, p. 56
10. Hastings, *The Secret War*, p. 473
11. A good example of a film that imagined the success of German spies in Britain is *The Next of Kin*, directed by Thorold Dickinson for Ealing Studios in 1942. In the film a special brigade is formed to carry out a raid on a port in northern

France where U-boat pens are being built. Two German agents are smuggled into Britain, one by parachute, one by submarine, and slowly piece together the details of the raid, which is undermined by lax security, especially among officers. To try to tighten things up, the security officer of the brigade briefs the men with a short speech in which he says, 'Remember, the enemy has highly trained agents. They may be in any walk of life – grocers, publicans, barbers, politicians – people who the enemy has bribed or blackmailed. Even people who admire Nazism so much they are prepared to betray their own country. Watch out for these people, all the time.' The film began as an army training film but was so powerful it was given a general release and became a big commercial success. No one at the time knew that the central premise of the film, that spies were everywhere, was completely false.

12. Howard, *Strategic Deception in the Second World War*, pp. 47–48

6. First US Army Group

1. Howard, *Strategic Deception in the Second World War*, p. 107
2. Roger Hesketh's plans for rebuilding Meols Hall were only finally completed between 1960 and 1964, making it, according to English Heritage, one of the most convincing country houses constructed since the war.
3. Howard, *Strategic Deception in the Second World War*, p. 110
4. Wheatley, *The Deception Planners*, p. 85
5. From the Harmer papers, quoted in Levine, *Operation Fortitude*, p. 203
6. Holt, *The Deceivers*, pp. 334–45
7. Roger Hesketh, *Fortitude*, pp. 19–25
8. Levine, *Operation Fortitude*, p. 208
9. Hesketh, *Fortitude*, p. 90

10. Levine, *Operation Fortitude*, p. 206
11. Howard, *Strategic Deception in the Second World War*, p. 106
12. Ibid., p. 121
13. Cruikshank, *Deception in World War Two*, p. 170
14. Howard, *Strategic Deception in the Second World War*, p. 115

7. *Patton*

1. Carlo D'Este, *Patton: A Genius for War*, p. 18
2. Alan Axelrod, *Patton: A Biography*, p. 13
3. D'Este, *Patton*, pp. 130–36
4. Ibid., p. 143
5. Ibid., *Patton*, p. 165
6. Stanley Hirshon, *General Patton: A Soldier's Life*, p. 123
7. D'Este, *Patton*, pp. 248–66
8. Ibid., *Patton*, p. 509
9. Ibid., *Patton*, p. 524
10. Many years later an American historian accused Patton of committing a war crime for encouraging men to kill prisoners; see James Weingartner, 'Massacre at Biscari: Patton and an American War Crime,' in *The Historian* 52, 1989. See https://www.tandfonline.com/doi/abs/10.1111/j.1540-6563.1989.tb00772.x
11. Hirshon, *General Patton*, pp. 376–78
12. D'Este, *Patton*, p. 533
13. Hirshon, *General Patton*, pp. 394–95
14. For an analysis of the different forms of shell shock and the military response to the problem in the First World War see Taylor Downing, *Breakdown: The Crisis of Shell Shock on the Somme* passim; for the details of the executions carried out in the different armies see pp. 234–56
15. Hirshon, *General Patton*, p. 393
16. D'Este, *Patton*, pp. 538–40
17. Stephen Ambrose, *The Supreme Commander*, p. 229

18. D'Este, *Patton,* p. 545
19. Dwight D. Eisenhower, *Crusade in Europe*, p. 182
20. D'Este, *Patton,* pp. 540–41
21. Hirshon, *General Patton*, p. 416
22. D'Este, *Patton,* p. 556
23. The comment was made to his full-time driver Kay Summersby, who was also probably Eisenhower's mistress, and it was recorded in Kay Summersby Morgan, *Past Forgetting*, pp. 165–66
24. D'Este, *Patton,* pp. 567–68
25. *The Times*, 22 April 1944
26. *The Washington Post*, 24 April 1944
27. Eisenhower, *Crusade in Europe*, p. 224
28. Omar Bradley, *A Soldier's Story*, p. 231
29. Breuer, *Hoodwinking Hitler*, p. 113
30. The intelligence officer was Lieutenant Colonel William Harris, and he said this in a lecture on deception planning at the General Staff College in 1947; quoted in Holt, *The Deceivers*, p. 587
31. Cruickshank, *Deception*, pp. 178–80
32. Irving, *Hitler's War*, pp. 683–84

8. *Shepperton*

1. Allen Eyles, *Odeon Cinemas*, pp. 7–11
2. Derek Threadgall, *Shepperton Studios*, p. 6. Seventy years later, in the early 2000s, the site was sold for around £35 million.
3. Norman Loudon was writing in *Picturegoer Weekly* in 1933, quoted in Morris Bright, *Shepperton Studios*, p. 6
4. Adrian Brunel, *Nice Work*, pp. 173–74
5. Steve Chibnall, *Quota Quickies*, p. 18
6. Bright, *Shepperton Studios*, p. 29
7. The film was produced by Alexander Korda, who thought the British Empire had been a thoroughly good thing, but directed

by his brother Zoltan, who had a left-wing critical view of imperialism. But Alexander's view prevails in the film, which is dedicated to the 'handful of white men whose everyday work is an unsung saga of courage and efficiency' represented by District Commissioner Sanders. It is rather surprising that the civil rights activist Paul Robeson agreed to appear in the film, but he wanted to give a sense of dignity to the Africans depicted. He later claimed he had been hoodwinked into appearing and said he hated the film and would never work with Korda again. Bizarrely, the future president of Kenya, Jomo Kenyatta, appeared in the film as an extra and claimed to be pleased with the final result. *Sanders* was the first of a quartet of films about Empire produced by Korda, including *Elephant Boy* (1937), *The Drum* (1938) and *The Four Feathers* (1939).

8. Threadgall, *Shepperton Studios*, pp. 16–19
9. Dobinson, *Fields of Deception*, p. 24
10. Ibid., pp. 25–28
11. Threadgall, *Shepperton Studios*, pp. 26–27
12. Jasper Maskelyne, *Magic – Top Secret*, p. 15
13. Reading his own account of his wartime experience, *Magic – Top Secret,* it would be possible to believe that the war could not have been won without the genius of Jasper Maskelyne. He makes grandiose claims for building dummy battleships and fleets of submarines. He writes about his 'Magic Gang' being more effective than any Ali Baba. He describes his work in helping to win the war in the Middle East and then in the Far East against the Japanese. In reality his work for Lt-Colonel Clarke was more focused on developing small escape devices for spies and agents. David Mure, in *Masters of Deception* p. 95–96, argues that most of the inventions that Maskelyne claimed as his own should in fact be credited to Clarke and that Maskelyne's work was marginal and 'largely notional'.

Various films on the subject of the *War Magician* have been mooted over the years, featuring among others Tom Cruise and Benedict Cumberbatch, but they all appear to have been dropped as the validity of Maskelyne's claims about his achievements has been increasingly challenged over recent years.

14. Hesketh, *Fortitude*, p. 85
15. Ibid., pp. 117–18
16. IWM Documents 14889: Hugh Clark's unpublished wartime memoirs
17. IWM Documents 17386: A.A. Southam's unpublished memoirs
18. Threadgall, *Shepperton Studios*, p. 28
19. NA: AIR 41/7 Photographic Reconnaissance Vol II May 1941 to August 1945, p. 146. See also Downing, *Spies in the Sky*, pp. 251–52
20. Threadgall, *Shepperton Studios*, p. 29

9. *Scotland*

1. Sefton Delmer, *The Counterfeit Spy*, pp. 117–19 & IWM: Documents 20170: 'The Story of the Fourth Army' by Colonel Rory MacLeod
2. IWM: Documents 20170: 'The Story of the Fourth Army' by Colonel Rory MacLeod
3. Howard, *Strategic Deception in the Second World War*, p. 111
4. For the full story of this remarkable mission and its consequences see Downing, *Spies in the Sky*, pp. 143–47
5. IWM: Documents 20170: 'The Story of the Fourth Army' by Colonel Rory MacLeod
6. Ibid.
7. Public Record Office, *Garbo*, p. 187
8. Ibid., p. 188

9. Howard, *Strategic Deception in the Second World War*, p. 116 & Levine, *Operation Fortitude*, p. 216
10. Hesketh, *Fortitude*, p. 68
11. Howard, *Strategic Deception in the Second World War*, p. 116
12. Ibid., p. 117
13. Levine, *Operation Fortitude*, p. 219
14. Wheatley, *The Deception Planners*, pp. 178–79
15. Hesketh, *Fortitude*, p. 166

10. More Tricks

1. Between January and May 1943, the Axis had lost 172 merchant ships in the Mediterranean, more than half a million tons of shipping. About a quarter of all guns lost by the Axis in this period were lost at sea. The Axis air forces had lost 2,329 aircraft in North Africa since November 1942, including 400 transport planes that were trying to bring in supplies, compared to Allied losses of 657 over the same period. The Allied propagandists called the collapse in Tunisia 'Tunisgrad' after the defeat at Stalingrad, and nearly three million leaflets were dropped over Germany mocking the humiliating German losses.
2. Helen Fry, *The Walls Have Ears*, pp. 100–7
3. Breuer, *Hoodwinking Hitler*, pp. 159–61
4. Cruikshank, *Deception in World War II*, p. 184
5. Dobinson, *Fields of Deception*, pp. 198–201
6. Cruikshank, *Deception in World War II*, p. 185
7. Downing, *Spies in the Sky*, pp. 91–92. After the war, Wavell asked the Air Ministry for some sort of recognition for the development and construction of his invention that saved so much time in measuring the height of radar and radio installations. After years of wrangling he eventually received a cheque for £25!

8. NA: AIR 41/7 Photographic Reconnaissance Vol II May 1941 to August 1945, p. 145
9. The word 'boffin' was the usually affectionate term used during the Second World War to describe the mildly eccentric scientist who did vital war work that only a few people could understand, although everyone knew was tremendously important. The origins of the word are obscure and several myths have grown up around it, some suggesting it came from the name of a strange long-necked bird that liked to strut about. More prosaically it probably came from some sort of abbreviation of 'back office intelligence.' Another name used to describe these scientists, the vast majority of which were men, was 'the back room boys.'
10. Range and Direction Finding, or RDF, was the British name used in 1940–41. When the Americans joined the war the acronym they used for RAdio Detection And Ranging provided the word 'radar,' which became the common term to describe this system to identify objects from the reflection of radio waves sent out to them.
11. The story of the development of radar, of the extraordinary and daring raid at Bruneval, and of the development of Window is told in Taylor Downing, *Night Raid*.
12. Ellis, *Victory in the West, Vol 1, The Battle of Normandy*, p. 103
13. Breuer, *Hoodwinking Hitler*, pp. 175–77
14. Jones's account of his role in the radar war in spring of 1944 is to be found in R.V. Jones, *Most Secret War*, pp. 400–13
15. M. Clifton James, *I Was Monty's Double*, pp. 105–6
16. Levine, *Operation Fortitude*, pp. 262–65; Holt, *The Deceivers*, pp. 561–62
17. James, *I Was Monty's Double*, p. 144
18. In 1954, James wrote up his story in *I Was Monty's Double*, which four years later was turned into a film starring John Mills and in which James played both himself and Monty.

As Joshua Levine has observed, this at least brought him enduring recognition and made him far better known than many of MI5's double agents who played a much more significant role in the Fortitude deception but remained unknown.

11. Reactions

1. Delmer, *The Counterfeit Spy*, p. 141
2. Howard, *Strategic Deception in the Second World War*, p. 117
3. Hesketh, *Fortitude*, p. 167
4. Antony Beevor, *D-Day*, p. 41
5. Basil Liddell-Hart (ed), *The Rommel Papers*, pp. 453–56
6. The giant concrete control centre, Le Coupole, can be visited today. See: https://www.lacoupole-france.co.uk/history-centre/history/the-special-constructions.html
7. It was said that many dummy minefields were laid out by local commanders just to get Rommel and other senior officers off their backs. They assumed if they put up the Danger signs no senior officer would actually cross them to check if mines really had been laid.
8. Liddell-Hart (ed), *The Rommel Papers*, p. 465
9. Holt, *The Deceivers*, p. 573
10. Howard, *Strategic Deception in the Second World War*, pp. 49–50
11. Levine, *Operation Fortitude*, pp. 241–42
12. From *Lagebericht West No 1199* [Summary Report No 1199], dated 9 March 1944, quoted in Hesketh, *Fortitude*, pp. 174–75
13. From *Ueberblick des Britischen Reiches No 28*, [Overview of British Empire No 28] dated 29 April 1944, quoted in Hesketh, *Fortitude*, p. 175
14. From *Ueberblick des Britischen Reiches No 29*, dated 15 May 1944, quoted in Hesketh, *Fortitude*, p. 178
15. From *Lagebericht West No 1199* [Summary Report No 1199], dated 9 March 1944, quoted in Hesketh, *Fortitude*, p. 186

16. Howard, *Strategic Deception in the Second World War*, pp. 128–29
17. Liddell-Hart (ed), *The Rommel Papers*, p. 470
18. For instance, Oshima had told Tokyo that he had concluded that the Pas de Calais was the most likely area where the invasion would take place and he itemised in some detail the defences along this area. Oshima also reported that General Dollman's Seventh Army had only eight divisions to guard the whole stretch of coast from the Seine to the Loire and that most of these were understrength. See Carl Boyd, *Hitler's Japanese Confidant*, pp. 110–22
19. Boyd, *Hitler's Japanese Confidant*, pp. 124–25
20. The Americans had broken the Japanese diplomatic codes in 1940 and called the intelligence they received from deciphering enemy signals 'Magic'. The British called the intelligence they received from enemy signals 'Ultra'.

12. *Standing By*

1. Alanbrooke, *War Diaries*, Danchev and Todman (eds), p. 554
2. *The Times*, 2 June 1944
3. Mollie Panter-Downes, *London War Notes*, p. 326 – Panter-Downes was a Londoner who wrote a weekly column for *The New Yorker*
4. The beaches were subdivided into smaller sectors, named firstly by letter D for Dog, E for Easy, F for Fox; and then by colour. So each section of beach was known, for example, as Dog Red, Easy Green, Fox White, and so on.
5. NA: AIR 41/7 Photographic Reconnaissance Vol II May 1941 to August 1945, pp. 142–46
6. Ellis, *Victory in the West, Vol 1, The Battle of Normandy*, p. 104
7. Downing, *Spies in the Sky*, pp. 236–253
8. Beevor, *D-Day*, p. 10
9. David Stafford, *Ten Days to D-Day*, pp. 160–61 & 177–78

10. Eisenhower, *Crusade in Europe*, p. 249
11. Ibid., p. 250
12. Group Captain Stagg later wrote an account of these dramatic days, see Stagg, *Forecast for Overlord*
13. Admiral Sir Bertram Ramsay, *The Year of D-Day*, p.
14. Summersby, *Past Forgetting*.
15. The first man to land in Occupied France was pathfinder Sergeant Bob Murphy of the 505th Regiment of the 101st Airborne. He landed by crashing into a greenhouse in a garden in Sainte Mere-Eglise. It turned out to be the garden of a school teacher, a 60-year-old woman who got up and went downstairs to her back door to see what all the noise was about. To her amazement she saw the blacked-up American paratrooper climbing out of her shattered greenhouse. Murphy stopped, looked at her as she stared at him, not having any idea who he could be or what army he belonged to. Murphy looked at the school teacher, put his finger to his lips in the gesture of silence, and disappeared into the night. The school teacher, who might well have thought she had seen a Martian land in her garden, went back to bed. Told to the author in an interview with Bob Murphy in 2001.
16. These were the guns captured by Captain Dick Winters of Easy Company of the 506th Regiment of the 101st Airborne. The capture of the guns forms a central part of the story of *Band of Brothers*, initially a book by Stephen Ambrose based on an unpublished memoir by Dick Winters, and then dramatised in the Stephen Spielberg–Tom Hanks HBO television series of the same name. Westpoint today still uses the example of the storming of Brécourt Manor to show how a small but highly motivated unit can overpower a far larger force in a well-defended emplacement.
17. The vinyl record on which this was recorded had to be sent back to England to be played down the line to Broadcasting House

before it could be broadcast, and so his words were not heard on the radio for about 24 hours.

13. The Day

1. These aerial photos provide a unique record of the progress of the D-Day invasion, hour by hour throughout the day. But as the invasion was a success no one needed to examine them in detail. So, within a few days, they were just filed away. Rediscovered, they formed the basis of a documentary, *D-Day: The Lost Evidence*, produced by Taylor Downing and David Edgar of Flashback Television for the History Channel in the US, the UK and worldwide to mark the 60th anniversary of D-Day in June 2004.
2. Ellis, *Victory in the West, Vol 1: The Battle of Normandy*, p. 169
3. Some 700 Americans had been lost when E-boats had got in among the ships in a practice landing off Slapton Sands in Devon in April. The losses were explained away at the time by a variety of other causes, and it was only decades later that the full story of the Slapton Sands disaster was pieced together.
4. The opening scenes of Stephen Spielberg's *Saving Private Ryan* (1999) accurately capture the horror of the Omaha landings. Veteran associations across the US reported that when many veterans saw the film, the sights and sounds were so realistic that they brought back terrible memories of the landings that day. For some weeks after the movie's launch extra counsellors had to be called in to help traumatised veterans.
5. Bradley, *A Soldier's Story*, p. 271
6. Casualties for D-Day itself are difficult to calculate, as few units reported a total for just a single day; most units reported figures over a longer period, say 6–20 June. Also, many of those classed as missing on D-Day later turned up in adjoining units, or had been evacuated to the UK wounded, or taken prisoner. Antony Beevor estimates British casualties as roughly 3,000 killed, wounded and

missing on the day, with 4,649 American killed, wounded and missing. See Beevor, *D-Day*, p. 151

7. Beevor, *D-Day*, pp. 141–42
8. Irving, *Hitler's War*, p. 639
9. Asa Briggs, *History of Broadcasting, Vol III, The War of Words*, p.597 & David Hendy, *The BBC*, pp. 266–70. The BBC defended themselves by saying they had announced only that there were 'reports' of an invasion and the formal and definite news that it had taken place did not occur until 9.32am as planned.
10. Kathleen Hey, *The View from the Corner Shop*, pp. 276–79
11. https://hansard.parliament.uk/Commons/1944-06-06/debates/e8874bd2-700f-4184-9abe-6fb13493f0dd/LiberationOfRomeLandingsInFrance
12. For making this statement, Churchill could later have been accused of knowingly misleading the House. But he never was.

14. Deception Continues

1. Howard, *Strategic Deception in the Second World War*, pp. 185–86
2. Hesketh, *Fortitude*, pp. 199–200
3. Public Record Office, *Garbo*, pp. 204–5
4. Howard, *Strategic Deception in the Second World War*, p. 188
5. Ellis, *Victory in the West, Vol 1: The Battle of Normandy*, pp. 261–62
6. Liddell-Hart (ed), *The Rommel Papers*, p. 479
7. Ibid., p. 478–79 & Beevor, *D-Day*, pp. 224–26
8. IWM: Documents 20170: 'The Story of the Fourth Army' by Colonel Rory Macleod & IWM: Documents 22394: Colonel Horn Papers
9. IWM: Documents 20170: 'The Story of the Fourth Army' by Colonel Rory Macleod
10. The opening scene of the first episode in the landmark 26-part television series *The World at War* (Thames Television, 1973–

74, series producer Jeremy Isaacs) is of Oradour-sur-Glane, which is very evocatively shot from the air and ground and made to stand for all the atrocities and massacres carried out by all armies during the war. The village is still maintained as a memorial to the victims, and an additional nearby Oradour Memorial Centre was opened by President Chirac in 1999.

11. Howard, *Strategic Deception in the Second World War*, pp. 189–90
12. Liddell-Hart (ed), *The Rommel Papers*, pp. 479–81 & Beevor, *D-Day*, pp. 236–37
13. Rommel's memo to Von Kluge complaining about the conduct of the war in Normandy by OKW fills four printed pages in Liddell-Hart (ed), *The Rommel Papers*, pp. 481–84. Rommel also sent a copy to Hitler, which only added to the Führer's suspicions about his commander in Normandy.
14. Beevor, *D-Day*, p. 234
15. Hesketh, *Fortitude*, pp. 421–23
16. D'Este, *Patton*, p. 613
17. Holt, *The Deceivers*, p. 586
18. Howard, *Strategic Deception in the Second World War*, p. 193
19. Eisenhower, *Crusade in Europe*, p. 288

15. Evaluation

1. Public Record Office, *Garbo*, pp 230–31
2. Aerial reconnaissance had spotted a German panzer unit resting up in fields near Arnhem, but British commanders refused to take this seriously and ordered the parachute drop to go ahead anyway. The paratroopers at Arnhem were soon fighting for their lives. The ground forces of XXX Corps under General Horrocks that were intended to drive forward at speed to link up with the captured bridges found the

going too difficult, and the men at Arnhem had to fight it out against vastly superior enemy forces until finally forced to withdraw or surrender. The Arnhem drop resulted in nearly 1,500 British and Polish deaths and 6,500 prisoners being taken.

3. Cruikshank, *Deception*, pp. 190–96
4. IWM: Documents: 18974; Rob Olver's memoirs: *A Doctor's Memories of R Force*
5. Cruikshank, *Deception*, p. 205
6. Alanbrooke, *War Diaries*, Danchev and Todman (eds), p. 461
7. Ibid., p. 463
8. Ibid., p. 554
9. Howard, *Strategic Deception in the Second World War*, p. 105

Epilogue

1. D'Este, *Patton*, p. 708
2. Ibid., p. 783
3. Liddell Hart (ed), *The Rommel Papers*, pp. 486–87
4. There has been a lively debate for 80 years as to who flew the Spitfire that attacked Rommel's car. It was either a pilot from 602 Squadron RAF or more likely a pilot from 412 Squadron Royal Canadian Air Force.
5. The *Gedenkstatte Deutscher Widerstand* in Berlin, the German Resistance Memorial Centre, is a centre for research and the publication of documents relating to the resistance movement against National Socialism. It calculates that up to 20,000 Germans were imprisoned or executed as a result of the July bomb plot. See: https://www.gdw-berlin.de/en/home/
6. Mure, *Master of Deception*, p. 260
7. Churchill, *The Second World War, Vol V, Closing the Ring*, p. 526
8. Cruikshank, *Deception*, p. 157

9. Holt, *The Deceivers*, p. 51
10. For instance, in the *Independent*, 23 May 2013, 'The Cross-Dressing Spy who was Arrested on a Secret Mission': https://www.independent.co.uk/news/uk/home-news/lieutenant-colonel-dudley-clarke-the-crossdressing-spy-who-was-arrested-on-a-secret-mission-8628513.html
11. In the 2022 BBC drama series *SAS: Rogue Heroes*, Clarke appears as an enigmatic figure who has a relationship with a female French spy in Cairo. He is played by Dominic West.
12. Dobinson, *Fields of Deception*, p. 218
13. Hesketh, *Fortitude*, pp. xii–xii, and Holt, *The Deceivers*, pp. 783–87
14. Wheatley, *The Deception Planners*, p. 228
15. NA: CAB 154/101 *Historical record of deception in the war against Germany and Italy*
16. Trevor-Roper, *The Secret World*, pp. 1–35
17. Ibid., pp. 86–88 & p. 109
18. Ben Macintyre, *A Spy Among Friends*, pp. 277–78
19. Public Record Office, *Garbo*, p. 277
20. Pujol and West, *Garbo*, p. 164
21. Ibid., p. 167
22. Macintyre, *Double Cross*, p. 349
23. Productions like Noël Coward's *In Which We Serve* (1942), using a naval ship with its divisions between captain and seamen as a stirring metaphor for class-divided Britain, and Launder and Gilliat's *Millions Like Us* (1943), capturing the spirit of the newly liberated 'mobile woman', proved immensely successful. *In Which We Serve* starring Noël Coward, Celia Johnson, John Mills, Bernard Miles and featuring the first screen appearance of Richard Attenborough was the second-most popular film at the box office in 1943 and was hugely popular in America, where it won a special Academy Award. *Millions Like Us*, starring

Patricia Roc, Gordon Jackson, Eric Portman and Megs Jenkins, was another box-office hit. The two films were produced with support both editorially and financially from the Ministry of Information.

24. Threadgall, *Shepperton Studios*, pp. 45–46

BIBLIOGRAPHY

Collections Of Documents

Gilbert, Martin (ed), *The Churchill Documents, Vol 17: Testing Times, 1942*. Hillsdale, Michigan: Hillsdale College Press, 2014.

Gilbert, Martin & Arnn, Larry P (eds), *The Churchill Documents, Volume 18: One Continent Redeemed*. Hillsdale, Michigan: Hillsdale College Press, 2015.

Gilbert, Martin & Arnn, Larry P (eds), *The Churchill Documents, Volume 19: Fateful Questions, September 1943 to April 1944*. Hillsdale, Michigan: Hillsdale College Press, 2017.

Liddell Hart, Basil H. (ed), *The Rommel Papers*. New York: Da Capo Press, 1953.

Public Record Office Secret History Files, ed Mark Seaman, *Garbo: The Spy who saved D-Day*. London: Public Record Office, 2000.

Primary Sources

Alanbrooke, Field Marshal Lord, *Field Marshal Lord Alanbrooke's War Diaries*, Alex Danchev and Daniel Todman (eds). London: Weidenfeld & Nicolson, 2001.

Brunel, Adrian, *Nice Work: The Story of Thirty Years of British Film Production*. London: Forbes Robertson, 1949.

Cadogan, Sir Alexander, *The Diaries of Sir Alexander Cadogan 1938–1945* (ed. David Dilks). London: Cassell, 1971.

Churchill, Sarah, *Keep on Dancing: An Autobiography*. London: Weidenfeld and Nicolson, 1981.

Churchill, Winston, *The Second World War*, 6 vols. London: Cassell, 1948–54.

Vol III: The Grand Alliance, 1950.

Vol IV: The Hinge of Fate, 1951.

Vol V: Closing the Ring, 1952.

Eisenhower, Dwight D., *Crusade in Europe*. New York: Doubleday, 1948 [republished by John Hopkins University Press, 1997].

Harriman, Averell and Elie Abel, *Special Envoy to Churchill and Stalin, 1941–1946*. New York: Random House, 1975.

Hesketh, Roger, *Fortitude: The D-Day Deception Campaign*. London: St Ermin's Press, 1999.

Hey, Kathleen, *The View from the Corner Shop: The Diary of a Wartime Shop Assistant* (eds Patricia & Robert Malcolmson). London: Simon and Schuster, 2016.

Ismay, General Hastings, *The Memoirs of General, the Lord Ismay*. London: Heinemann, 1960.

James, M.E. Clifton, *I Was Monty's Double*. London: Rider and Company, 1954.

Jones, R.V., *Most Secret War*. London: Hamish Hamilton, 1978 [republished by Penguin Books, 2009].

Kennedy, Major-General Sir John, *The Business of War*. London: Hutchinson, 1957.

Macmillan, Harold, *War Diaries: Politics and War in the Mediterranean, January 1943–May 1945*. London: Macmillan, 1984.

Martin, Sir John, *Downing Street: The War Years*. London: Bloomsbury, 1991.

Maskelyne, Jasper, *Magic – Top Secret*. London: Stanley Paul, 1949.

Masterman, J.C., *An Oxford Tragedy*. London: Victor Gollancz, 1933.

Masterman, J.C., *The Double Cross System in the War of 1939–1945*. London: Yale University Press, 1972.

Montgomery, Field Marshal Viscount, *Normandy to the Baltic*. London: Hutchinson, 1947.

Montgomery, Field Marshal Viscount, *Montgomery and the Battle of Normandy: A Selection from the Diaries, Correspondence and Other Papers of Field Marshal the Viscount Montgomery of Alamein, January to August 1944*, Brooks, Stephen (ed). Stroud, Gloucestershire: History Press for the Army Records Society, 2008.

Moran, Lord, *Churchill at War, 1940–1945*. London: Robinson, 2002.

Morgan, Lieutenant-General Sir Frederick, *Peace and War: A Soldier's Life*. London: Hodder and Stoughton, 1961.

Mure, David, *Masters of Deception: Tangled Webs in London and the Middle East*. London: William Kimber, 1980.

Panter-Downes, Mollie, *London War Notes 1939–1945* [edited by William Shawn]. London: Longman, 1972.

Pujol, Juan and West, Nigel, *Operation Garbo: The Personal Story of the Most Successful Double Agent of World War Two*. London: Weidenfeld and Nicolson, 1985.

Ramsay, Admiral Sir Bertram, *The Year of D-Day*. Hull: University of Hull Press, 1994.

Stagg, John, *Forecast for Overlord*. London: Ian Allen, 1971.

Summersby Morgan, Kay, *Past Forgetting: My Love Affair with Dwight D. Eisenhower*. New York: Simon and Schuster, 1976.

Trevor-Roper, Hugh, *The Secret World: Behind the Curtain of British Intelligence in World War II and the Cold War*, Harrison, Edward (ed). London: I.B. Tauris, 2014.

Wheatley, Dennis, *The Deception Planners: My Secret War*. London: Hutchinson, 1980.

Official Histories

Briggs, Asa, *The History of Broadcasting in the United Kingdom, Vol III, The War of Words*. Oxford: Oxford University Press, 1995.

Dobinson, Colin, *Field of Deception: Britain's Bombing Decoys of World War II*. London, Methuen, 2000. Published by the English Heritage Monuments Protection Programme.

Ellis, Major L.F., *Victory in the West: Vol I, The Battle of Normandy*. London: HMSO, 1962. [Reprinted by the Imperial War Museum, London and The Battery Press, Nashville, 1993].

Gilbert, Martin, *Road to Victory: Winston Churchill 1941–1945*. [Volume 7 of the 8 volume official biography of Winston Churchill.] London: Heinemann, 1986.

Harrison, Gordon, *United States Army in World War II: The European Theater of Operations, Cross-Channel Attack*, Office of the Chief of Military History, Department of the Army, The Pentagon, Washington DC, 1951.

Howard, Michael, *Strategic Deception in the Second World War*. London: Norton, 1995. [Originally published as *Volume 5* of *British Intelligence in the Second World War*. London: HMSO, 1990].

Secondary Sources

Ambrose, Stephen, *The Supreme Commander*. London: Cassell, 1970.

Ambrose, Stephen, *Band of Brothers*. New York: Touchstone, 1992.

Axelrod, Alan, *Patton: A Biography*. London: Palgrave Macmillan, 2006.

Barr, Charles, *Ealing Studios*. London: Cameron & Tayleur, 1977.

Beevor, Antony, *D-Day: The Battle for Normandy*. London: Viking, 2009.

Bishop, Patrick, *Operation Jubilee: Dieppe, 1942: The Folly and the Sacrifice*. London: Penguin, 2022.

Boyd, Carl, *Hitler's Japanese Confidant: General Oshima Hiroshi and MAGIC Intelligence, 1941–1945*. Kansas: University Press of Kansas, 1993.

Breuer, William B., *Hoodwinking Hitler: The Normandy Deception*. Westport, Connecticut: Praeger, 1993.

Chibnall, Steve, *Quota Quickies: The Birth of the British 'B' Film*. London: BFI Publishing, 2007.

Cruikshank, Charles, *Deception in World War Two*. Oxford: OUP, 1979.

Delmer, Sefton, *The Counterfeit Spy*. London: HarperCollins, 1971.

D'Este, Carlo, *Patton: A Genius for War*. New York: HarperCollins, 1995.

Downing, Taylor, *Churchill's War Lab: Code-breakers, Boffins and Innovators: The Mavericks Churchill led to Victory*. London: Little, Brown, 2010.

Downing, Taylor, *Spies in the Sky: The Secret Battle for Aerial Intelligence during World War Two*. London: Little, Brown, 2011.

Downing, Taylor, *Night Raid: The True Story of the First Victorious British Para Raid of World War II*. London: Little, Brown, 2013.

Downing, Taylor, *Breakdown: The Crisis of Shell Shock on the Somme, 1916*. London: Little, Brown, 2016.

Downing, Taylor, *1942: Britain at the Brink*. London: Little, Brown, 2022.

Eyles, Allen, *Odeon Cinemas: 1. Oscar Deutsch Entertains Our Nation*. London: Cinema Theatre Association, 2002.

Fort, Adrian, *Archibald Wavell: The Life and Times of an Imperial Servant*. London: Jonathan Cape, 2009.

Fry, Helen, *The Walls Have Ears: The Greatest Intelligence Operation of World War II*. New Haven: Yale University Press, 2019.

Hastings, Max, *The Secret War: Spies, Codes and Guerrillas 1939–45*. London: William Collins, 2015.

Hendy, David, *The BBC: A People's History*. London: Profile, 2022.

Hirshson, Stanley P., *General Patton: A Soldier's Life*. New York: HarperCollins, 2002.

Holland, James, *Sicily '43: The First Assault on Fortress Europe*. London: Bantam Press, 2020.

Holt, Thaddeus, *The Deceivers: Allied Military Deception in the Second World War*. New York: Scribner, 2004.

Horne, Alistair, *The Lonely Leader: Monty 1944–1945*. London: Macmillan, 1994.

Irving, David, *Hitler's War*. London: Hodder and Stoughton, 1977.

Keegan, John (Ed). *Churchill's Generals*. London: Weidenfeld & Nicolson, 1991.

Lewin, Ronald, *Churchill as Warlord*. London: Batsford, 1973.

Levine, Joshua, *Operation Fortitude: The Greatest Hoax of the Second world War*. London: HarperCollins, 2012.

MacKay, Robert, *Half the Battle: Civilian Morale in Britain during the Second World War*. Manchester: Manchester University Press, 2002.

Macintyre, Ben, *Operation Mincemeat: The True Spy Story that Changed the Course of World War II*. London: Bloomsbury, 2010.

Macintyre, Ben, *Double Cross: The True Story of the D-Day Spies*. London: Bloomsbury, 2012.

Macintyre, Ben, *A Spy Among Friends: Philby and the Great Betrayal*. London: Bloomsbury, 2015.

Moorhead, Alan, *Montgomery: A Biography*. London: Hamish Hamilton, 1946.

Overy, Richard, *The Bombing War: Europe 1939–1945*. London: Allen Lane, 2013.

Smyth, Denis, *Deadly Deception: The Real Story of Operation Mincemeat*. Oxford: Oxford University Press, 2010.

Stafford, David, *Ten Days to D-Day: Countdown to the Liberation of Europe*. London: Little, Brown, 2003.

Threadgall, Derek, *Shepperton Studios: An Independent View*. London: BFI Publishing, 1994.

Todman, Daniel, *Britain's War, A New World 1942–1947*. London: Allen Lane, 2020.